YALE HISTORICAL PUBLICATIONS, MISCELLANY, 129

Confidence Men and Painted Women
A Study of Middle-class Culture in America, 1830–1870

KAREN HALTTUNEN

Yale University Press
New Haven and London

Designed by Sally Harris
and set in Baskerville type by
Coghill Composition Co.

Library of Congress Cataloging in Publication Data

Halttunen, Karen, 1951–
Confidence men and painted women.

(Yale historical publications. Miscellany; 129)
Bibliography: p.
Includes index.
1. Middle classes—United States—History—19th
century. 2. United States—Moral conditions. 3. Social
values. 4. Hypocrisy. 5. Sincerity. I. Title. II. Series.
HT690.U6H34 1982 305.5′5′0973 82–8336
AACR2
ISBN 0–300–02835–0
0–300–03788–0 (pbk.)

7 9 10 8

To John L. Thomas

"Why do you tremble at me alone?" cried he, turning his veiled face round the circle of pale spectators. "Tremble also at each other! Have men avoided me, and women shown no pity, and children screamed and fled, only for my black veil? What, but the mystery which it obscurely typifies, has made this piece of crape so awful! When the friend shows his inmost heart to his friend; the lover to his best beloved; when man does not vainly shrink from the eye of his Creator, loathsomely treasuring up the secret of his sin; then deem me a monster, for the symbol beneath which I have lived, and die! I look around me, and, lo! on every visage a Black Veil!"

Nathaniel Hawthorne, "The Minister's Black Veil"

"For, comparatively inexperienced as you are, my dear young friend, did you never observe how little, very little, confidence, there is? I mean between man and man—more particularly between stranger and stranger. In a sad world it is the saddest fact. Confidence! I have sometimes almost thought that confidence is fled; that confidence is the New Astrea—emigrated—vanished—gone." Then softly sliding nearer, with the softest air, quivering down and looking up, "Could you now, my dear young sir, under such circumstances, by way of experiment, simply have confidence in me?"

Herman Melville, The Confidence-Man: His Masquerade

We live amid surfaces, and the true art of life is to skate well on them.

Ralph Waldo Emerson, "Experience"

Contents

List of Illustrations

All illustrations furnished courtesy of The Newberry Library, Chicago.

Preface

The Victorians, according to Lytton Strachey and other more objective historians of nineteenth-century England, were hypocrites. As a generation, they were true to the example set by Dickens's famous fictional hypocrite, Mr. Pecksniff: they sacrificed sincerity for bourgeois propriety, claimed to be moral and pious in ways they were not, and shut their eyes to whatever was ugly and unpleasant around them. On Sundays, these nineteenth-century Pharisees attended church though they had lost all religious faith, and on Mondays, they returned to the service of Mammon and resumed without scruple their exploitative economic activities. And while spending their days professing allegiance to the sexual ideals of purity and self-restraint, Victorian men spent their nights prowling through the underworld of prostitution and sexual deviancy revealed in the pages of Victorian pornography. "Was the whole age a hollow sham?" asks W. L. Burn in *The Age of Equipoise*. "It would not be difficult to produce evidence for the argument that it was; that the habit of church attendance, the use of religious phraseology, the overt practice of the conventional abstinences were no more than a veneer over sadism and lust and greed; essential to a good reputation among the pushing middle-classes and an assistance to professional success."[1] Anxious to make their mark in an age of dramatic industrial capitalist development, hemmed in by the rigorous demands of bourgeois propriety, and afflicted by at least as much innate depravity as the vilest Puritan who ever lived, nineteenth-century English men and women simply became hypocrites.[2]

Influenced by this view of English Victorianism, historians of American Victorianism have defined sentimentalism, the cult of feelings that dominated middle-class literature and culture from 1830 to 1870, as a form of hypocrisy. Sentimentalism, they argue, was a technique for evading the harsh social realities of expansive industrial capitalism. While romanticism, according to E. Douglas Branch, recognizes reality, passes judgment on it, and clings nonetheless to myth, sentimentalism refuses to recognize reality or is unable to pass judgment on it, and then clings to myth. In the view of Ann Douglas, sentimentalism "asserts that the values a society's activity denies are precisely the ones it cherishes. . . . The sentimentalization of theological and secular culture was an inevitable part of the self-evasion of a society both committed to laissez-faire industrial expansion and disturbed by its consequences." In shaping their culture around sentimental platitudes, these historians have suggested, the American middle classes indulged in bourgeois self-congratulation and endeavored to disguise the evils of the nineteenth-century industrial social order they were helping to usher in.[3]

One noted historian of English Victorianism has, however, pointed to a flaw in this critique of nineteenth-century middle-class culture. No twentieth-century attack on Victorian hypocrisy can match the intensity of the Victorian self-condemnation. "Of all Victorian attitudes," Walter E. Houghton writes, "none was so often attacked by the Victorians themselves as hypocrisy."[4] And those who charge themselves with this offense are not easily convicted. Hypocrisy may or may not have been the primary offense of the English Victorians, but, as Houghton clearly demonstrates, hypocrisy was regarded by them as a critical problem. This problem as defined by the Victorians themselves assumes particular significance for the study of nineteenth-century American middle-class culture, for American Victorians condemned hypocrisy as a major social threat. In the vast literature of advice on personal conduct published in America after 1830, middle-class concerns about the problem of hypocrisy assumed the form of an extended attack on two archetypal hypocrites, the confidence man and the painted woman. Antebellum advice manuals warned young men against joining the ranks of the confidence man, who prowled the streets of American cities in search of innocent victims to deceive, dupe, and destroy. Advice books, fashion magazines, and etiquette manuals cautioned young women against emulating the arts of the painted woman, sometimes a prostitute but more often a woman of fashion, who poisoned polite society with deception and betrayal by dressing extravagantly and practicing the empty forms of false etiquette. The hypocrisy of the confidence man and the painted woman did not lie simply in a discrepancy between what they practiced and what they preached. Their art, as depicted in the conduct-of-life literature, was far more subtle: they could manipulate facial expression, manner, and personal appearance in a calculated effort to lure the guileless into granting them confidence. The fear of hypocrisy expressed in mid-nineteenth-century conduct manuals ran deep: these archetypal hypocrites threatened ultimately, by undermining social confidence among men and women, to reduce the American republic to social chaos.

The first major question I address is not Why were American Victorians hypocrites? but rather, Why did nineteenth-century conduct manuals represent hypocrisy, personified in the confidence man and the painted woman, as a major threat to American society? The conduct manuals were aimed at an audience of aspiring men and women who hoped to fulfill the promise of the allegedly open society of Jacksonian America, either by entering the ranks of the middle class from below or by rising within those ranks to higher and higher levels of gentility. Published largely in the major urban centers of the Northeast, they were aimed more specifically at those who sought their social fortunes in the booming cities of the young nation. The problem of hypocrisy symbolized by the confidence man and the painted woman arose out of a crisis of social identity faced by these men and women who were on the move both socially and geographically. In what was believed to be a fluid social world where no one occupied a fixed social position, the question "Who am I?" loomed large; and in an urban social world where many of the people who met face-to-face each day were strangers, the question "Who are you really?" assumed even greater significance. In an open, urban society, the powerful images of the confidence man and the painted woman expressed the deep concern of status-conscious social climbers that they themselves and those around them were "passing" for something they were not.

The second major question I consider is, How did the conduct manuals propose to meet the dangerous threat of hypocrisy to their readers' social lives? The figures of the confidence man and the painted woman were offered as antitypes of proper conduct in mid-nineteenth-century America. Throughout the hundreds of advice books, etiquette manuals, fashion magazines, and mourning guides published in the antebellum period ran one central dictum: proper conduct was to demonstrate above all a perfect sincerity or "transparency" of character. In response to the poisonous hypocrisy being spread by the confidence man and the painted woman, the conduct manuals concocted a sentimental antidote in the personal ideal of sincerity. More important, they insisted that the social forms and rituals adhered to in "polite society," where the proper people met face-to-face, ensure the sincerity of all participants. This insistence on the sincerity of formal social behavior among middle-class Americans defined sentimental "culture" in the broadest sense of the term. In response to the hypocrisy they saw operating in the marketplaces and streets of the city, the arbiters of genteel conduct in sentimental America determined to ensure perfect sincerity in the society of the middle-class parlor.

The first section of this study (chapters 1 and 2) explores the social origins of the problem of hypocrisy as personified in the evil figure of the confidence man as he appeared in conduct-of-life literature from 1830 to 1860. The confidence man is examined as a symbolic expression of two social problems facing ambitious men and women in antebellum America: the problem of establishing and recognizing social identity in a republic based theoretically on the boundless potential of each individual, and the problem of securing success in the anonymous "world of strangers" that was the antebellum city. The second section (chapters 3, 4, and 5) examines the cultural effort to resolve the problem of hypocrisy with the sentimental ideal of sincerity, which shaped genteel codes of dress, etiquette, and social ritual during the antebellum period. The last section (chapter 6, the conclusion, and the epilogue) examines the decline of the sentimental ideal of personal conduct after midcentury, summarizes the social significance of sentimental culture during its ascendancy, and follows the image of the confidence man in American success mythology into the twentieth century.

This book is not a social history of the urban middle classes, although it does draw on the work of the new social historians on nineteenth-century social mobility. What follows is a cultural history of the sentimental ideal of social conduct that defined in essentially moral terms what it was to be middle-class in the antebellum period. Popular advice manuals offered social aspirants a "sincerity" system, composed of hundreds of rules for polite conduct in proper parlor society and designed to establish the legitimacy of their claims to genteel standing. By donning "sincere" dress, adhering to "sincere" forms of courtesy, and practicing "sincere" bereavement, the socially ambitious could demonstrate that they were not mere confidence men and painted women "passing" as genteel, but were true ladies and gentlemen deserving of the higher social place to which they aspired. The sentimental ideal of sincerity that shaped the norms of middle-class conduct in the antebellum period was central to the self-conscious self-definition of middle-class culture during the most critical period of its development.

To support the point that the "Age of Equipoise" might be condemned as "a hollow sham," W. L. Burn offers a portrait in Victorian hypocrisy that puts Mr. Pecksniff's example to shame:

> William Palmer, the Rugeley poisoner, a man without pity or remorse, was a regular attender at church and a subscriber to a missionary society. His wife, whom it can scarcely be doubted he poisoned for the sake of the insurance moneys payable on her death, died on September 24, 1854; on Sunday October 8th he attended church and took communion; almost exactly nine months later his maid-servant bore a child to him.[5]

Like the moustache-twirling, black-caped villain of late Victorian melodrama, Palmer the Rugeley poisoner was undoubtedly a hypocrite. American Victorianism also produced an exemplary hypocrite in the Reverend Henry Ward Beecher, who, after vigorously condemning the blandishments of the seducer in an advice manual for young men, himself seduced (how thoroughly is not entirely clear) a Mrs. Elizabeth Tilton of his congregation.[6] The hypocrisy of either of these notorious Victorians can scarcely be challenged. But the hypocrisy of American sentimental culture in the nineteenth century is far more open to question. For at the heart of the sentimental value system was a deep fear of the hypocrisy that was believed to be poisoning American social relations. The broadest significance of sentimental culture between 1830 and 1870 lay in the powerful middle-class impulse to shape all social forms into sincere expressions of inner feeling. Whether or not twentieth-century historians of Victorian America can or should charge sentimentalists with hypocrisy in any ultimate moral sense, they should recognize the powerful anxieties of nineteenth-century middle-class Americans concerning the problem of hypocrisy in an open, urban society. Those anxieties were central to the emergence of genteel social forms during an important period in the development of American middle-class culture.

My greatest thanks go to John L. Thomas, whose superb teaching and scholarship first stimulated my interest in antebellum American culture; and to David B. Davis, who supervised this project in its early stages and whose brilliant critical scrutiny benefited it at every step. For helpful suggestions and readings of various drafts along the way, I am grateful to Sydney E. Ahlstrom, Burton J. Bledstein, T. H. Breen, William K. Breitenbach, Nancy F. Cott, George M. Fredrickson, Joseph F. Kett, Edmund S. Morgan, George H. Roeder, Jr., Carl S. Smith, David Van Zanten, and Gordon S. Wood. Robert H. Wiebe's penetrating criticism and advice have proved invaluable. For financial assistance of various kinds, I am indebted to the Whiting Foundation, the Northwestern University Research Grants Committee, and the Northwestern Department of History. I am grateful to The Newberry Library for permission to use the illustrations in this volume and to Peter Weil for taking the photographs. At Yale University Press, I would like to thank my editor, Charles Grench, and my copy editor, Barbara Hofmaier.

Jane H. Hunter, Lucy K. Marks, Debra Raskin, and Michael L. Smith have offered help in countless ways and have always been there when I needed them. To B. J. T. Dobbs and Sarah Maza, I am grateful for their guidance and encouragement during the final writing stages. Finally, I would like to thank my parents, Nancy E. Halttunen and Olavi H. Halttunen, and my sister, Lisa M. Halttunen, for their support and their unwavering faith throughout several decades of my education.

The Era of the Confidence Man

During the first half of the nineteenth century, unprecedented numbers of young men were leaving their rural homes and families to seek work in the booming cities of industrializing America. As thousands of young Americans broke away from traditional restraints on their conduct, middle-class moralists began to grow alarmed. Who would guide the conduct of America's rising generation as they wandered far beyond the surveillance of their families, their towns, and their churches? After 1830, a number of clergymen, teachers, and sentimental writers confronted the moral problem generated by this mass migration in dozens of manuals of advice to American youth. In these manuals, they offered advice on manners, morals, personal appearance, mental development, and work habits; they instructed their readers where to live, what to eat, how to entertain themselves, and when and whom to marry. Their books were enormously popular; William A. Alcott's *Young Man's Guide*, first published in 1833, had gone through twenty-one editions by 1858, and the first edition of Daniel Eddy's *Young Man's Friend* sold ten thousand copies. By 1857, Albert Barnes noted "the unusual number of books that are addressed particularly to young men." More specifically, the advice manuals were addressed to the youth between the ages of fourteen and twenty-five who had just left home and now stood poised on the threshold of a new life in the city.[1]

In a very literal sense, antebellum advice literature focused on that moment when the inexperienced young man first set foot in the city. As Eugene Arden has observed, the literary image of the

1

raw but ambitious youth striding into the city achieved legendary proportions in the nineteenth century: "Knapsack in hand, clothing coarse and homespun, the bloom of outdoor health on his cheeks, the rustic hero entered [the city] to seek fame and fortune."[2] The imaginative power of this image owed much to one of the greatest moments in American autobiography, when a dirty runaway apprentice named Benjamin Franklin awkwardly entered colonial Philadelphia with two large bread rolls tucked under his arms and a third fast disappearing down his throat.[3] But nineteenth-century advice writers added a significant new dimension to this powerful image. In the pages of antebellum advice manuals, the youth just entering the city was immediately approached by a confidence man:

> The moment the inexperienced youth sets his foot on the sidewalk of the city, he is marked and watched by eyes that he never dreamed of. The boy who cries his penny-paper, and the old woman at her table professedly selling a few apples and a little gingerbread, are not all who watch him. There is the seducer in the shape of the young man who came before him, and who has already lost the last remains of shame. There is the hardened pander to vice who has as little remorse at the ruin of innocence as the alligator has in crushing the bones of the infant that is thrown into his jaws from the banks of the Ganges: and there is she—who was once the pride and hope of her parents—who now makes war upon virtue and exults in being a successful recruiting-officer of hell.[4]

Although the term *confidence man* does not appear in the advice manuals, it accurately identifies the villain of the piece. The seducer—whether rake or pimp, gambler or thief—begins his assault on the innocent youth by winning his confidence through an offer of friendship and entertainment. In the classic antebellum tale of seduction, he then leads the youth into a gorgeous theater—the seducer's natural habitat, for he himself is a skilled actor. He takes him to a fashionable club where he coaxes his prey into accepting his fatal first drink and gradually draws him into a card game. Finally, he lures his victim to a brothel where, if the theater and the alcohol and the gambling have failed to win him to a life of vice, illicit sexuality succeeds. The youth's character has been destroyed, step by fatal step, because he has been tricked into offering his confidence to a man without principle, a man whose art it is to deceive others through false appearances.

The figure of the confidence man was not entirely new within American success mythology. A century before he made his appearance in the antebellum advice manuals, he had approached Ben Franklin in the person of Governor Keith of Philadelphia, who falsely promised to set up the naive youth as the colony's printer. Franklin also met up with some confidence women on a boat to New York, two friendly young ladies who turned out to be thieves.[5] But Franklin's deceivers, unlike their nineteenth-century counterparts, did not deliberately direct their confidence games toward the total destruction of the young man's character. What distinguished the nineteenth-century confidence man was his position at the center of the anxieties that advice manuals expressed about American youth. Henry Ward Beecher, in the introduction to his *Lectures to Young Men*, stated clearly that his entire purpose in writing the manual was to warn American youth against the arts of the seducer:

> Having watched the courses of those who seduce the young— their arts, their blandishments, their pretences;—having witnessed the beginning and consummation of ruin, almost in the same year, of many young men, naturally well disposed, whose downfall began with the appearance of innocence; I felt an earnest desire, if I could, to raise the suspicion of the young, and to direct their reason to the arts by which they are, with such facility, destroyed.[6]

In the nineteenth century, the raw country youth entering the city to seek his fortune was coming to symbolize the American-on-the-make. And in the central drama of antebellum advice literature, that inexperienced young man had just set foot in the city when he was approached by a confidence man seeking to dupe and destroy him. Why did this archetypal villain pop out of the shadows just as the American youth entered the city in search of fame and fortune? What were the symbolic connections between the youth's effort to rise in the world and the confidence man's evil game? A full understanding of popular American attitudes toward social mobility during the "era of the common man" must begin with a careful examination of the many layers of meaning conveyed in the image of the confidence man.

In their efforts to warn youthful readers against the evil power of the confidence man, the manuals offered a detailed picture of how the confidence game worked. The game depended, first of all, on the malleability of the youthful character. Within prevailing Lockean psychology, the youth's character was like a lump of soft wax, completely susceptible to any impressions stamped upon him: "Everything leaves its impress on the young: the countenances they look at, the voices they hear, the places they visit, the company they keep, and the books they read."[7] The term *character*, in fact, could apply not to the lump of wax itself but to the impression made upon it: "The primary meaning of the word *character* is a mark made by cutting or engraving on any substance, as wood, stone, or metal. Hence, as applied to man, it signifies the marks or impressions made upon the mind."[8] The youth was said to be especially vulnerable to impressions made by the company he kept: "Young men, to an extent greater or less, are chameleon-like. They take a tinge, so to speak, from the company they keep; especially if it is *much* kept. Nay, they are often affected for life by the society of an individual for merely half an hour."[9] This susceptibility to the mark of his companions was reinforced by the inexperienced youth's confiding nature. Because he had known only the open trust of the domestic circle, he was "generous and confiding. He mingles feelings without suspicion, and is ready to believe all sincere who proffer him their friendship."[10] Malleable and confiding by nature, the youth proved easy prey.

The confidence man acted upon the waxen character of his youthful victim through a mysterious force called influence. Within the sentimental culture of Victorian America, influence was believed to be the power by which any person's character affected the characters of others, for good as well as for evil.[11] "You will have *associates*," David Magie told his readers, "and you will feel their influence." He continued, "The link is mysterious which binds human beings together, so that the heart of one answers to the heart of another, like the return of an echo; but such a link exists. . . . The influence is often silent and unperceived, like the rolling in of a wave in a quiet sea; but like that same wave it is mighty and resistless."[12] As a force for good, influence was spoken of as a moral gravitation, a personal electricity, a cosmic vibration. But as a force for evil, influence was compared to a poison, a disease, a source of contamination and corruption. The impressions made by wicked companions were "like poison, taken into the physical system, and will be sure, sooner or later, to reveal its bitter results."[13] Henry Ward Beecher expressed his horror lest his son fall under the libertine's influence by saying he would "rather see him rot in a lazar-house, than putrify with such corruption."[14] The "very presence" of the profligate was said to be "polluting to the soul."[15] In fact, so powerful was the force of evil influence that a young man could be contaminated merely walking the streets:

> Feel as they may, contact with evil it is impossible to avoid. If they walk the streets of the city, or tread the floors of the hall, it is to see sights, and hear sounds, and be subjected to influences, all of which, gradually and imperceptibly, but surely and permanently, are drawing the lines of deformity on their hearts.[16]

This belief in the contaminating powers of influence owed much to the popular pseudoscience of mesmerism and to the miasmic theories of the cholera epidemics that swept the United States in 1832 and 1849.[17] The licentious man was said to be "a pestilence in the community" who could infect everyone around him because "his breath blights every innocent thing."[18]

Although simple contact with evil was enough to begin the ruin of youthful character, the confidence game worked not simply through contagion but through seduction. The confidence man launched his seduction subtly: "The young are seldom tempted to outright wickedness; evil comes to them as an enticement."[19] His skill in enticing his victim rested on his mastery of the art of disguise; the "seducer was a man of wealth and fashion, and professed to take a deep interest in the youth, and to be anxious to promote his welfare. He had a pleasant address, was mild and courteous in his manner,—but within him was the spirit of a fiend."[20] After introducing his victim to a few attractive and apparently innocent pleasures, the seducer drew him farther and farther into sin. "From pleasures which may be termed innocent, to those deeply criminal, there is an approximation which is not the less fatal because it is gradual and unperceived. There is a sort of shading off in this criminal process of seduction that keeps the mind inattentive to its progress from comparative innocence to the dark and deepening colors of guilt."[21] The confidence man knew exactly how to lure his victim from one stage of guilt to the next, because he was a master of human psychology, who specialized in the passions and caprices of youth: "These wild gushes of feeling, peculiar to youth, the sagacious tempter has felt, has studied, has practiced upon, until he can sit before that most capacious organ, the human mind, knowing every stop and all the combinations, and competent to touch every note throughout the diapason."[22]

The object of the confidence man's game was thus not simply to corrupt the youth, but to achieve total mastery over him. The youth was warned that "the first sacrifice of conscience and principle is like Samson giving up his locks,"[23] and once these were gone, he had lost all power of self-mastery. He was "ensnared," "taken captive." "He may, in his moments of meditation and remorse, strive to tear the manacles from his limbs, and break the chains that bind him to his cruel task-masters [bad habits]." But he was helpless before the power of the "tyrant vice."[24] In Beecher's view, the young men who fell under the power of the confidence man were the victims of a monstrous breed of slave traders:

> Men there are, who, without a pang or gleam of remorse, will coolly wait for character to rot, and health to sink, and means to melt, that they may suck up the last drop of the victim's blood. . . . The agony of midnight massacre, the phrenzy of the ship's dungeon, the living death of the middle passage, the wails of separation, and the dismal torpor of hopeless servitude—are these found only in the piracy of the slave-trade? They are all among US! worse assassinations! worse dragging to a prison-ship! worse groans ringing from the fetid hold! worse separations of families! worse bondage of intemperate men, enslaved by that most inexorable of all taskmasters—sensual habit![25]

From that first enticement through the many subtle stages of deepening guilt, the confidence man had one ultimate purpose: the total enslavement of his victim.

To what extent did advice literature confront a real flesh-and-blood villain in the confidence man? The term *confidence man* was probably first coined by the New York press in 1849 during coverage of the arrest of a swindler named William Thompson. Thompson was a man of genteel appearance whose trick was to approach a gentleman on the street, chat with him briefly, and then ask whether he had the confidence to lend his watch to a stranger. Upon being handed the watch, Thompson walked off laughing. In this fashion, he succeeded in tricking several New Yorkers out of expensive gold watches before being spotted one day by a previous victim, named Thomas McDonald, who apparently did not share the trickster's sense of humor and had him thrown into the Tombs. In its extensive coverage of Thompson's case, the press suggested that he was not the only criminal of this kind operating in the city.[26] In 1857, Herman Melville published his own fictional confidence game, *The Confidence-Man: His Masquerade* (which may have been inspired in part by the Thompson case), and one reviewer noted that America was filled with confidence men: "One of the indigenous characters who has figured long in our journals, courts, and cities, is 'the Confidence Man'; his doings form one of the staples of villainy, and an element in the romance of roguery. Countless are the dodges attributed to this ubiquitous personage."[27] Two years later, the notoriety of this breed of criminal achieved recognition in *The Rogue's Lexicon*, a dictionary of crime published by the *National Police Gazette*.[28] But the most reliable evidence that confidence men did in fact roam American cities in the mid-nineteenth century lies in police records. A survey of New York police captains in the 1860s estimated that of 2,500 professional criminals in the city, 100 were confidence men operating games such as the "Spanish Prisoner" racket; another 100 were "damper sneaks," men who posed as businessmen and engaged in elaborate negotiations or simply loitered around places of business to steal unguarded bonds and cash; and 25 were forgers.[29] Police thus estimated that nearly one out of ten professional criminals in New York in the 1860s was a confidence man. The proliferation of moveable wealth, especially negotiable paper, in the early nineteenth century, and the growing confusion and anonymity of urban living, had made possible for the first time a wide variety of swindles, frauds, forgeries, counterfeiting activities, and other confidence games.[30] Ironically, the new law-enforcement officer who emerged during this period to handle this sophisticated new breed of urban crime himself often resorted to the arts of the confidence man. The police detective was said to be "dishonest, crafty, unscrupulous, when necessary to be so. He tells black lies when he cannot avoid it, and white lying, at least, is his chief stock in trade. He is the outgrowth of a diseased and corrupted state of things, and is, consequently, morally diseased himself."[31]

The most notorious and possibly the most numerous class of confidence men were the gamblers. In 1825, the first successful gambling house in New York City opened, and by 1835, the New York *Herald* could report that "there is a small and select number of very splendid hells in this city where young men with property are sent to perdition in no time."[32] Policemen and politicians learned to look the other way as professional sharpers set up operation all over the city and enjoyed between 1835 and the Civil War their most prosperous period in New York history. "Thimble-riggers, Three-Card-Monte throwers and other sure-thing tricksters worked openly in the streets."[33] Most houses cheated, and some establishments known as "second-class skinning houses" operated only when a "sucker" was on hand. To keep a steady stream of suckers coming to their tables, many houses employed "steerers" or "ropers in," "men of considerable address" who "make a flashy-genteel appearance, very impressive and taking with greenhorns."[34] "They worm themselves into the confidence of strangers; show them every thing worth seeing in the city; and finally introduce them to their employers, the gambling-house proprietors."[35] Given the skill of these and other confidence men, it is not surprising that nineteenth-century urban guidebooks warned newcomers to beware "the goodnatured civilities of persons you have never seen before. Gratuitous offers of assistance or advice, or good fellowship, are suspicious, to say the least. Do not be persuaded to go anywhere with these casual acquaintances."[36]

When antebellum advice manuals delivered similar warnings against "the goodnatured civilities of persons you have never seen before," their concerns for youthful readers were clearly grounded in reality. But the villain whose confidence game was so elaborately described in the advice manuals was far more dangerous than the "watch-stuffer," the "damp sneak," or the "steerer." In the confidence game, an impressionable youth fell under the power of a villain who corrupted his character, enticed him into a life of vice, and finally reduced him to slavery. The intellectual framework of this nineteenth-century melodrama was eighteenth-century republican ideology. At the center of the radical Whiggism that had fueled the American Revolution was the belief that politics was fundamentally a matter of the disposition of power, which meant "the dominion of some men over others, the human control of human life: ultimately force, compulsion."[37] The central characteristic of power was its aggressiveness; it preyed on liberty, which was fundamentally passive, vulnerable. Radical Whigs were obsessed with the intoxicating desire of men for domination over others. In itself, they believed, power was not evil, but it was made malignant by the nature of man. No man could withstand the corrupting effect of power, which acted like a strong liquor on those who held it. If corrupt rulers were suffered to encroach upon the liberty of the people, they soon became tyrants and reduced the people to slavery. To eighteenth-century republicans, slavery meant "a force put upon humane nature, by which a man is obliged to act, or not to act, according to the arbitrary will and pleasure of another."[38] But the people had one sure defense against enslavement by tyrants: their virtue. So long as they practiced the republican virtues of industry, sobriety, frugality, and simplicity, their liberty was safe. Once they were corrupted by the poisonous love of luxury, their vigilant watch over their liberty would relax and they would be reduced to slavery. The republican mind-set was highly conspiratorial: within their paranoiac fear of encroachments against their liberty, American Whigs interpreted all events as part of a systematic plot to corrupt and enslave them.[39]

All the major elements of eighteenth-century republican ideology—the struggle between liberty and power, the danger of corruption and decay, the ultimate threat of tyranny and enslavement—were present in the nineteenth-century confidence game. In it, the passive liberty of the American youth falls victim to the self-aggrandizing power of the confidence man. The youth loses his liberty because he surrenders his vigilance and abandons his republican virtue for a riotous life of luxury and sin. Once the liberty of the rising generation was lost, the advice writers feared, the American republic would be in grave danger. Along with eighteenth-century republicans, the advice writers believed that the republic "depends upon the personal character we individually possess. There is no charm in free institutions to sustain themselves and to bless a nation. Liberty, where the individual is the slave of his neighbor's opinion, or still worse, of his own passions and appetites, is a mere sound."[40] America was passing through a critical period when its character was not yet formed, "and great are the responsibilities that rest upon her, and critical the trial through which she must pass."[41] Since the Revolution, Americans had stressed that what made a republic great was the character and spirit of its people. The ultimate threat of the confidence man was thus his power to subvert the American republican experiment.

The writers of advice to young men were addressing a generation of Americans deeply anxious about the future of the republic: "No sooner did Americans create their Union than they began to speculate fretfully about how long it would last."[42] As the self-proclaimed sons of the nation's founding fathers, many Americans in the first half of the nineteenth century felt a powerful sense of their responsibility to preserve their inheritance of liberty and transmit it to future generations. But after John Adams and Thomas Jefferson died on the fiftieth anniversary of American independence, the American people entered what George Forgie has called the post-heroic age, and began to fear that they were betraying the sacred trust bequeathed to them.[43] Themes of doom and decline and vivid rhetorical images of a violent breakdown of social order began to dominate discussions of the state of the republic.[44] "Countersubversion movements," dedicated to exposing the enemies of American liberty, began to accuse groups such as Masons, Mormons, and Catholics of secretly plotting to overthrow the republic.[45] Andrew Jackson's war against the Bank was presented as part of a larger struggle to protect republican values against betrayal by a conspiratorial "money power," which used "ill-gotten gains to corrupt and dominate the plain republican order."[46] The fatal disease of luxury, it was widely feared, was once again contaminating the character of the American people. "Should our grand experiment of self-government ultimately fail," said Lauren Persus Hickok, a professor at Union College, "it will doubtless be because our prosperity is greater than our virtue can bear."[47] In the midst of this crisis, Americans came to believe that the republic's only chance for survival lay in the character of the rising generation. As George Forgie has argued, "The connection between child rearing and the future of the Republic elevated child rearing to a concern of the highest order."[48] Significantly, in the 1840s, Americans began to refer to the republic itself as a growing youth. "Republicanism," as Gordon Wood has observed, "was the concomitant of youth," just as monarchy and aristocracy were the product of age and social decay.[49] The American Revolution had been the nation's season of youth, which had to be preserved if nineteenth-century Americans were to ensure the survival of the republic.[50] The spectre of the confidence man was very compelling to antebellum Americans. The confidence game was not simply a literary device intended to persuade young men not to consort with gamblers and dandies and pimps. It was a symbolic expression of deeper fears about the direction of American society. But what was the nature of the crisis confronting the new nation? The confidence game played on eighteenth-century republican fears about the threat of self-aggrandizing power. Exactly what kinds of power were represented by the nineteenth-century image of the confidence man? Who was this alleged villain who lurked in the dark corners of society plotting to corrupt and enslave American youth and thus bring down the republic? By nature, the confidence man defied social definition; he was a man of shifting masks and roles, without fixed status or profession. But for purposes of discussion, three types of confidence men may be distinguished that suggest more specifically what kinds of power this villain represented: the youth's urban companion, the demagogue, and the gambler. With these three portraits, the advice writers revealed the nineteenth-century meaning behind their eighteenth-century republican drama by expressing implicitly their concerns about the major social, political, and economic forces transforming the American nation in their own time.

The most common portrait was the youth's urban companion. He was the stranger who approached the young man just entering the city, at the precise moment when all familial and communal restraints were falling away. The urban stranger began his confidence game with an offer of friendship: "Practiced in the arts of temptation, they make a gradual advance upon the ingenuous and unsuspecting youth. They insinuate themselves into his confidence and friendship."[51] Because he knew his way around the city, this stranger proved attractive to his innocent victim, who soon began to defer to him:

> Drawn, as they soon are, into fellowship with those who have gone there before them, and accustomed, as they are, to look up to them as their superiors, they naturally conform to their habits and practices, and fall an easy prey to the corrupt and corrupting examples by which they are surrounded. They have not firmness to resist the enticements of depraved companions.[52]

The youth's attractive, witty companion knew how to lead his victim gradually down the steps into corruption without arousing the youth's suspicions until it was too late. With the first sacrifice of principle, the young man was at his seducer's mercy: "He has carried his point; and one breach of obligation, he well knows, will make way for another, until your character and your destiny become identified with his own.[53] The evil companion thus acted as a recruiting agent for the ranks of confidence men. Out of fear of this archetypal false companion, the advisers pleaded with the rising generation to avoid bad company. "If I could persuade you, my reader, to shun bad company as you would the poison that destroys even by contact,—to be more careful of your company than of almost anything else, I should rejoice."[54]

Why did antebellum advice books reflect such anxiety concerning the American youth's companionship in the city? To answer that question it is necessary to examine briefly the mass migration of young men to the city in the late eighteenth and early nineteenth century. In the eighteenth century, the population of the American colonies had resulted at an average rate of 3 percent annually, and this rapid growth had increased in an agricultural crisis, for within the system of partible inheritance, average farm holdings underwent a steady rate of decline. At the same time, the increasing efficiency of technological agriculture reduced the demand for manpower. As a result, many farmers' sons became landless agricultural laborers, craftsmen, or small home manufacturers. Gradually, as regional agricultural specialization spurred the development of commercial cities, alternatives to farming expanded, and thousands of young men swarmed into cities such as Boston, New York, Philadelphia, Rochester, New Haven, and Lowell to work as insurance clerks and brokers, storekeepers and traders, skilled and semiskilled artisans, merchants, professional men, innkeepers, drivers, stablers, and dock hands. With all these push-and-pull factors encouraging the farmer's son's migration, the age at which young men left home began to decline. Between 1750 and 1820, the average age of departure dropped from the mid-twenties to the late teens, despite continued encouragement from parents and counselors that young men stay home until the age of twenty-one. Antebellum advice books, written for young men who had just left their families for the perils of an unsupervised life in the city, often specifically addressed readers as young as fourteen.[55]

In the patriarchal family of the seventeenth and early eighteenth century, the father had exercised great control over the lives of his children, who depended on him for the land and capital goods needed to begin their own families. But as farmers became less able to provide sufficient farm holdings for their sons and as new opportunities opened to young men, the patriarchal family began to lose its power to shape the lives of its children. The demands of the commercializing economy for new financial and technological skills were undermining the traditional paternal task of teaching sons how to make a living, and the family's role as educational institution began to give way to a growing reliance on self-education. Even the apprenticeship system, which had been designed to extend and formalize the family's authority over young men, was in decline. The traditional master-servant relationship had stressed reciprocal obligations of moral watchfulness and deferential obedience, broad educational guidance and personal service, but by the mid-eighteenth century the moral elements of the agreement were disappearing, and by the early nineteenth century the entire system was breaking down under the impact of mercantile capitalism and the factory system. Through the first several decades of the nineteenth century, young men in the cities found themselves increasingly less inhibited by traditional restraints on the social conduct of single workingmen. They were moving out of their rooms above the shops of their masters and into hotels and boarding houses, where their employers could not supervise their leisure activities. In Rochester, New York, in the 1820s and 1830s, home-centered work relations broke down as workingmen were removed from the homes and the domestic discipline of their master craftsmen into working-class neighborhoods, where a lawless disregard for middle-class morality prevailed. Although the Rochester pattern may not have been universal, the gradual breakdown of small shop work-organization was under way in antebellum America. In the early nineteenth-century interval between an apprenticeship system and later institutional structures for containing adolescents, there was "a very real crisis of youth in the nineteenth-century city."[56]

As the ties between family generations weakened and as traditional controls over young workingmen declined, older patterns of social deference were giving way to the new significance of relations between peers. The growing importance of women's friendships between 1780 and 1835, according to Nancy F. Cott, suggests a new sense of the desirability of peer relationships, an ideal that owed much to the egalitarianism of republican ideology and Christian revivalism.[57] But the writers of advice to young men were not nearly so sanguine about peer group contact. The decline of parental and employer authority, they feared, had given free rein to what later generations would call peer pressure. Cut off from the family discipline of their own homes and those of their shop masters, young men were clustering in boarding houses and hotels. With their leisure time freed from employer supervision, they were banding together to attend the theaters, the gambling saloons, and the brothels of the early industrial city. What peer contact meant to middle-class moralists was the moral contamination of innocent young men by their vicious companions. Into the figure of the confidence man as urban associate, the advisers cast broader anxieties about the replacement of traditional, hierarchical social relationships based on deference with peer relations among social equals.

A second type of confidence man set forth in antebellum advice literature was the demagogue, whose game was to profess an interest in the public good in order to disguise and carry out his own selfish purposes. He was a man of shifting faces, a man without fixed principles: "For a profitable popularity he accommodates himself to all opinions, to all dispositions, to every side, and to each prejudice. He is a mirror, with no face of its own, but a smooth surface from which each man of ten thousand may see himself reflected."[58] His aim was to shape the political character of any youth who had failed to form independently his own political opinions, and had thus become "a fit subject for the unprincipled demagogue, to be moulded and managed at his will."[59] One special type of demagogue was the amoral "PARTY MAN," who would lie, slander, place wicked men in office, support the liquor traffic, and even deny his religion, in order to secure victory for his party. The party man was a hypocrite of the deepest dye, a man who had two distinct characters. In his inner character, he was a man of principle, but when he donned his political character, he was a man of deceit:

> All the requisitions of his conscience he obeys in his private character; all the requisitions of his party, he obeys in his political conduct. In one character he is a man of principle; in the other, a man of mere expedients. As a *man* he means to be veracious, honest, moral; as a *politician*, he is deceitful, cunning, unscrupulous,—*anything* for party.[60]

The political confidence man, in his efforts to deceive American youth and mold them into "tools of demagogues," presented a grave threat to the republic.[61] In a republic each citizen was a sovereign and thus needed "the same independence of mind, the same personal virtues, and sense of personal responsibility, as he would if clothed in purple, and wearing a diadem."[62] If the rising generation were to be successfully "moulded" and "managed" by demagogues, their liberty would be lost. And within Jeffersonian political theory, in which land ownership was to protect the independent yeoman from political enslavement to unscrupulous demagogues, this danger was particularly pronounced. The landless young men drifting into the early industrial cities of America seemed to be at the mercy of political confidence men.

Such repeated warnings against the evil machinations of the demagogue reflect an uneasiness with the emergence of mass

politics in Jacksonian America. The early republican period between 1789 and 1840 marked the gradual transition from traditional deferential politics focusing on the political leader to modern
egalitarian politics focusing on the electorate. An eighteenth-
century disapproval of parties as evil associations put together by
factious men bent on self-aggrandizement was giving way to the
more modern view, held by new professional politicans such as
those of the Albany Regency, of parties as democratic associations
providing beneficial political competition. By the end of the 1820s,
the consensus tradition of American politics, defended in a last-
ditch effort by the People's Party of New York, had been utterly
defeated. "By 1840 the parties were so meticulously organized
down into every ward and precinct and were so successful in
mustering the citizenry in huge numbers to the polls that we may
finally speak of the full emergence, in modern terms, of mass
political parties, the first in the world."[63]

The new mass political parties met with great hostility from the
religious community. Pious evangelical conservatives such as Lyman
Beecher and Ezra Stiles Ely had few quarrels with democracy itself,
but they condemned political factionalism for disrupting man's
efforts to establish divine law as the foundation for worldly government. Behind this distrust lay their justifiable fear that politicians
were commanding more public attention than were religious leaders and winning this attention in ways unacceptable to the clergy.
"The whole array of democratic trappings, from chauvinistic drum-
beating to secret bribes, appalled the religious community, used to
the deferential ways of the past."[64] The new professional politician,
as depicted by Lyman Beecher's son, Henry Ward Beecher, was
selfish, godless, and unprincipled.

The demagogue's confidence game was most dangerous, however, not because he was personally wicked, but because his authority over the American people rested illegitimately in his direct
appeal to a slavish political mob. His "insidious attacks" were directed at the "multitude, ignorant, prejudiced, inflamed and infuri-
ated by unseen guides, till they trample on law, order, property and
life."[65] In condemning the demagogue's appeal to the mob, the
advisers expressed deep concern about what Alexis de Tocqueville
called the "tyranny of the majority": "And is this a condition of
liberty, to hold my property, my opinions, my life, subservient to
the dictates of the mass; let those dictates be what they will? No!"[66]
More than this, however, the figure of the demagogue reflected

concern about the new professional men whose business was to exploit that tyranny for selfish ends. This critique rested not simply on the emergence of partisan politics in the Age of Jackson, but on the massive transformation in the social relations of power that accompanied the new politics. In the 1820s and 1830s, political success increasingly demanded new techniques for organizing a mass electorate through patronage and manipulating the party press, techniques that contributed steadily to the nationalization of the power of the majority. In the new era of mass politics, political power flowed out of local communities and state capitals into the national arena.[67] As professional politicians learned to shape public opinion, various groups in American society began to oppose what they saw as an illegitimate and dangerous manipulation of the ignorant masses from the national level. One example of this resistance was the early Whig opposition to Jackson's bank veto of 1832 as an act of executive usurpation that infringed "upon the accustomed powers of established, locally based political leaders."[68] Significantly, Jackson's veto had been addressed not to the legislature or to the Court, but directly to the voters themselves, while the proto-Whig response appealed to the authority of established political leaders. Another example of local opposition to the nationalization of public opinion were the anti-abolitionist mobs of the 1830s. The "gentlemen of property and standing" who led these mobs feared that the manipulation of national public opinion by the abolitionist press threatened to usurp local control by appealing directly to an emotionally susceptible people without deference to local authorities.[69] For the writers of antebellum advice literature, too, the dangerous direction of American politics seemed equally clear: hypnotic, charismatic demagogues were rising up to enslave a generation of American youth for selfish, unprincipled gain. Through the art of the confidence game, they were usurping the prerogative of local authorities to shape the character of the rising generation, and in so doing they were threatening to destroy the American republic.

A third common form assumed by the confidence man of antebellum advice manuals was the gambler. The gambler, like his two evil fellows, was regarded as a serious competitor for the power of influence over the rising generation, and so horrible was his influence that one clerical adviser expressed the graphic wish to see his son die rather than fall victim to this confidence man:

Rather than have a child of mine seduced by the flatteries and black treachery of these foul destroyers, I would see him struggling with death—his eye sinking, his breast heaving, his heart throbbing—throbbing with its last pulsations. . . . I would return from his grave thankful that he rests,—*rests* there, rather than lives to mingle with gambling fiends, to feel the damning influence of their oaths and curses, and to imbibe their horrible principles.[70]

The gambler's confidence game was unvarying: he approached the unsuspecting youth with a smile and an offer of friendship, lured him into granting him confidence, drew him gradually into fashionable gambling society, and then thoroughly fleeced him. But the evil of gambling was not simply that young men could be cheated out of all their worldly goods at the card table. Gambling was evil because it produced nothing: "In gambling, it is true, property is shifted from one individual to another, and here and there one probably gains more than he loses; but nothing is actually *made*, or *produced*."[71] In fact, gambling undermined all desire to practice industry, for the gambler inevitably came "to regard the moderate but constant and certain rewards of industrious exertion as insipid."[72] Because it brought gain without production and without industry through a game of chance, gambling was a kind of speculation: "Indeed, a Speculator on the exchange, and a Gambler at his table, follow one vocation, only with different instruments."[73]

Into the image of the confidence man as gambler, the advisers cast their antipathy for capitalist speculation. Speculation, Henry Ward Beecher warned his readers, was a game of skill that produced nothing of benefit, but instead encouraged an aversion to steady industry. Even worse, the reckless speculator, like the gambler, cheated himself and those around him: "He defrauds himself, his family, the community in which he dwells; for all these have an interest in that property."[74] By encouraging fraud, speculation undermined the "principle of *mutual confidence*"[75] upon which commerce rested. And it was commerce alone that bound all human society together, just as "the great law of gravitation"[76] bound together the world of matter. God had created commerce "for the development of the benevolence and all the noble qualities of the human heart."[77] But the archetypal speculator, the gambler, was the "cool, calculating, essential *spirit* of concentrated avaricious selfishness."[78] When this speculative spirit of pure selfishness ran amuck and produced a panic in 1837, then the ties of commercial benevolence were completely severed, as debtors wrote tricky pledges and cheated their creditors: "Fidelity seemed to have forsaken men. Many that had earned a reputation for sterling honesty were cast so suddenly headlong into wickedness, that man shrank from man. Suspicion overgrew confidence, and the heart bristled with the nettles and thorns of fear and jealousy."[79]

Behind this extended attack on the gambler/speculator lay an uneasiness with the dramatic expansion of the American market economy in the first decades of the nineteenth century. After 1790, success in the export sector stimulated urbanization, and growing urban demands for foodstuffs and labor began to draw people out of self-sufficiency into the money economy. After 1815, the transportation revolution made possible greater regional specialization and the growth of interregional trade. The scope of the domestic market expanded as the West produced food, the South grew cotton, and the Northeast provided banking services, insurance, brokerage, transport, manufacturing, imports, and, most important, capital. As the growth of the national market stimulated manufacturing in New England and the Mid-Atlantic states, capital shifted from shipping into textiles; increasing social overhead investments were made in transportation facilities, banking, insurance, and warehousing; and a distribution system for imports developed. In the expanding domestic market of early nineteenth-century America, speculative economic activity was rapidly on the rise.[80]

In their moral opposition to games of chance, the advice writers presented a critique of capitalistic speculation, a critique rooted in the *mentalité* of the Northern agricultural society of pre-industrial America. The populations of the small rural communities of the eighteenth century, as James A. Henretta has argued, did not display the strong entrepreneurial mentality attributed to them by previous historians of colonial New England. In the small eighteenth-century towns, the lack of transportation and of markets made subsistence the primary way of life and thus necessarily circumscribed human goals. Without a market for his surplus, the eighteenth-century farmer lacked any real incentive to produce more than he could sell locally. In the absence of an external market, the system of exchange was predominantly local and usually involved direct exchange not for profit but for the acquisition of necessities. The basic social unit of production, of capital formation, and of property transmission was the family, which was defined along extended intergenerational lines. The eighteenth-century agricultural emphasis on the welfare of the family line, Henretta argues, inhibited the emergence of economic individualism, and local face-to-face economic exchange was directed largely toward the maintenance of the community's established social relationships.[81]

In the early nineteenth century, this limited economic exchange, which was integrally tied up with the social relationships of the family and the immediate community, was giving way to an expanding market economy that appeared to many Americans as a giant, threatening game of hazard. Jacksonian Democrats succeeded in harnessing some of this anxiety in their war against the Bank by accusing a "money power" of constructing a "mysterious, swaying web of speculative credit" in "a false, rotten, insubstantial world" of corrupt finance in an effort to destroy the Jeffersonian republic of industry and simplicity.[82] The Jacksonians thus appealed to a growing sense of helplessness before the vicissitudes of a vast and unpredictable market. "Men of business are, like threads of a fabric, woven together, and subject, to a great extent, to a common fate of prosperity or adversity," and the reckless speculator could carry whole communities with him to ruin. To Henry Ward Beecher, economic prosperity built upon speculation was itself a kind of cosmic confidence game:

> Upon a land—capacious beyond measure, whose prodigal soil rewards labor with an unharvestable abundance of exuberant fruits, occupied by a people signalized by enterprise and industry,—there came a summer of prosperity which lingered so long and shone so brightly, that men forgot that winter should ever come.

But suddenly, in the Panic of 1837, "men awoke from gorgeous dreams in the midst of desolation." Merchants were ruined, clerks were discharged, mechanics stood idle, and farmers stared at useless wheat surpluses. Economic historians have tended to play down the severity of the Panic of 1837, but to Beecher the devastation was incalculable: "The world looked upon a continent of inexhaustible fertility, (whose harvest had glutted the markets, and rotted in disuse,) filled with lamentation, and its inhabitants wandering like bereaved citizens among the ruins of an earthquake, mourning for children, for houses crushed, and property buried forever." Economic expansion built on speculation was, in Beecher's view, groundless, hazardous, overcommitted, and uncontrolled. The benevolence of commerce had given way before "the gambling of commerce," and all men were now threatened with financial ruin by the confidence man as speculator.[83]

In these three portraits in villainy—the youth's urban companion, the demagogue, and the gambler/speculator—the writers of antebellum advice literature expressed a deep disenchantment with the direction of historical change in early nineteenth-century America. In the figure of the urban associate, they cast their fears of the major social forces transforming American society: a high rate of geographical mobility and particularly of migration to the city, the decline of social deference and a loosening of ties between family generations, the breakdown of traditional restraints over single workingmen, and in general a replacement of traditional hierarchical social relationships with modern peer relations. In the image of the demagogue, they expressed anxieties regarding the political changes of their time: the growing dominance of party politics and techniques of mass politics, the new tyranny of the majority, the nationalization of public opinion, and the decline of "natural" local leadership in the face of the manipulative, charismatic leadership of new professional politicians. Finally, in the spectre of the gambler/speculator, they embodied their fears of the economic forces shaping the young American republic: the rapid expansion of the national market and of speculative economic activity.

How accurate was the advice literature's implicit assessment of the historical forces transforming American society in the early nineteenth century? As I have suggested, their views of social, political, and economic change as expressed in their portraits of the confidence man did reflect a certain awareness, however crude and simplistic, of some major changes taking place. In very general terms, the advice writers were addressing the gradual emergence in the early nineteenth century of a system of horizontal social relations that replaced the vertical social relations dominant in seventeenth- and eighteenth-century American life. As James E. Henretta has observed, most Northern Americans throughout the seventeenth and most of the eighteenth century lived their lives within the bounds of three social institutions—the family, the local community, and the church. Though largely autonomous and independent, all three were traditional, vertical institutions in which the lines of force radiated downward, from the father, the selectmen, and the minister, and the prevailing pattern of social relationships was authority and deference. But this traditional framework underwent severe strain throughout the eighteenth century from the powerful forces of demographic growth and economic development, which gradually tended to pry the individual loose from the "tight social, psychological, and ideological bounds of the traditional systems of elite control."[84] By 1815, when the increasingly complex preindustrial economy had reached full maturation, the ties of kinship, community, and religion were receding: "The centrifugal forces of trade and war, of geographic migration and political participation had shattered the tiny self-contained cosmos of the agricultural village."[85] Because the traditional vertical institutions could not contain the new complexity of national social life, new social organizations emerged that were formed along the horizontal lines of economic class and social status—organizations such as medical societies, mechanics' institutions, benevolent fraternities, charitable associations, and political clubs. Membership in these new organizations was not hereditary or compulsory, but voluntary; the pattern of authority was not one of mastery and deference, but one of equality.

To the clergymen, educators, and popular moralists who wrote advice manuals, the meaning of this transformation was alarmingly clear: "We have fallen on a period of social disorders, agitations, and excitements. There are signs of a spirit of anarchy in the very midst of us, which makes us sometimes tremble for the weal of our institutions."[86] Although they revealed some crude awareness of the forces of social, political, and economic change at work around them, they could only understand those forces within a declension framework. Their sense of history rested fundamentally on the belief that the golden age of American social relations was past. Once, they believed, young men had deferred without question to their fathers, their town authorities, and their clergymen; intergenerational family ties had been unbreakable, political opinion had been determined by the proper local authorities, and economic transactions had been characterized by honesty and plain dealing. The social history implicitly woven throughout the advice manuals was an extended jeremiad on America's declension from a more ordered and virtuous era. When the advice writers deplored the decline of deference among the rising generation, they were echoing a complaint that had been voiced by New England clergymen as early as the Reforming Synod of 1679.[87] Within their declension framework, the advice writers were using the confidence man as a scapegoat for the loss of a mythical era when American social relations had known nothing but integrity, harmony, and obedience to legitimate authority.

When the clerical Jeremiahs of 1679 lifted up their voices against the perilous apostasy of their generation, they were expressing in part a fear that their own authority over the New England people was in decline, and the antebellum advisers of youth, in their denunciations of "a spirit of anarchy" in their midst, were revealing a similar concern. Ever since the Great Awakening, the official power and prestige of the American clergy had been in a state of decline. With the coming of the American Revolution, and especially by the nineteenth century, ministers had begun to shore up their failing status by claiming major responsibility for forming the character of the rising generation in the young republic.[88] But in the confidence man, they found what they perceived to be a serious competitor for the power to shape the character of American youth. Nowhere was their concern about this competition more evident than in the advice manuals' direct attack on the pernicious literature believed to be dragging thousands of young men to their ruin. Evil writers, too, were seen as confidence men, whose trick was to cloak their villainous characters in the garb of virtue. "The most abandoned knaves are presented to the reader, as gentlemen of honor. The apostate from religion and the hypocrite are favorite characters with this class of writers."[89] The influence of such literature was incalculable: "The deadly streams from such a fountain flow through the streets, enter the houses, shops, stores and public institutions, penetrate into the chamber and retired apartment, and thousands at the same time partake of the fatal fluid."[90] Having warned their readers against the poison of pernicious literature, the advice writers went on to urge American youth to read good literature. A good book, they stressed, preserved its reader from evil companions, for he "has no inducement to resort to bad company, or the haunts of dissipation and vice; he has higher and nobler sources of enjoyment in himself. At pleasure, he can call around him the best of company,—the wisest and greatest men of every age and country."[91] Presumably, the wisest and greatest men in antebellum America included the advice writers themselves. The youth who passed by a French novel in favor of an advice manual, in other words, erected a kind of literary barrier against the machinations of the confidence man.

In their exaggerated assessment of the influence of bad books, the advice writers betrayed professional jealousy of the confidence man's power over American youth. According to Henry Ward Beecher, the young men of a given community actually belonged to their parents and guardians, their employers and political leaders, and their clergymen: "We grade our streets, build our schools, support all our municipal laws, and the young men are *ours;* our sons, our brothers, our wards, clerks, or apprentices; they are living in our houses, or stores, or shops, and we are their guardians, and take care of them in health, and watch them in sickness." But this prerogative of ownership was continually under challenge from a "whole race of men, whose camp is the Theatre, the Circus, the Turf, or the Gaming-table . . . a race whose instinct is destruction, who live to corrupt, and live off of the corruption which they make." This evil race of men acted as if the young men belonged to them: "and when they offer to corrupt all these youth, we paying them round sums of money for it, and we get courage finally to say that we had rather not; that industry and honesty are better than expert knavery—they turn on us in great indignation with, *Why don't you mind your own business—what are you meddling with our affairs for?*"[92] Beecher's heavy irony made his own view unmistakably plain: it was the confidence man, not the parents and masters and clergymen, who was the meddler, who was usurping the prerogative of shaping the rising generation.

Within the advice writers' declension framework, American society was falling into anarchy in part because the American clergy were no longer heeded and respected by the rising generation. But as Beecher's tirade suggests, the advice writers' attack was directed against a new and dangerous form of social authority emerging in America. The collapse of familial, communal, and clerical influence over American youth had left a vacuum into which flowed the confidence man. According to Henretta's historical schema, this fear that a new kind of social leadership was emerging in the early nineteenth century was well founded. The clear authority exercised within the hierarchical social institutions of seventeenth- and eighteenth-century America was giving way to the more tenuous authority possible within the egalitarian social organizations of the nineteenth century. In the emerging social system, authority could be seized by any charismatic figure who emerged from the masses as a man of magnetic personal power.[93] The most compelling heroes and antiheroes, both real and fictional, of antebellum American culture were just such charismatic men: Andrew Jackson, whose iron will was claimed by his followers to embody the collective will of the American people; Charles Grandison Finney, the revivalist, whose magnetic eye drew thousands to rebirth in Jesus; Captain Ahab of Herman Melville's *Moby Dick,* whose monomaniacal obsession made his will the law of the *Pequod,* and Hollingsworth of Nathaniel Hawthorne's *The Blithedale Romance,* whose dark countenance and philanthropic single-mindedness held the people of Blithedale under his spell; Napoleon, who had forcefully imposed his military vision upon much of Europe, and Lord Byron, who had persuasively imposed his sexual desires upon many of Europe's women.[94] Whether vetoing the Bank bill, hunting white whales, or seducing scores of helpless women, these men held the fascinated attention of the American people because, in the absence of a clearly defined, hierarchical authority structure, they used the power of charisma to bend others to their will.

For the writers of antebellum advice manuals, however, charisma was an unacceptable criterion for the exercise of authority over the rising generation. The confidence man's greatest offense was that he usurped power from the legitimate leaders of American society. The illegitimacy of his own power was conveyed symbolically in his nature as a trickster. As anthropologist Mary Douglas has pointed out, the trickster figure who pervades the mythology of many cultures is a marginal man, without a fixed place in the social structure. As such he represents the threat of social disorder, the dangers of formlessness; and because he is socially marginal, great powers of contamination are attributed to him. To be more specific, the trickster is a source of contamination because he dwells in the less structured or inarticulated areas of the social system. For example, the witches of primitive cultures are "social equivalents of beetles and spiders who live in the cracks of the walls and wainscoting," and the "powers attributed to them symbolise their ambiguous, inarticulate status."[95] The inarticulate powers of contamination vested in socially marginal figures contrast sharply with the articulate powers vested in those men who clearly wield legitimate social authority.

The confidence man of antebellum advice literature, who invariably approached his victim with an offer of friendship that proved to be part of a confidence trick, was a modern industrial version of the trickster. Like Douglas's trickster, he was a marginal man: "an outcast from society . . . who has no sympathies or feelings in common with the rest of mankind," a man who "wander[ed] up and down without ties of social connection, and without aim, except of money to be gathered off from men's vices."[96] Like the trickster, too, he carried enormous powers of contamination: his mere presence could infect youthful character. Within Douglas's theory, the confidence man's power to pollute young men resided in the threat he presented to the legitimate leaders of the American republic. The villains of antebellum advice literature were all represented as tricksters because they threatened to usurp the traditional authority exercised by the legitimate leaders of preindustrial America. Here lay the ultimate danger of the new horizontal society: by leveling the traditional, vertical social structures, it made authority a function not of fixed social status but of fluid self-aggrandizement. In the horizontal society, any man could seize authority over others: the licentious youth who rose from nowhere to become a leader among his youthful peers, the unprincipled demagogue who rose from nowhere to manipulate the passions of the mob, the avaricious gambler/speculator who rose from nowhere to seize control of the economic lives of those foolish enough to play his game.

How was the young man to escape ruin in a society swarming with marginal men who threatened to contaminate and destroy him? In primitive cultures, precautions against the trickster are taken through ritual defense or the observation of taboo. In antebellum America, young men were urged to defend themselves through character formation. Since the trickster threatened to assume the task of shaping the youth's malleable character, the young American was told he must assume complete command of his own moral destiny by forming his own character from within. Here lay the moral meaning of the "*self*-made man": by exercising self-possession, self-government, and, above all, self-reliance, he placed himself beyond evil influences and became a law unto himself. "You must be a law to yourselves, in the mart of trade, the cabin of the steamboat, and the crowded inn, or you will soon make shipwreck of faith and a good conscience. No shield less strong can quench the darts of Satan and bad men."[97]

Most important to the self-reliant character was the cultivation of firm principles, which provided "the foundation and framework of character . . . the mainspring of purpose and action."[98] Principle was what made the youth a fixed law unto himself and placed him beyond the need to seek guidance from those around him. The meaning of principle was often captured in navigational metaphors: principle was the compass that kept the youth on course through the voyage of life, the beacon that guided him through storm and night, the ship's helm to which he clung though mast and cargo were lost. The character without principle was like a ship without a rudder, "imperfect and unstable—liable to be changed by every wind, broken by every wave, and to fall into a deep, dark moral chaos."[99] Only principle could banish chaos from the young man's personal universe: the youth who lacked it was "a wild, a chainless and a dangerous thing—wandering forth, like some terrible principle in nature, not bound into the fixed paths of the planets, or subject to any known law of order, threatening to commingle and crush worlds."[100] The advice manuals were seldom specific concerning exactly what principles were to be cultivated. What was important about principles was their fixity: God judged men's principles "according as these are stable or fluctuating—are right or wrong."[101]

According to the advice manuals, the fixed principle was the right principle because the youth who held fast to it could not be led astray by false companions. Like Martin Luther at Worms, he could not be manipulated or moved: "Efforts are made, at one time, to win him over by flatteries; at another, to move him by threats. But his granite nature resists every assault. His purposes cannot be shaken; his iron will cannot be broken."[102] In a world filled with confidence men, every youth had to hold tight to his principles or become the tool of others:

> O, do not sacrifice a just principle for worlds! Do not put by your convictions of truth, of right, at every nod and beck of others! ... If you do, you will go through life a weak, a vacillating, and a despised man,—perhaps a tool and a stepping stone for others. Preserve, then, an independent, a *truly* independent mind.[103]

The youth who vacillated, who stopped to listen to the flatteries of other men, who approached when they beckoned, was lost. Fixity, in other words, was the youth's only defense against the powers of marginality. The self-reliant youth who cultivated firm principles stood as a fixed point of moral certainty in a chaotic world roamed by tricksters who worked to contaminate the unwary with their own social formlessness.

The advice literature's formula for the American youth's self-defense against the confidence man contained, however, one serious flaw. The youth threatened with contamination by the trickster was himself a marginal man in passage from one social state to another. Anthropologist Arnold van Gennep defined *rites de passage* as "rites which accompany every change of place, state, social position and age" and isolated three phases of the rite: separation from an earlier fixed point in the social structure, marginality or liminality (from the Latin *limin*, meaning threshold), and aggregation, when the passage or transition is completed.[104] The antebellum American youth just entering the city was in a condition of liminality in every sense cited by van Gennep. First of all, he was geographically liminal, in transit from his home in the country to a new place in the city. Second, he was in passage from a dependent or semidependent state to a position of independence. Third, he was socially liminal as an ambitious youth just beginning his quest for social and economic advancement. Finally, he was in passage from boyhood to manhood. But in the early nineteenth century, as Joseph Kett has observed, American culture did not offer clearly defined rites for a boy's passage to manhood: between the ages of ten and twenty-one, he oscillated between dependence and independence, and "no consensus existed as to the moment when a boy became a man."[105] The American youth thus not only had to endure a prolonged condition of liminality; he had to do so without the assistance of rituals to lend meaning to that ambiguous and confusing condition in which "persons elude or slip through the network of classifications that normally locate states and positions in cultural space."[106] If a fixed character alone could protect the youth against the contaminating powers of the trickster, then the young man addressed by the advice manuals was in fact no match for the confidence man. For he, like his enemy, was a liminal man.

Ever since Benjamin Franklin's dramatic entrance into colonial Philadelphia, the image of the American youth standing hopefully on the urban threshold had captured the spirit of the American Dream. Because of his complete liminality, he was the archetype of the American-on-the-make. Only in the first few decades of the nineteenth century did the convention established by Franklin achieve full power over the American middle-class imagination. Eighteenth-century champions of the self-made man, Franklin included, had stressed his usefulness as a leader within the republican community; not until the nineteenth century was the self-made man celebrated solely for his individual social and economic advancement.[107] By the early nineteenth century, explains John G. Cawelti, "under the impact of a rapidly growing economy and the expansive mood of manifest destiny, with the prospect of a vast supply of cheap land, rapidly expanding markets, an increasingly more efficient transportation system, and high wages continuing into the indefinite future, it was easy to believe that if individuals were sufficiently enterprising and society put no artificial barriers in their way, the general welfare would take care of itself."[108] The American cult of the self-made man was entering its heyday. By 1840, both political parties had adopted the rhetoric and symbols of the open society and were loudly professing their devotion to the interests of the self-made man. Popular biographies of self-made men—politicians, businessmen, even artists and intellectuals—proclaimed the faith that, in the boundless American social environment, any man might rise to any position in life.

The advice manuals for young men written between 1830 and 1860 were not intended solely as guides to success. In fact, direct discussion of the young man's work life comprised but a small proportion of the advice offered. William A. Alcott's *Young Man's Guide*, for example, which provided a relatively lengthy discussion of business management, also covered such topics as marriage, amusements, criminal behavior, and social, moral, and mental improvement. The writers of antebellum advice literature were not primarily successful businessmen but clergymen such as John Todd, Joel Hawes, and Henry Ward Beecher, educational reformers such as William A. Alcott and Horace Mann, and popular sentimental writers such as Timothy S. Arthur. Middle-class moralists all, they were less interested in constructing a success ethic than in ensuring the formation of moral character.

Nonetheless, character formation was the nineteenth-century version of the Protestant work ethic. Through personal exertion and resolve applied steadfastly to molding his character, the youth was told, he might overcome his lack of endowed faculties and advantages to triumph over circumstance and become anything he chose. "*You may be,*" said one advice manual, "*whatever you will resolve to be.*"[109] In the American republic, with its rapid property turnover in the absence of hereditary honors, most "real men—men of force of character—men who command respect—men who do good in the world—are self-made men."[110] In the boundless, open society of the young American nation, the advice writers believed, the only limitations on the individual's ultimate station in life seemed to lie in his character, which might be deliberately molded into the shape of success.

Recently the new social history has challenged this faith in the boundlessness of the Jacksonian social environment and has begun to piece together a picture of what Edward Pessen has called "the surprising immobility of the 'era of the common man.' "[111] Such studies serve to underline the vitality of the antebellum American faith in the cult of the self-made man. Stuart Blumin explained the discrepancy between myth and reality by arguing that "the American Dream is fed, not by such mundane matters as mobility matrices but by isolated cases of spectacular success."[112] Alternatively, Stephen Thernstrom has suggested that even the small property gains made by some hardworking laborers may have been sufficient to maintain the faith expressed by Calvin Colton in 1844, that "this is a country of *self-made men*."[113] Whether fed by a few dramatic stories of men who rose from rags to riches or by many stories of men who worked hard all their lives to buy a modest little house of their own, the cult of the self-made man thrived in antebellum American culture. And its fundamental assumption was that all Americans were liminal men, in passage from a lower to a higher social status. This assumption was best expressed in a new nineteenth-century usage of the term *middle class*. In the eighteenth century, the term *middling class* referred to people who occupied a static social position between the extremes of peasantry and aristocracy, a position believed to offer only modest opportunities for advancement. But by the 1830s, middle class no longer meant a point of equilibrium between two other fixed classes; to be middle-class was to be, in theory, without fixed social status. Members of the middle class imagined themselves on a social escalator to greater wealth and prestige. They lived suspended between the facts of their present social position and the promise, which they took for granted, of their economic future.[114] In reality, as Stuart Blumin's study of antebellum Philadelphia, for example, has shown, the middle-class escalator was at least as likely to go down as up. Whether rising or falling, however, middle-class Americans were defined as men in social motion, men of no fixed status. And the middle class was believed to include a vast majority of Americans who were neither very wealthy nor very poor. This view of the composition of American society thus ascribed to most Americans a permanent condition of liminality and offers support for Victor

Turner's argument that liminality in modern societies can be virtually institutionalized:

> What appears to have happened is that with the increasing specialization of society and culture, with progressive complexity in the social division of labor, what was in tribal society principally a set of transitional qualities "betwixt and between" defined states of culture and society has become itself an institutionalized state. . . . Transition has here become a permanent condition.[115]

This idea that all Americans were liminal men was clearly expressed in the various regional characters of American legend and folklore, many of whom were confidence men. From the West came the backwoodsman, with his gift for masquerade and his mastery of the tall tale. Mike Fink, the Mississippi boatman, and Davy Crockett, the frontier hunter, told endless lies about their strength and prowess and delighted in anecdotes of their own trickery.[116] From the Southwest came a variety of legendary confidence men, from the cardsharp and the horse-race "fixer" to the bogus lawyer and doctor and banker and long-lost relative. "Avaricious, cruel, and utterly ruthless, always operating on the edge of the law, he moved through the land like a flight of seven-year locusts, leaving empty wallets behind him." His "supreme incarnation" was regional humorist John Jones Hooper's creation Simon Suggs, whose motto was *"It is good to be shifty in a new country."*[117] But the master trickster of all came out of New England. He was the Yankee, famed for maintaining a laconic silence or answering all questions with other questions, while he peddled warming pans in the West Indies and pills made of white paper to cholera victims in Canada. Seba Smith's Jack Downing was the most famous fictional Yankee of his era.[118] But it was a flesh-and-blood Yankee named P. T. Barnum who fully captured the American imagination with his sharp entrepreneurial dealings and self-admitted bunkum. Barnum dedicated his autobiography, somewhat awkwardly, to "The Universal Yankee Nation, of which I am proud to be one."[119] By the time *The Life of P. T. Barnum* was published in 1854, the Yankee had been transformed from a regional character into a national myth. Constance Rourke has argued that the Yankee absorbed some of the attributes of the backwoodsman: "I am Sam Slick the Yankee peddler," a London broadside announced, "—I can ride on a flash of lightning and catch a thunder-bolt in my fist."[120] But in this era of dawning industrial capitalism, the Eastern entrepreneurial sharper got the upper hand of the preindustrial Westerner, and emerged as the dominant symbol, not just of the American confidence man, but of American national character.

Despite the vast differences between the Yankee and the back-woodsman, the two figures held one quality in common that permitted their merger into a single American national character. That quality was identified by a British traveler named Lady Emmeline Stuart Worthey, who toured America in the 1840s. "It is said," she wrote, that "if you ask a Connecticut Yankee in any part of the world how he is, he will, if not 'sick,' answer 'moving, Sir,' equivalent to saying 'well'; for, if well, he is sure to be on the move."[121] In all his guises, the American confidence man displayed an abundance of what George Pierson has called the "M-factor" that has shaped the American national character: movement, migration, mobility. He was, first of all, a wanderer, independent of any fixed social nexus of community, family, or permanent friends. His geographical mobility determined a second distinguishing characteristic: his upward social mobility. As Pierson argues, "In a new community (frontier or town) family and past performance hardly count. Everyone has to make his own mark, and stands equal with his fellow-strangers. The social competition, as it were, starts over, with all the camaraderie and 'gamesmanship' of a new catch-as-catch-can."[122] As a wanderer, the confidence man was eternally self-aggrandizing. Blessed with superior wit, skill in the use of resources, adaptability and enthusiasm, he was a one-man enterprise, inspired as much by the beauty of his scheme as by the need for aggrandizement.[123] In the theoretically fluid, open social world of the Age of Jackson, the trickster emerged as the archetypal American because the trickster represented man-on-the-make.

The image of the Yankee, as William R. Taylor has argued, was ambiguous.[124] On the one hand, he was mercenary, hypocritical, philistine, an evil genius of duplicity whose sharp practices exploited the confidence placed in him by his fellow men. But on the other hand, he was thrifty, industrious, ascetic, "a cracker barrel mentor, a Romantic rustic given to apothegms on trust in oneself, in one's fellow man, and in the benevolence of 'Natur.' " In his more attractive guises, he was not simply a confidence man, but a "man of confidence," uniquely suited to represent the American nation in an age of democratic patriotism, Romanticism, and expanding capitalism.[125] At first glance, this attractive Yankee figure appears vastly different from the confidence man of the advice manuals who threatened to destroy the character of the rising generation. But the scenario of the confidence game as sketched in antebellum advice literature carried its own ambiguities. The contaminating powers of the confidence man sprang from his social formlessness, his marginality, but his youthful victim was also socially formless, liminal. The confidence man was selfish, self-aggrandizing, but the youth too was seeking to make his fortune in the "open society." It is most significant that the confidence man's final purpose was to recruit the American youth to his own ranks, to lure his victim "until your character and destiny become identified with his own." Here lay the deepest fear buried in the confidence game of antebellum advice literature: that the youth himself might become a confidence man, that his worst enemy lurked not in the city streets but within his own breast. And here lay also the attractive powers of the confidence man. For the youth to become successful, he himself might have to learn the tricks of the confidence man.

Historians of American success mythology have recognized that, although antebellum Americans threw themselves into the cult of self-improvement, many nonetheless expressed anxiety about the American pursuit of the main chance. In *Apostles of the Self-Made Man,* John G. Cawelti argues that many were uneasy about the conflict between the pursuit of individual success and traditional social and religious ideals. Alternatively, Fred Somkin, in *Unquiet Eagle,* has stressed the republican foundation of popular concerns about America's growing prosperity, which raised the old spectre of luxury and extravagance.[126] But the anxieties about social mobility that were expressed in the scenario of the confidence game went far deeper than Cawelti and Somkin have suggested. The confidence man served as a symbolic expression of the dangers of marginality in a society of placeless men. In this "era of the common man," when most Americans claimed to be middle-class, and when to be middle-class was to be socially fluid, a majority of Americans appeared to be liminal men who defied social classification. And the American youth entering the city in pursuit of fame and fortune symbolically captured the liminality of the placeless American. It was his liminality that made him susceptible to the seductions of confidence men, and ultimately threatened him with recruitment to their ranks. Somehow, the middle-class culture of social mobility emerging in America after 1830 would have to come to terms with this fearful spectre of the confidence man.

Hypocrisy and Sincerity
in the World of Strangers

In warning the American youth not to be seduced by the evil confidence man, antebellum advice manuals were cautioning him above all not to become a confidence man himself. And in warning him against the contagious moral leprosy of the confidence man, the advice manuals focused on a single evil trait: hypocrisy. The youth who was successfully recruited into the ranks of confidence men became a "fiend of hell, disguised in the robes of honor and purity," who destroyed his victims "by his fascinating arts and deep hypocrisy."[1] The advisers' broadest fear was not simply that a small corps of confidence men roamed American society, but that an entire generation of Americans was being tainted with hypocrisy:

> Instead of acting in open daylight, pursuing the direct and straight-forward path of rectitude and duty, you see men, extensively, putting on false appearances; working in the dark, and carrying their plans by stratagem and deceit. Nothing open, nothing direct and honest; one thing is said, and another thing meant. When you look for a man in one place, you find him in another. With flattering lips and a double heart do they speak. Their language and conduct do not proceed from fixed principle and open hearted sincerity; but from a spirit of duplicity and management.[2]

The confidence man personified the pervasive duplicity of the rising generation.

As shown in chapter 1, the young men streaming into the cities of antebellum America were viewed as potential tricksters because of their social formlessness, their liminality. But the fear that young Americans were a generation of hypocrites arose more specifically from a concern about the conditions surrounding their drive toward success. The youth addressed by the advice manuals made his bid for fame and fortune among strangers in the city. In this world of strangers, the advice writers feared, appearances were valued more than realities, and surface impressions proved more important than inner virtues. Hypocrisy, in other words, seemed to pay off, and the aspiring youth was in danger of emulating the urban trickster whose own success at manipulating surface impressions for selfish gain was unquestionable.

In addressing the problem of hypocrisy in the world of strangers, the advice writers were confronting a dilemma that lay at the heart of urban middle-class culture in Victorian America. How were the aspiring middle classes to secure success among strangers without stooping to the confidence man's arts of manipulating appearance and conduct? The question revealed deep anxieties about the destructive potential of hypocrisy in the American republic. To Victorian Americans, hypocrisy was not merely a personal sin; it was a social offense that threatened to dissolve the ties of mutual confidence binding men together. To meet this threat the advice writers urged upon their readers the importance of sincerity. If young Americans would learn to practice perfect sincerity in all aspects of their personal conduct, the evil influence of the confidence man might be defeated, and all men might be securely knit together by benevolence. In the 1830s, this cult of sincerity was emerging as the highest ideal of the sentimental middle-class culture that would dominate Victorian America. An understanding of how the cult of sincerity shaped middle-class culture in mid-nineteenth-century America must begin with a discussion of the problem of hypocrisy in the new world of strangers.

In the small towns of colonial America strangers were the exception rather than the rule. Most inhabitants knew the other members of their community, and the arrival of a stranger was a special event that initiated certain traditional responses. Ship captains often reported the names of newcomers; inhabitants were expected to inform the authorities whenever they gave lodgings to a stranger; and certain large towns appointed special officials to watch for unknown visitors. Only those strangers "known to be of an honest conversation and accepted by the major part of the Town" were to be accepted as residents.[3]

As the city gradually replaced the town as the dominant form of social organization, however, the stranger became not the exception but the rule. By the mid-eighteenth century in New England, population growth and geographic mobility were making official surveillance of strangers increasingly difficult;[4] and by the early nineteenth century, an urban explosion was propelling vast numbers of Americans into what urban sociologist Lyn Lofland has called the "world of strangers," whose inhabitants know nothing of the majority of their fellow residents.[5] The period between 1820 and 1860 demonstrated the fastest rate of urban growth in all American history: the proportion of people living in cities rose by 797 percent while the national population increased only 226 percent.[6] In an admittedly arbitrary gesture Lofland has defined the world of strangers, in which traditional ways of "coding" or identifying strangers are impossible, as an urban area with a population of roughly eight thousand to ten thousand or more.[7] Between 1820 and 1860, American cities of ten thousand or more increased over eightfold,[8] and a high rate of residential mobility within cities probably reinforced the impact of anonymity. In Boston, for example, the residential mobility rate between 1830 and 1857 was 85.5 percent; the figures suggest that one-half of Boston's population would disappear and be replaced over one or two years. Although many moves within the city involved only short distances, the extraordinary rate of residential mobility must have contributed to popular awareness of the city as a world of strangers.[9] Finally, the physical pattern of urban growth during this period exacerbated the problems of living among strangers. Areal expansion could not keep pace with population increases, and the result was an increasing density of the urban population. The growth of Boston, for example, was limited by the shoreline; the city annexed few suburbs until after the Civil War.[10] Similarly, booming antebellum Philadelphia made no innovations in its preindustrial physical structure, but remained a city with a grid street pattern, narrow house lots, interior alleys behind row houses, and shacks or smaller houses in the rear yards. As population increased, older blocks were simply subdivided, new alleys and tiny houses were added, and traffic problems became terrible. Not until after 1860, when population density peaked, did the new street railways open the suburbs.[11]

Antebellum Americans who were confronting the world of strangers for the first time often experienced great shock. After many months in New York City, Lydia Maria Child was still not accustomed to the vast anonymity of that metropolis: "For eight weary months, I have met in the crowded streets but two faces I have ever seen before. . . . At times, I almost fancy I can feel myself turning to stone by inches."[12] Two years earlier, Edgar Allan Poe had registered his own dark fascination with the great mass of urban strangers in "The Man of the Crowd." It is the story of a man who becomes obsessed with a single demonic face in the "dense and continuous tides of population" flowing past his coffeehouse window and pursues the stranger through the streets out of "a craving desire to keep the man in view—to know more of him." He gives up after an entire night and a day only when he recognizes that the stranger is *the man of the crowd,* who wanders constantly among the urban masses because he "refuses to be alone." "It will be in vain to follow," the narrator concludes, "for I shall learn no more of him, nor of his deeds."[13] In this study in compulsion Poe drew on his generation's shock at realizing that the urban stranger cannot be known. Even one's neighbor next door, as a visitor to Pittsburgh commented in 1818, might be a stranger: "A next door neighbor is, with them, frequently unknown, and months and years pass, without their exchanging with each other the ordinary compliments of friendship and goodwill."[14] In an exposé of New York entitled *The Secrets of the Great City,* James Dabney McCabe told the story of two men who lived next door to each other for twelve years as perfect strangers until one of them noticed that they had the same last name. During the course of their first conversation they discovered that they were long-lost brothers.[15] The power of this urban myth derived from the unexpectedness of discovering an intimate relationship in the anonymous city.

The need to come to terms with the stranger clearly did not disappear along with the traditional methods used in the small towns of preindustrial American society. In all social groups people require information about those they meet, in order to avoid both psychological and physical damage. The city thus presented a serious problem: how could one identify strangers without access to biographical information about them, when only immediate visual information was available? In the preindustrial city, according to Lyn Lofland, strangers were coded largely on the basis of personal appearance. Costume, manner, body markings, and linguistic patterns could indicate status or rank, occupation, nationality, and, because of the practice of punitive mutilation, even moral character. With the Industrial Revolution, however, the rising classes began to imitate the dress and conduct of the older elites, legal regulation of dress styles declined, bodily mutilation for moral offenses disappeared, and language grew more standardized. Identifying the urban stranger on the basis of personal appearance thus became almost impossible.

In the cities of early industrial America, preindustrial methods of ordering the world of strangers were becoming very unreliable. According to Francis Lieber, the absence of privileged classes encouraged many Americans "to elevate themselves, in matters of appearance, to the level of others, from whom, in Europe, they would be perfectly willing to keep a respectful distance."[16] Lieber and other foreign travelers in the United States were surprised at how eager Americans were to imitate their social betters in dress and manner. This concern about the standardization of personal appearance was expressed by Americans in the figure of the well-dressed, well-mannered, and charmingly articulate confidence man. A popular urban myth told of the foreign impostor, a bogus count or baron, who gained admittance to the wealthiest parlors in the city by virtue of his polished appearance. Well-dressed, smoothly courteous, and quietly dignified, he soon succeeded in winning the hand of some bourgeois heiress, received a handsome marriage settlement, and abruptly disappeared before the wedding.[17] In contemporary descriptions the antebellum city was presented as the natural habitat of hypocrisy and deceit, "the theatre of humbugs," where righteous men deplored "the unclean appetites that are slicked over with fashion, and the beastliness that assumes the name of 'gentlemen.' "[18] Very popular were the numerous sensationalist exposés that purported to rip the mask of hypocrisy from the face of the depraved city itself, books with such titles as *Sunshine and Shadow in New York, Philadelphia in Slices, New York Naked,* and *The Secrets of the Twin Cities; or, The Great Metropolis Unmasked. A Startling Story of City Scenes in Boston and New York.*[19] As Richard Wohl has argued, the popular adulation of rural life that took shape in early industrial America rested on the fundamental assumption that "it is in the country that things and people are what they seem, but in the city appearances are dangerously deceiving."[20]

In the cities of early industrial America, the personal appearance of a stranger did not offer reliable clues to his identity. Lyn Lofland argues that in the modern city, where people tend to look alike, the stranger can be identified according to his location in the city. As cities expanded and transportation facilities improved, spatial seg-

THE FATE OF HUNDREDS OF YOUNG MEN.

1. LEAVING HOME FOR NEW YORK. **2.** IN A FASHIONABLE SALOON AMONGST THE WAITER GIRLS—THE ROAD TO RUIN. **3.** DRINKING WITH "THE FANCY"— IN THE HANDS OF GAMBLERS. **4.** MURDERED AND ROBBED BY HIS "FANCY" COMPANIONS. **5.** HIS BODY FOUND BY THE HARBOR POLICE.

The young man's seduction by confidence men (the gamblers) and painted women (the waiter girls) after his arrival in the evil city.

regation of activities and of persons by class, caste, age, and ethnicity became possible. The non-elite middle classes actively sought such segregation in an effort to insulate themselves from the "dangerous classes," who threatened not only their persons and property but their status as well, by jeering and insulting them on the streets.[21] But in antebellum American cities, preindustrial methods for coding the urban stranger on the basis of appearance were not immediately replaced by modern methods based on the stranger's location in the city. The structure of the antebellum American city remained more preindustrial than modern and offered little spatial segregation of activities or of people. Until the introduction of street railways in the 1850s, American cities were predominantly "walking cities," without extensive and efficient public transportation that would enable settlement to spread into a larger area and thus become segregated by persons and activities. In antebellum Philadelphia, most areas were a jumble of occupations and classes, of shops and homes, of immigrants and native-born Americans. Only around 1860 did Philadelphia see the beginning of concentration—a downtown area, a few manufacturing clusters, a small slum, a few blocks dominated by blacks, an occasional class and ethnic enclave—but such spatial segregation was not yet the dominant pattern. Similarly, Boston in 1850 remained a tightly packed city of pedestrians, in which the area of settlement hardly exceeded a two-mile radius from City Hall. Although the peripheral communities of the walking city—including Charlestown, parts of Cambridge, East Boston, and nearby sections of Roxbury—filled between 1830 and 1850, these were not early models of the middle-class residential suburb; they mixed Boston commuters with local workers, and residences with factories.[22] The anonymity of the antebellum world of strangers was particularly great because preindustrial methods of coding the stranger had become useless before modern methods became possible.

Whenever daily social life is characterized by frequent face-to-face contact with strangers, the fleeting impressions made by surface appearances become of great importance. As urban sociologist Robert Park has observed, "the individual's status is determined to a considerable degree by conventional signs—by fashion and 'front'—and the art of life is largely reduced to skating on thin surfaces and a scrupulous study of style and manners."[23] To the many young Americans just entering the world of strangers, the urban art of "skating on thin surfaces" of style and manners was, of course, virtually unknown. So the advice manuals offered instruction on the importance of surface impressions. "It is certainly true," advised William Alcott in 1834, "that the impressions which a person's first appearance make upon the minds of those around him are deep and permanent."[24] What "thin surfaces of style and manners" were to be learned? Alcott discussed at great length the importance of dress, courtesy, cleanliness, modesty, good personal habits, and the restraint of anger. He particularly impressed upon his readers the importance of "little things" like proper salutations and modes of dress and assured them that no considerations of behavior or appearance were too trifling for their consideration. Aspiring young men were urged to be conscious of what sociologist Erving Goffman has called the "presentation of self in everyday life,"—that construction and maintenance of a consistent, idealized self in the presence of others that is especially important in societies characterized by social mobility.[25] On this question the advice manuals were backed up by hundreds of other guides to personal conduct, including manuals on good manners and proper dress, diet and physical self-culture, health and personal grooming. The art of engineering all outward expressions of the self in order to impress others had become a central concern of antebellum popular self-improvement literature.

Surface impressions were essential to success in the world of strangers, according to the advice writers, because appearances revealed character. In a theory that may be called the sentimental typology of conduct, they asserted that all aspects of manner and appearance were visible outward signs of inner moral qualities. In every detail of his conduct and appearance, the youth gave off clues to his inner identity, clues which would shape his destiny. As Rufus Clark wrote, the word character literally meant "a mark made by cutting or engraving,"[26] and inner virtues and vices cut their mark on the outward man. "We may form some opinion of a man's sense and character from his dress," wrote one anonymous adviser, and William Alcott added specifically that "cleanliness of the body has . . . a connection with mental and moral purity."[27] Most important, a man's inner character was believed to be imprinted upon his face and thus visible to anyone who understood the moral language of physiognomy:

Thus the habits of the soul become written on the countenance; what we call the expression of the face is only the story which the face tells about the feelings of the heart. If the heart is habitually exercised by malice, then a malicious expression becomes habitually stamped upon the face. The expression of the countenance is a record which sets forth to the world the habitual feelings, the character of the heart.[28]

In a sense, the sentimental typology of conduct represented the advisers' effort to establish that it was possible to know something about the character of a stranger. "Men may disguise their actions," one adviser assured his readers, "but not their inclinations and though it is not easy to guess, by the muscles of the countenance, what a man will do, it is hardly to be concealed what he wishes to have done."[29] Horace Mann even suggested that the laws of sentimental typology identified evil men better than the preindustrial method of branding criminals: "Rogues have had the initial letter of their initial title burnt into the palms of their hands; even for murder, Cain was only branded on the forehead; but over the whole person of the debauchee or the inebriate, the signatures of infamy are written."[30] With the decline of punitive mutilation in the early industrial city, Mann may have been trying to convince himself and others that criminals were still recognizable at a glance. Even as Mann and others asserted the sentimental typology of conduct, however, they had to admit that appearances could be deceiving: "Neither the young nor the old," wrote one, "have any certain method of knowing character by externals."[31] Surface impressions, they reluctantly conceded, could be manipulated by unscrupulous men. But, according to Timothy S. Arthur, man had not always possessed the ability to disguise evil intent with a pleasant appearance: he had learned to act the hypocrite through the Fall of Adam. Prelapsarian man had exhibited a perfect correspondence between heart and countenance:

His face was the index of his mind—the table upon which all he felt and thought was written; and we have good reason to believe that he had no need of oral speech for the conveyance of his ideas, but found language dumb in comparison to the wonderful play of the innumerable muscles of his face and lips, which were in perfect correspondence with all his feelings and thoughts, and gave to them a full and beautiful utterance; his eye, the perfect mirror of his mind, at a single glance sealing his lips into silence.[32]

In this myth of man's lapse from perfect sentimental typology, Arthur expressed an unconscious recognition of the decline of preindustrial methods of coding the urban stranger. Once again, the advice writers were coming up smack against the spectre of the confidence man. The confidence man represented the new urbanite who could sever the connection between inner character and outward appearances by consciously manipulating the impression he made on others. His art was to cultivate a "fair exterior and winning manner";[33] he was usually mild and courteous, sociable and generous; his taste seemed impeccable, his clothing was beautiful, and his accomplishments were great. But though "gifted in intellect, eloquent in speech, beautiful in person, commanding in attainments, captivating and shining in all that he does," all his accomplishments were like "the beautiful hues on the back of the serpent, the more hideous in proportion to their power to charm the victim."[34] Even moral physiognomy was subject to the manipulations of the social hypocrite. The face of the "polished Libertine" was "mild and engaging," and smiles were wielded for self-interested deception: "The importance and influence of smiles and good words are so well known that thousands, and thousands, and thousands, play the hypocrite through this very medium."[35] The hypocrisy of the confidence man destroyed the sentimental typology of conduct by severing the link between surface appearances and inner moral nature.

In the world of strangers, surface impressions are always a significant part of face-to-face social behavior, but in the cities of early industrial America, where preindustrial methods of coding the urban stranger were breaking down before modern methods could replace them, the importance of "front" was unusually great. The art of what Erving Goffman has called "impression management" was particularly important to the thousands of young men new to the city and not accustomed to the urban significance of surface impressions.[36] According to the sentimental typology of conduct, the young man who carefully cultivated the little things was simply learning to display his inner moral qualities. At the same time, however, the advice writers uneasily acknowledged that appearances could be deceiving, that perfect sentimental typology had been destroyed in the Fall of Adam. Fallen man was capable of manipulating surface impressions to deceive the strangers he met, and this was precisely the evil art of the confidence man. The advisers of antebellum youth thus found themselves in a moral dilemma. The youth had to learn to cultivate good surface impressions in order to make his way in the city. But by doing so, he was learning the arts of the confidence man, whose "fair exterior and winning manners" were designed for deception. The youth who learned to master the little things thus walked a thin line between moral self-improvement and hypocrisy. For the advice writers, it was one thing to assert that appearances are important because they reveal inner character; it was quite another to say that appearances might be deceitfully manipulated to convince others of inner character. The young man who concentrated solely on engineering an acceptable front to the world was guilty of cultivating what the advice writers condemned as "the mere surface of character."[37] The outward display of inward virtue was, in a sense, an integral part of character itself; character was "the revelation that we make to the world of our inward forces, virtues, and principles."[38] But that revelation had to be a simple translation of inner qualities into their outward expression. The youth who cultivated "the mere surface of character" without cultivating the inner moral principles that lay beneath the surface was a confidence man. In assuming a mask of virtue for an urban audience, he was practicing the dangerous art of hypocrisy. Why did the advisers of antebellum youth have difficulty in distinguishing an attention to surface impressions from the confidence man's game? Why did they believe an urban concern for personal appearance threatened to transform a generation of young Americans into hypocrites? These anxieties cannot be understood without attention to the Puritan attitudes in which the advice literature was steeped.

Puritan piety was shaped by the eternal question "Am I saved?" and the Puritan's religious life was largely devoted to answering that question in the affirmative. According to the doctrine of predestination, the Puritan could do nothing to alter the divine decree concerning his eternal destiny. He could, however, endlessly search his conduct for signs that he had been granted saving faith in Christ. By the time Massachusetts Bay Colony was founded, two generations of Puritan writers had devoted themselves to describing the processes through which God's free grace operates in the salvation of men. From the many autobiographies, sermons, and treatises on the subject there had emerged a morphology of conversion, a pattern of steps by which unregenerate man moved toward saving faith. The conversion experience fell into roughly five stages: knowledge of the law, conviction of sin, faith in Christ's saving power, combat with doubt and despair, and, finally, assurance of salvation. The New England Puritans, who introduced tests of saving faith for church membership in the 1630s, early acquired a reputation as English Protestantism's most sophisticated students of the signs and stages of the conversion process.[39]

Even for New England Puritans, however, the morphology of conversion presented a problem. The assurance of salvation wrought by grace was easily confused with the false assurance or security of the unregenerate. Even in fallen men, they believed, some faculties exist that can produce actions similar to those which result from faith. Thus the man who relied unhesitatingly on the signs of his conversion, who abandoned all doubts of his own election, succeeded only in demonstrating that he had never had saving faith to begin with. Such a man fell into the chief sin of pride, a high valuation of self. His self-deception rested on the error of relying on his individual merit rather than on Christ. It was not enough, therefore, that a Puritan scrutinize carefully his conduct for signs of saving faith. He must seek out the sources and motivations of his conduct; he must examine his innermost heart. Spiritual autobiography provided the arena for this ongoing process of self-examination. According to Daniel B. Shea, Jr., the "thematic cornerstone" of spiritual autobiography was the "distinction between easy self-righteousness and the new birth of saving grace."[40]

From John Bunyan on, Puritan autobiographers often focused on the problem of rooting out false self-confidence through a "pilgrimage through the deceits of the heart."[41] The Puritan autobiographer ruthlessly sought to root out all signs of his own self-righteousness, which he usually termed hypocrisy. In *Grace Abounding to the Chief of Sinners,* Bunyan called himself "a poor painted Hypocrite" because he craved his neighbors' admiration for his outwardly moral life.[42] Cotton Mather similarly condemned himself as a "Refined Hypocrite."[43] Like many other Puritans, Mather had gone through a bout with spiritual pride during his adolescence. Reverend Aaron Burr was eighteen when he discovered that "there never was such a Bottomless Depth of Pride and Hypocrisy, Such an amazing Scene of the Most vile and abominable Thoughts indulged in the Heart of any Sinner as there was in mine."[44] Many Puritan autobiographers deplored what was essentially an adolescent lapse into the heresy of Arminianism, which asserted that salvation could be achieved through good works without the merits of Christ. Samuel Hopkins, for example, had "had a very good outside, and rested entirely on [his] Duties," until he realized the self-righteous foundation of his hope; and even then he continued to have "a Secret hope of *recommending* myself to God by my religious Duties."[45] In his pride Hopkins had become confident of the power of his own faith, and had concluded that his Christian work was at an end.

For the anxious Puritan probing his life for assurance of his own election, hypocrisy offered the surest evidence that his hopes were in vain. Thomas Shepard expressed powerfully the Puritan's loathing for the hypocrite who cloaked his sinfulness with the appearance of virtue:

> What though thy life be smooth, what though thy outside, thy sepulcher, be painted? O, thou art full of rottenness, of sin, within. Guilty, not before men, as the sins of thy life make thee, but before God, of all the sins that swarm and roar in the whole world at this day, for God looks to the heart; guilty thou art therefore of heart whoredom, heart sodomy, heart blasphemy, heart drunkenness, heart buggery, heart oppression, heart idolatry; and these are the sins that terribly provoke the wrath of Almighty God against thee.[46]

The Christian who fell into this terrible sin of spiritual pride was, in an important sense, the victim of a confidence game played by Satan, the Prince of Liars. In John Milton's *Paradise Lost,* Satan is represented as a master of guile, who affects an attitude at odds with his true inner state in order to ruin mankind: "Th' infernal Serpent; hee it was, whose guile / Stirr'd up with Envy and Revenge, deceiv'd / The Mother of Mankind." So skilled was he in his hypocrisy that he deceived even the archangel Uriel:

> So spake the false dissembler unperceiv'd;
> For neither Man nor Angel can discern
> Hypocrisy, the only evil that walks
> Invisible, except to God alone,
> By his permissive will, through Heav'n and Earth.[47]

Satan's confidence game was to lead men to destruction by encouraging their false confidence in their salvation. When Aaron Burr passed through his period of false self-righteousness, he "forsook every thing But what the D[evi]l and my own deceitfull Heart flatered [sic] Me was right."[48] So crafty was the demonic confidence man, according to Jonathan Edwards, that he could actually counterfeit the Spirit's saving operations in the exact order of their appearance, and thus lure men into thinking they were saved.[49]

Their false confidence was hypocrisy, which ensured their damnation.

Just as seventeenth- and eighteenth-century Puritans had condemned the "painted sepulcher" of outward moral conduct, nineteenth-century advisers of youth warned their readers against the hypocrisy of cultivating the "mere surface of character." In the nineteenth-century world of strangers, however, what had been primarily a theological problem took on new social meaning. The social and economic importance of surface impressions was far greater in the cities of antebellum America than it had been in the small towns of the colonial period. The most difficult aspect of the urban problem of hypocrisy for the advisers of young men was the new importance of reputation. The youth addressed by advice literature no longer lived in the town where he had grown up, where the people he met knew him and his name and his abilities. Because he was a stranger, and because no stable apprenticeship system could ensure the value of personal recommendations, reputation was becoming a major prerequisite for his success. Repeatedly he was warned that "the reputation now established must and will go with him, when he begins business for himself."[50] Within the nineteenth-century version of the Protestant ethic, the moral qualities of industry, sobriety, and frugality were believed to result inevitably in material success. But in reality such virtues were worthless unless displayed to the right people. As Paul E. Johnson has said, "Society chose its own self-made men," and the personal values stressed under the new industrial work ethic were useless to the self-made man unless employers decided to reward them.[51] Bluntly stated, the growing importance of reputation in the world of strangers suggested that the youth's inner moral state mattered less than his standing in the eyes of others. The advice writers were forced once again to confront the problem of hypocrisy in the world of strangers. For a man of good reputation, they believed, was not necessarily a man of inner virtue: "A fair reputation among men," wrote one, "is no certain index of the heart towards God."[52] Reputation without virtue, Artemus Muzzey warned his readers, was worthless: "Could we by art and caution sustain a good name with a hollow and false character, what would it profit us?"[53]

Muzzey's implicit fear was that a good reputation, with or without moral foundation, would in fact profit a young man—not spiritually but financially. For the urban marketplace rewarded not virtue but apparent virtue. Self-interest, not fixed moral principle, guided the behavior of most businessmen: "Men are honest while they can thereby promote their worldly interests, secure customers, and increase their reputation. The principle with such persons is a matter of cold calculation, and purely selfish interest."[54] The selfish motive behind such integrity, the advisers warned, would one day stand revealed, for these men—mere "counterfeits" of honesty—would sell their integrity when the price was right. Their virtue was "stock in trade" which they would bring "to market the moment there is an opportunity to dispose of it for as much as they think it worth."[55] The virtues of a fundamentally dishonest man in pursuit of wealth were "marketable commodities, and may be hung up, like meat in the shambles, or sold at auction to the highest bidder."[56] The businessman who cultivated reputation rather than self-reliant virtue, like the confidence man, dealt in confidence for a profit.

In condemning the cultivation of virtue as marketable commodity, the advisers revealed grave concern about the impact of market values on personal conduct. At the same time, however, they recognized the importance of establishing a good reputation in the world of strangers. Reputation, in the words of one adviser, *"makes friends; it creates funds; it draws around him patronage and support; and opens for him a sure and easy way to wealth, to honor and happiness."*[57] Reputation was that aspect of the youth's character that won the confidence of others: "Were I to define what I mean by character, I say *it is that which makes free and intelligent beings have confidence in you.*"[58] The youth of good character, not unlike the confidence man as gambler or pimp, dealt in confidence for financial gain, for only confidence could induce a stranger to invest capital in the economic ventures of an enterprising young man. In fact, the advice writers at times spoke of character as a kind of capital: "Character is like stock in trade; the more of it a man possesses, the greater are his facilities for making additions to it. Or, it is like an accumulating fund,—constantly increasing in value, and daily acquiring to itself fresh accessions of stability and worth."[59] By investing in virtues, principles, and habits rather than in stocks, a man ensured

a safe, a certain investment. How much is a single unalloyed virtue in the soul of a young man worth? It was founded in secret, and was to outward appearance a small thing. But once founded, the first sum recorded, the principal invested, every year will enhance its value. Temptations, the frowns of the wicked, and the smiles of contempt; envy, jealousy, malice and all the powers of darkness may be leagued against him, but the assault will be vain. Stronger than the bolts and locks that shut on the bank's deep vault,—better than endorsements, bonds and pledges,—stronger than all earth and sin combined, is that deep, Christian, unfaltering principle, whose germ was planted by the hand of self, and in the dew of youth. May you each, my young readers, probe this by personal experience. Without this possession you can never be secure against a moral bankruptcy.[60]

On the issue of reputation, the antebellum advisers of youth found themselves caught between a rock and a hard place. To be heard by this generation of young Americans they had to acknowledge the importance of character as reputation, as moral capital. As heirs to Puritan theological concerns about hypocrisy, however, they were anxious about the moral implications of a concentrated effort to appear moral in the eyes of men. In order to advise young men on the importance of a good reputation, the writers had to establish a firm connection between a man's worldly standing before other men and his spiritual standing before God. They began their theological apology for reputation with the simple Arminian assertion that character formation and religion were one and the same: "Religion, pure and undefiled religion, as it is before God even the Father, is the perfection of human character and attainment."[61] As religion acted on man's inner moral character, it necessarily boosted his reputation before men: "For you will mark . . . that, in general, even the vicious and irreligious do, in truth, respect a man whom they believe to be sincerely religious."[62] John Todd went so far as to say that God had ordained that all men must honor a virtuous man and despise a vicious one. Such a law ensured that a good reputation gave sound evidence of a virtuous heart. For this reason, in Todd's somewhat cyclical view, it was God's commandment that men look to their reputations: "On your own character, then, for this life and for the next, depends the decision of the question whether you shall be despised; and I beg that you will understand that God has written over your chamber door, in letters of light—to be read when you enter it, and to be read when you leave it—'let no man despise thee.' "[63]
Within this theological view of reputation, the advisers were stressing the efficacy of piety in improving a man's reputation before other men, and urging their readers to respect the spiritual

significance of a man's reputation among others. They went on to affirm, in an even greater departure from their theological heritage, that to be in a state of grace was to enjoy a good reputation with God. God too judged man by his character: "If you possess character, you will never be overlooked by God or man."[64] Just as the young man's worldly task was to make a good impression upon his fellows, his religious responsibility was to please God. "This conscientious desire to do every thing that is pleasing to God, is the evidence of a 'new heart.' "[65] Like the youth's fellows in the world of strangers, God scrutinized every aspect of his behavior, only his was an "omniscient eye" that "sees all thoughts, hears all words, witnesses all actions."[66] The major difference between God's and men's judgment of character was, of course, that God's discernment was greater: a dishonest businessman, for example, might "escape the censure of the world, and pass through life with an unsullied reputation, and yet be totally unfit to stand before Heaven's tribunal, where the secrets of all hearts will be revealed, and the great Judge 'will render to every man according to his deeds.' "[67] While men could only look upon one another's faces to read character, God's eye penetrated into the character of the human heart: "Before God, every heart has a character. We cannot see into the bosom, but God can. All things are transparent to Him, and he looketh on the heart as we do upon one another's faces: and to Him, every heart is as distinctly marked as men's countenances are to us."[68] Even though God could scrutinize the innermost heart, he was presented as merely another reader of character, and the youth was warned to behave himself in the presence of this "Great Judge of Character."

Aaron Burr's Puritan sense of disgust at his "Secret hope of *recommending* myself to God" was nowhere to be found in the advice literature's view of the spiritual value of reputation. The youth who diligently guarded his reputation before man and God, according to the manuals, did recommend himself to God and thus secured his heavenly reward. In their efforts to link reputation with spiritual state, the advisers were trying to hold together two conflicting definitions of character. Character meant, on the one hand, self-reliant virtue based on fixed inner principle. At the same time, character meant reputation, the youth's outward demonstration of inner virtue; not his principles, but his standing in the eyes of others; not his self-reliance, but his efforts to please an audience of strangers. The concept of character represented an effort to reconcile two different views of human nature: the premodern concept of soul, which focused on man's inner spiritual being as he confronted God alone, and the modern concept of personality, which turned attention to man's external standing before other men.[69] The nineteenth century's use of the term *character* demonstrates the transition from the premodern farmer's spiritual reliance on God for economic judgment, for agricultural success or failure, to the modern salesman's secular reliance on other men as the buyers who determined his worldly fate, his success or failure in the marketplace. In their encouragement of self-reliant virtue, the advice writers aimed to place the young man beyond capricious circumstance in a threatening modern world and thus betrayed their nostalgia for a static, hierarchical social order and a fixed reference point for personal conduct. But in their emphasis on reputation, they acknowledged the importance of how the youth represented himself to others and thus helped propel him into the modern world.

Ultimately, the writers of advice had to accept the conditions of success operating in the early industrial world of strangers. As William Alcott wrote, "We are compelled to take the world, in a great measure, as it is. We can hardly expect men to come and buy our wares, unless we advertise or expose them for sale. So if we would commend ourselves to the notice of our fellow men, we must set ourselves up."[70] For a young man to get ahead among strangers, Alcott admitted, he had to learn to cultivate the right impressions, to guard carefully his reputation with other men. But these were the arts of the confidence man, the arch-hypocrite of the world of strangers. How, then, was the youth to succeed in this world without succumbing to hypocrisy, without being recruited into the ranks of confidence men?

In the broadest sense, the problem of hypocrisy revealed a serious crisis in urban middle-class norms of social conduct. Who could be trusted in the treacherous city where any offer of friendship might result in a calculated betrayal? How could strangers meet without being contaminated with the hypocrisy of confidence men? As a man on the make and as a newcomer to the city, the inexperienced youth represented an entire generation of urban middle-class Americans striving for higher social status. They, like the youth represented in the advice manuals, wandered in a kind of social vacuum respecting the norms governing face-to-face conduct. They had left behind them the traditional conventions of a

familiar social world, where character unfolded slowly within relatively stable social relations and men came to know one another
gradually and well. But they had not yet developed new conventions for the world of strangers, where character had to be assessed
quickly within relatively fleeting relationships and men often came
to know very little of one another. Caught between old norms and
expectations and new social demands on conduct, the urban middle
classes confronted what they perceived to be a serious crisis.

This is not merely to say that they did not know how to behave in
the world of strangers. In their view, the widespread hypocrisy that
was poisoning social relations among the rising generation threatened to destroy those relations, to dissolve the ties of confidence
that bound men together in society. These ties, they believed, were
fundamentally sentimental: affection, not coercion, linked man to
man, heart to heart, in the American republic. Before the Fall,
wrote Rufus Clark, the law of love that bound mankind together
had been strong. But with mankind's first deception, "each heart
was separated from the other, and sought to build up a distinct
kingdom within the narrow enclosure of its own private interests."[71]
As each human heart was thus isolated from its neighbor, men had
learned to protect their self-interest through duplicity. Widely
practiced, the advisers feared, such deceitfulness threatened to tear
the social fabric asunder. As David Magie wrote in 1853, "The
whole *frame-work of society* is upheld and kept in order by truth, and
nothing but truth. Let deception become universally prevalent, and
communities as such could scarcely exist, much less flourish and be
happy." Deception destroyed the social bonds among men, within
this view, by contaminating the sources of sociability: "the stream of
social enjoyment would be poisoned at its very fountain."[72] Duplicity, within the sentimental view of social relations, was capable of
reducing the American republic to a state of anarchy: "Suspicion
now takes the place of confidence, and the abodes of human beings
are turned into so many dens of ravenous beasts."[73]

This crisis in social relations called for the establishment of a new
code of conduct, within which men could meet without suspicion,
without fear of betrayal by confidence men. The advice manuals
met this need with the cult of sincerity. The most important quality
to be cultivated in all personal conduct, they instructed their readers repeatedly, was sincerity. First of all, young men were never to
be guilty of telling lies. But the demand for sincerity went far
beyond verbal truth-telling: the advisers insisted on "a faithful

correspondence between the heart and the lips, the feelings and the words, the inward consciousness and the outward expression."[74] Sincerity meant not just integrity but candor—the perfect outward revelation of all inward truth:

> Candour is opposed to many other vices, all of which are unfriendly to truth. Disingenuousness, which would conceal the truth by some deceptive veil; artifice, which could make falsehood pass for truth; improper concealment, which could hide the truth where it is required; moral cowardice, which makes one fear the truth, these mean yet dangerous and besetting vices are all opposed to candour.[75]

Perfect candor was a matter not simply of the spoken word but of the entire personal manner and appearance. The sincere youth was supposed to have a frank, open countenance and an ingenuous manner. In short, the advisers of American youth urged them to cultivate nothing less than "a perfectly transparent character."[76] If all men would embrace the virtue of transparent character, then sentimental typology would be restored to its prelapsarian perfection, and hypocrisy would be no more. Perfect sincerity would collapse the distance between moral traits and their visible signs in conduct and appearance, between the state of a man's soul and his reputation among men. Transparent man cultivated no Machiavellian mask to disguise his thoughts and feelings, no cloak to hide his evil heart. The sincere youth was in reality exactly what he appeared to be. When Alcott told his readers that men must "set ourselves up" to be noticed by others, he hastily added, "not for something which we are not;—but for what, upon a careful examination, we find reason to think we are."[77] Even as he encouraged them to "advertise and expose their wares," he insisted on the sincerity of their personal statement. In Alcott's view a virtuous youth could strive to make the right impressions on other men, but only within a scrupulous adherence to the cult of sincerity. If all men would conform to a strict code of sincerity, then social confidence would be secured, and the republic would be rescued from a descent into anarchy.

The cult of sincerity set forth in the pages of antebellum advice manuals was not new to Anglo-American culture. The introspective religious impulse of seventeenth-century Puritanism, with its central attack on the sin of spiritual hypocrisy, had given rise in English thought to what Leon Guilhamet has called the "sincere ideal."[78]

When the Puritan asked himself "Am I saved?" he implicitly questioned whether or not he was sincere. According to John Howe, a post-Restoration Puritan leader, "Sincerity is a most God-like excellency; an imitation of his truth, as grounded in his all-sufficiency; which sets him above the necessity or possibility of any advantage by collusion or deceit; and corresponds to his omnisciency and heart-searching eye."[79] As the Puritan ideal of sincerity was adopted by a variety of English intellectuals in the late seventeenth and early eighteenth centuries, it was extended from the realm of religious piety to all aspects of daily conduct. The latitudinarian Archbishop John Tillotson wrote,

> And with the sincerity of our piety towards God, let us join the simplicity and integrity of manners in our conversation with men. Let us strictly charge ourselves to use truth and plainness in all our words and doings; let our tongue be ever the true interpreter of our mind, and our expressions the lively image of our thoughts and affections, and our outward actions exactly agreeable to our inward purposes and intentions.[80]

The Dissenter Isaac Watts, the liberal theologian Benjamin Hoadly, the Deist Earl of Shaftesbury, the Augustan Joseph Addison, the sentimental novelist Samuel Richardson—all found common intellectual ground in the sincere ideal.[81] Many could echo Daniel Defoe's complaint in 1709 that "this Sir, is an Age of Plot and Deceit, of Contradiction and Paradox. . . . It is very hard under all these Masks, to see the true countenance of any Man."[82] In attacking their own "Age of Plot and Deceit," eighteenth-century proponents of the sincere ideal asserted that if men would learn to act without guile, they might recapture their prelapsarian condition of uncorrupt sincerity and establish social utopia. When Timothy S. Arthur informed his readers that Adam had communicated not through the spoken word but through the language of a transparent physiognomy, he was expressing an eighteenth-century view of the Edenic nature of perfect sincerity.

In antebellum American advice literature, however, sentimental formulation of the cult of sincerity took on a new note of urgency. Sincerity here was not simply a lovely utopian ideal toward which all men should strive; it was the only hope of a social framework threatened by the pervasive hypocrisy of the American people. In the dangerous world of strangers, where evil confidence men stalked the streets seeking to dupe and destroy their fellow men, only sincerity could ensure the survival of sentimental social bonding. But the nineteenth-century American cult of sincerity contained one serious flaw: the young man upon whose candor rested the fate of the republic still inhabited a society poisoned by deceit. It must be remembered that the ease with which the confidence man seduced his innocent victim owed much to the youth's ingenuous, confiding nature. "The most open hearted are the most liable to be imposed upon by the designing."[83] Even as the advice manuals encouraged readers to cultivate transparency of character, they advised them that "in general, it is the best way to say as little about ourselves, our friends, our books, and our circumstances as possible."[84] It was most important, the manuals warned, "not to disclose our hearts to those who shut up theirs from us."[85] Even "a tell-tale countenance" could place the unguarded youth at a dangerous disadvantage, because the confidence man was a master psychologist who would use the transparent youth's innermost feelings against him in the seduction process. Thus the youth who "cannot hear displeasing things without visible marks of anger or uneasiness, or pleasing ones without a sudden burst of joy, a cheerful eye, or an expanded face, is at the mercy of every knave; for either they will designedly please or provoke you themselves, to catch your unguarded looks, or they will thus seize the opportunity to read your very heart, when any other shall do it."[86] According to this anonymous writer, the only sure defense against such knaves was the cultivation of

> an artificial insensibility of fear, anger, sorrow, and concern of any sort whatever. He that actually feels either pain or pleasure cannot help expressing it some way or other; and whoever makes the discovery has the springs of the affections at his command, and may wind them up or let them down at pleasure; whereas, he that witnesses no sensation of the mind, betrays no weakness, and is wholly inaccessible.[87]

In urging his readers to cultivate a mask of insensibility to protect themselves against knavery, this anonymous writer displayed a cynicism unusual among the sentimentalist advice writers. But many other manuals advised their readers not to wear their hearts on their sleeves, to tell the truth but not the whole truth, to choose their intimate friends with great caution. Perfect transparency of character, they admitted, could prove very dangerous if practiced freely among strangers.

Ironically, sincerity made the youth more susceptible to seduction and thus to recruitment into the ranks of the hypocrites. The cult of sincerity obviously offered the only solution to the problem of hypocrisy in the world of strangers. But sincerity could not be practiced safely in the streets and marketplaces of the antebellum city where the problem of hypocrisy had taken form. The cult of sincerity was to take shape in an entirely different social arena, where it would be enforced not by men but by women.

Sentimental Culture
and the Problem of Fashion

A profound middle-class distrust of the city as a realm of hypocrisy and deceit surfaced in English literature nearly a century before 1830. One of the most famous heroines of eighteenth-century literature was the victim of a confidence game played in the world of strangers that was London: Samuel Richardson's Clarissa is a poor country girl who meets her downfall because, as Ian Watt has observed, she never knows "what duplicities are hidden in the behaviour of the people she meets, or what horrors are being perpetrated behind the walls of [the city's] houses." As Clarissa herself confesses, "I knew nothing of the town and its ways." Watt has argued that the response of Richardson and other eighteenth-century writers to urbanization was to retreat from the dangers of a world "so large and various that only a little of it can be experienced by any one individual" into "the new domain of private experience" offered by the novel.[1] This emerging literary form drew its readers into an imaginative world of intensely personal relationships and offered them a psychological haven from the dangers of public life among strangers who hid their real intentions behind urban masks and disguises. Samuel Richardson's fear of the city launched a literary tradition that would culminate in the popular sentimental fiction of nineteenth-century America. The sentimental genre that first emerged in response to eighteenth-century London achieved its greatest popularity among American readers during the urban explosion of the decades before the Civil War.[2]

The central premise underlying all the sentimental fiction that poured off the American press in the nineteenth century was that private experience was morally superior to public life. Sentimentalists assigned value to private experience in proportion to its emotional intensity, or what they termed *sensibility*. Sensibility was the *summum bonum* of literary sentimentalism: "Blest Sensibility!" wrote one enthusiast. "Exquisite meliorator of the mind! Touched by the magic of thy wand, the heart finds grief delicious!"[3] Sensibility meant the responsiveness of a delicate heart to the slightest emotional stimulus. The nerves of the woman or man of sensibility responded immediately and fully to "the least twitch on the spider-fine filaments of memory and pity."[4] Although such a finely tuned nervous system could belong to a man as well as a woman, sentimentalists believed that generally women were endowed with superior sensibility. Woman was defined as a creature of the heart, who acted largely from her affections; man, as a creature of the mind, who was moved primarily by his reason. As one sentimentalist wrote, woman possessed in abundance "all the virtues that are founded in the sensibility of the heart. . . . Pity, the attribute of angels, and friendship, the balm of life, delight to dwell in the female breast."[5]

Because she was endowed with superior sensibility, according to the sentimentalists, woman was naturally more sincere than man. For sensibility meant not merely the intense feelings of the private heart; it referred as well to the body's sympathetic response to those affections, to the outward physical manifestations of the heart's contents. The woman of sensibility involuntarily expressed her feelings in swoons, illness, trances, ecstasies, and, most important, tears, the "infallible signs of grace in the religion of the heart."[6] Sentimentalists thus insisted that true women were constitutionally transparent, incapable of disguising their feelings: "With her heart on her lips and her soul in her eyes— / What more could I ask in dear woman than this."[7] Even her complexion offered evidence of her inner emotions as she reddened or grew pale in the intensity of her sensibility. This quality of involuntary candor was seen as one of woman's finest attributes: even the historian Hannah Adams, who led an unusually public and intellectual life for a woman of her time, was eulogized on the grounds that "her sensibility, the warmth of her affections, her sincerity and candor, call forth a flow of feeling that cannot be restrained."[8] As Adams's eulogy suggests, the sentimental retreat from the public urban world represented in large part an effort to delineate a realm of experience where hypocrisy would be impossible.

In the sentimental view, the natural sincerity of woman granted her a special responsibility for counteracting the pervasive deceit of the larger society lying outside the realm of private experience. Because she was involuntarily transparent, she served as a natural foil to the villainous confidence man, who was dangerous insofar as he contrived to be emotionally opaque. With his "fair exterior and winning manners,"[9] he artfully disguised the illicit passions, hatreds, and torments of a fiend and thus severed the natural connection between outward appearances and inner emotional realities, the sentimental typology of conduct on which social confidence rested. But the true woman was believed incapable of such disguise. In every tear, blush, glance, smile, and gesture she affirmed the sentimental typology of conduct and thus helped restore confidence to social relations. In the sentimental view, even the best of men could only expose the duplicities of other men in the world of strangers. "I went forth," said one of Lydia Sigourney's heroes, "amid the jarring competitions and perpetual strifes of men. I adjusted their opposing interests, while I despised them and their concerns. I unravelled their perplexities. I penetrated their subterfuges. I exposed their duplicity."[10] But the men who moved in the dangerous public arena, as discussed in chapter 2, could not meet hypocrisy with sincerity, because any transparent display of feeling would expose them to seduction by confidence men. Only women, ensconced in their private realm of sensibility, could safely embrace the sentimental idea of sincerity.

The special responsibility of women to counteract the hypocrisy of a deceitful world was part of the larger social role assigned them within what historians have called "the cult of domesticity."[11] Between 1780 and 1835, as American society underwent a transition from preindustrial to modern industrial work patterns, the middle-class home was gradually deprived of its productive role in the economy. Because the home defied economic rationalization and eluded the cash nexus, it came to be seen as a separate social sphere, a retirement or retreat from the larger world. With the rapid expansion of industrial capitalism, what had been a premise of sentimental literature was becoming the foundation of a powerful social ethic. "The central convention of domesticity," writes Nancy Cott, "was the contrast between the home and the world,"[12] and that contrast was generally understood in sentimental terms. Middle-class Americans in the early nineteenth century began to idealize the home as "a treasury of pure disinterested love, such as is seldom found in the busy walks of a selfish and calculating world."[13] The woman's main social responsibility was to preserve the home as a realm of sensibility where "heart meets heart, in all the fondness of a full affection."[14] Unless he had a strong tie to this realm of domestic sensibility, according to Catharine Beecher, the man who "spent his life in the collisions of the world, seldom escapes without the most confirmed habits of cold, and revolting selfishness."[15] As keeper of sensibility in a heartless world, the American woman was to rescue the American man from such selfishness; and as keeper of sincerity in a world poisoned by hypocrisy, she was to guard the home as a retreat where he could find "reciprocated humanity . . . unmixed with hate or the cunning of deceit."[16]

The belief that women were naturally more sincere than men suggested that women might offer a solution to the problem of hypocrisy in American society. But the domestic isolation that protected transparent women from the confidence man's game also threatened to ensure their powerlessness over social relations outside the home. By definition the domestic sphere was closed off, hermetically sealed from the poisonous air of the world outside.[17] Although domestic sincerity might offer some psychological compensation for the deceitfulness of public urban life, it could not resolve the problem of hypocrisy in the larger social world. Hypocrisy was a problem where men met as strangers; within the domestic circle, where family members were presumed to know one another intimately, the problem of hypocrisy lost much of its significance. Needed was a third social sphere, lying between the public world of strangers where sincerity was dangerous and the private family circle where the sincere ideal was virtually meaningless. This middle social sphere was found in the parlor.

The parlor was the front room of the middle-class home where friends, acquaintances, and carefully screened strangers met formally "in society." Geographically, it lay between the urban street where strangers freely mingled and the back regions of the house where only family members were permitted to enter uninvited. Within the cult of domesticity, the parlor provided the woman of the house with a "cultural podium" from which she was to exert her moral influence over American society.[18] There she ruled as a kind of constitutional monarch whose responsibility was to enforce the hundreds of rules governing polite social intercourse. Central in this vast body of social legislation was the sentimental ideal of sincerity. Within the Victorian parlor sentimentalism was not a mere abstraction: it was a prescriptive norm that shaped all aspects of dress, etiquette, and social ritual. The key to all these cultural forms was the sentimental typology of conduct, the belief that every aspect of social behavior should transparently display the contents of the heart. "Sentimentalism" defined nineteenth-century middle-class *culture* in the broadest sense of the term: not simply as a body of literature or as a lofty ideal of personal conduct, but as a set of assumptions that determined, for example, what kind of bonnet a woman should wear, when a man should remove his glove to shake hands, and how men and women should shed tears over their dead. Through a scrupulous adherence to the cult of sincerity in the parlor, middle-class men and especially women were to turn back the tide of hypocrisy that seemed to be engulfing American society.

Sentimental culture represented the efforts of urban middle-class Americans in the decades before the Civil War to confront the serious social crisis symbolized by the confidence man. The confidence man represented, first of all, the dangers of liminality in a fluid society; and second, the dangers of life in the urban world of strangers where ambitious men deceitfully manipulated surface impressions in order to rise in the social scale. Social mobility in general, and urban social mobility in particular, made many middle-class Americans uneasy about the welfare of the American republic. Unable to understand the historical forces at work modernizing their society, they identified the problem in simplistic, moral terms: Americans were becoming hypocrites. The solution easily followed: the most naturally sincere portion of the population, women, were to ensure that hypocrisy was barred from polite middle-class social intercourse. The problem of hypocrisy, which had arisen in the streets and marketplaces of the world of strangers, would be confronted and resolved in the parlor of the middle-class home.

In drawing the battle lines for their war on hypocrisy in the parlor, however, middle-class Americans had to face a new enemy. For the parlor itself was in grave danger of invasion by confidence men and, even more horrifying to the Victorian mind, by their female counterparts, painted women. The parlor was by no means immune to the hypocrisy that poisoned social relations in the world outside the home, for even in the parlor the powerful aspirations of men and women on the make were evident. The parlor was the arena within which the aspiring middle classes worked to establish their claims to social status, to that elusive quality of "gentility."[19] As the next three chapters demonstrate, the conventions governing dress, etiquette, and social ritual in the parlor represented the middle-class effort to establish sincerity as the guiding force behind polite social conduct. But first it is necessary to examine what was perceived as the greatest threat to the sincerity of parlor society: the hypocrisy of fashion.

Before the Industrial Revolution fashion was primarily the province of the court-based aristocracy: the nobility set fashions in dress and determined the rigid rules of "courtesy" for the European upper classes.[20] In colonial America, aristocrats imitated the fashions set by the London court. But over the course of the eighteenth century, the increasing power of the middle classes gradually undermined the court's domination of fashion. In England, a wealthy and powerful oligopoly accepted the worldly advice of that wily diplomat, the Earl of Chesterfield, and began to imitate aristocratic dress and etiquette.[21] Even as fashion was becoming the aristocrat's only possible means to distinguish himself from the wealthy but untitled bourgeois, fashionable forms of dress and conduct were increasingly adopted by the middle classes. The aristocracy endeavored to stay one step ahead of the fashion-conscious middle classes, and the rate of fashion change accelerated. But with the coming of the French Revolution, according to sociologist René König, fashion at last became "a universal formative principle of society."[22] Once the revolution had abolished the distinctions of birth as illegitimate, the middle classes seized upon fashion as a means to segregate themselves from the less deserving lower classes. Nowhere was this phenomenon more pronounced than among the American middle classes in the Age of Jackson. The vociferous egalitarianism of the republic apparently made middle-class aspirants all the more anxious to pursue fashion in an effort to distinguish themselves from the democratic mob. As Alexis de Tocqueville insightfully observed,

> In democracies, where the members of the community never differ from each other and naturally stand so near that they may all at any time be fused in one general mass, numerous artificial and arbitrary distinctions spring up by means of which every man hopes to keep himself aloof lest he should be carried away against his will in the crowd.[23]

For the rising middle classes of the nineteenth century, fashion served both as a barrier which had to be surmounted by those entering the more privileged bourgeois circles and as a standard which could be applied to the claims of those seeking admission from below.[24] According to European observers of democratic manners and morals, the social conduct of the American middle classes clearly demonstrated the first function of fashion as barrier. In their eagerness to enter the more privileged bourgeois circles above them, middle-class Americans strived to pass the fashion barrier by dressing stylishly and practicing ceremonial etiquette to a degree condemned by many visitors as absurd. The social supremacy of the Chestnut Street set within Philadelphia society, reported Harriet Martineau, her tongue in cheek, rested on the practice of rising thrice on the toes before the curtsey; Arch Street residents rose only twice.[25] American efforts to enter higher social spheres often led them to imitate European fashions, with what foreign travelers regarded as ridiculous results. Francis Grund was struck, for example, by the efforts of a beautiful sixteen-year-old social aspirant who,

> throwing her head back and her breast forward, imitated by a sudden jerk of her body one of those ludicrous bows which the Gallo-American dancing-masters have substituted for the slow, graceful, dignified courtesies of old; and which fashionable women in the United States, who are generally in advance of the most grotesque fashions of Paris, are sure to turn into a complete caricature.[26]

Charles Dickens scornfully reported that fashionable young ladies in America "sang in all languages—except their own. German, French, Italian, Spanish, Portuguese, Swiss; but nothing native; nothing so low as native."[27] Worst of all, Americans anxious to crash the fashion barrier assumed false titles, lionized or cultivated titled nobility, and engaged in "toad-eating" or "toadying," the obsequious flattering of their social superiors.

Fashion-conscious behavior among middle-class Americans also demonstrated the importance of fashion as a standard that might be applied to the social claims of the less fortunate. The middle-class American who succeeded in crossing the fashion barrier, in other words, could then use fashion to exclude applicants who followed. Americans were merciless, according to European observers, in their scrutiny of the *parvenu* seeking admission to what was called society. "Claims are canvassed and pretensions weighed," wrote Thomas Hamilton; "manners, fortune, tastes, habits and descent undergo a rigid examination."[28] To distinguish themselves from the egalitarian masses below them, Americans wielded invitations and calling cards to barricade the vulgar from their social presence. Above all, they learned to "cut" former acquaintances as they improved their social status. Good manners in America, wrote Francis Grund, were aimed at making their victims "as uncomfortable as possible" to prove their inferiority. "In order to be 'genteel,' " he observed, "it is necessary, in the first place, to know nobody that is *not* so; and our fashionable women and girls have a peculiar talent for staring their old friends and acquaintances out of countenance, as often as they take a new house."[29]

Many of the European visitors who attacked the follies of American fashion-hunters revealed at least as much about their own sense of social superiority as they did about the snobbery of the American middle classes. Francis Grund's contempt for the fashionable American was not untypical: "This aristocracy here is itself nothing but a wealthy overgrown *bourgeoisie,* composed of a few families who have been more successful in trade than the rest, and on that account are now cutting their friends and relations in order to be considered fashionable."[30] Grund, along with many other European visitors to the United States, criticized the middle-class pursuit of fashion primarily for its ridiculous pretentiousness. But for American middle-class moralists, such as the writers of advice to young men, the problem of fashion was far more serious. In the view of men such as Rufus Clark, young men and women of fashion led

> a mere butterfly existence, sporting from flower to flower, and chasing one shadow after another, with no adequate views of the responsibilities and duties of life. Their greatest excitement is derived from the most trivial sources. The changes in the weather, the last novel, a new fashion, afford them the highest mental stimulus.[31]

The life of fashion, in other words, undermined all moral self-improvement. Fashion was regarded as the art of surface illusion, and the youth who mastered this art was advised sternly "to turn himself inside out and see the vile and empty chambers of his soul, and then put on his airs."[32] Young men and women of fashion were learning to cultivate a showy appearance at the expense of moral character: they "put on the tinsel" to emulate the "show and glitter" of the wealthy; they struggled hard "to *seem* to be what they really are not."[33] In the view of American moralists, the middle-class pursuit of fashion was not merely a ridiculous pretension; it was an act of hypocrisy. The greatest evils of fashion were symbolized in the "bland, smooth-tongued, genteel, fashionable companion," the confidence man.[34]

Fashion, in short, seemed to be infecting middle-class parlor society with the immoral practices of the worldly confidence man. Once again, the figure of the confidence man served to focus the anxieties of middle-class Americans concerning upward social mobility. For the advisers of youth recognized that behind the fashion impulse lay the middle-class American's desire to set himself or herself apart from the democratic masses by establishing artificial social distinctions. With less sophistication than Tocqueville, William Alcott essentially echoed the French critic's theory: a peculiarly American "shame of being thought poor" fueled the American pursuit of fashion, and the "dread of what is called falling in the scale of society" was so great that many Americans were driven to insanity and even suicide.[35] Alcott thus confronted what he considered to be a grave crisis: the pursuit of fashion, by which middle-class Americans attempted to establish their claims to gentility, was simply a parlor version of the confidence game that was poisoning social relations in the world outside the home.

Worst of all, the fashionable confidence game was being played primarily by that group of Americans most responsible for preserving the parlor as a sacred realm of sincerity: women. Of fashion-hungry women, Alcott wrote despairingly that "dress, personal appearance, equipage, style of a dwelling or its furniture, with no other view, however, than the promotion of mere physical enjoyment, is the height of their desires for self-improvement!"[36] Freed from many of the productive economic tasks performed by women in the earlier agricultural households, and often released from many domestic responsibilities by servants, the middle-class woman in the nineteenth century assumed the responsibility of elevating her family's social position as her husband struggled up the ladder of economic status.[37] It was she who worked to gain admittance into the finer bourgeois social circles by crossing the fashion barrier, and it was she who excluded the less deserving from her own set by raising the fashion standard. The American woman, whose highest moral responsibility was to preserve sincerity in the parlor, threatened to poison parlor society with the hypocrisy of fashion.

Middle-class women were thus caught in a conflict between two important social roles: how were they to act both as keepers of sincerity and as arbiters of fashion in the parlor? Fashion was condemned by sentimentalists as a form of hypocrisy, but fashion was increasingly viewed as a necessary evil in a society established on the promise of social mobility. This conflict between the sincere ideal and the growing power of fashion over middle-class life was a powerful force shaping the conventions of polite parlor conduct in the three major areas of sentimental culture: dress, etiquette, and social ritual. Of the three the most obvious area was women's dress: no other aspect of middle-class conduct was so completely shaped by the capricious dictates of fashion. The task of mediating the conflict between sentimental sincerity and fashionable hypocrisy thus had to be confronted in the pages of America's leading fashion magazine, *Godey's Lady's Book,* which began publication in 1830. By 1860, at least 150,000 women were regularly consulting *Godey's* to learn how to dress in the latest styles.[38] Significantly, even *Godey's Lady's Book* expressed great anxiety about the moral evils of the fashionable life: throughout the 1830s and 1840s, and into the 1850s, the fashion columns, articles, and short stories of *Godey's* were dominated by the moral critique of fashion as hypocrisy. In embracing the sentimental critique of fashion, the editors and contributors to *Godey's* set themselves two very difficult tasks: they had to articulate a sentimental rationale for a woman's attention to fashion, and they had to explain how particular dress styles conformed to the sentimental ideal by enhancing woman's sincerity. First, it is important to examine the critique of fashion offered by *Godey's Lady's Book.*

"How little stress is to be laid on personal appearance!"[39] Here was an odd message for a fashion magazine to proclaim, but in the first few years of *Godey's* publication, this maxim was echoed repeatedly. "It is always the mark of a weak mind, if not a bad heart," warned one contributor, "to hear a person praise or blame another on the ground alone that they are handsome or homely."[40] A woman's homely personal appearance or unstylish clothing, according to *Godey's,* too often led others to overlook her inner moral worth. Once a famous authoress, wearing an ugly, "leaf-colored" pelisse, had arrived incognito at a dinner party, and some of the guests had snubbed her for her poor taste. After watching this scene for as long as they could, those who knew her identity finally announced who she was, and the embarrassed guests learned, predictably, that a beautiful flower might be found under a dead leaf.[41] Dress, according to America's leading fashion magazine in its first years of publication, did not matter. What mattered was character.

Throughout the 1830s, *Godey's* noted with growing alarm the encroachments of fashion on the everyday lives of middle-class Americans. In 1837, the "Editor's Table" deplored the decline of simplicity in American social life and the rise of an extravagant life devoted to fashionable dress and entertainment.[42] Like the advice manuals for young men, *Godey's Lady's Book* condemned fashion for distracting attention from inner self-improvement toward frivolous and ephemeral matters:

> Oh! It is grievous to see a being standing upon the threshold of an immortal existence, created for glorious purposes, and with faculties to fulfil them, discussing the merits of a ribbon, or the form of a bow, or the width of a frill, as earnestly as if the happiness of her race, or her soul's salvation depended upon her decision.[43]

Above all, *Godey's* attacked fashion's destruction of sincerity in social intercourse. Under the powerful sway of fashion, society was being transformed into one great masquerade:

> The exterior of life is but a masquerade, in which we dress ourselves in the finest fashions of society, use a language suited to the characters we assume;—with smiling faces, mask aching hearts; address accents of kindness to our enemies, and often those of coldness to our friends. The part once assumed must be acted out, no matter at what expense of truth and feeling.[44]

The characters of men and women of fashion were not shaped from within, but assumed for the occasion; fashionable "character" was a part to be played, a mask to be donned. In a stock plot line of sentimental fiction, an ingenuous young girl enters "ultra-fashionable society," where she learns to assume "the mask of fashion."[45] The heroine in a story entitled "A Life of Fashion" chastises her old friend for thus succumbing to social hypocrisy: "I remember, Fanny, when falsehood was a stranger to your lips, when your ingenuous countenance was a true index of your pure mind, and now, though you have not yet seen your five and twentieth summer, the whitest-haired diplomatist in Europe might envy you your perfect power over every feature, and every tone."[46] In assuming the mask of fashion, Fanny was practicing the art of parlor hypocrisy and thus was guilty of destroying the sentimental typology of conduct. As *Godey's* intoned, "Many are men's hypocrisies, and countless are the conventional falsehoods that float about in the bustle of society."[47]

The attack of *Godey's Lady's Book* on fashion revealed a powerful republican bias in its focus on the fashionable excesses of the Old World aristocracy. "Throughout the old world," a *Godey's* editorial noted with disapproval, "the fashions are set by the *courts*, and those who consider themselves the porcelain towers of society."[48] Within those porcelain towers, according to republican ideology, men of power conspired to undermine the liberty of the people by seducing them from their simplicity and virtue. One of the aristocracy's techniques was to enslave the people to fashion: "Fashion is the voluntary slavery which leads us to think, act, and dress according to the judgment of fools and the caprice of coxcombs."[49] Once again, the American republican tendency to see plots against liberty being hatched everywhere was accompanied by the deep-seated conviction that appearances are deceiving and that the enemies of liberty often come in disguise. In numerous articles on the history of costume, *Godey's Lady's Book* observed that, in the eighteenth-century courts of the Old World, fashion had functioned as a form of disguise. Men and women of the court had assumed masks—not the nineteenth-century physiognomic "mask of fashion," but actual masks, half-size and full, held in place by a button grasped between the teeth. They had coated their faces with white enamel paint, thick powder, and black beauty patches. They had assumed towering hair styles laden with ribbons and artificial flowers and trappings of every imaginable kind, or they had worn powdered wigs. And they had buried their persons in padding and artificial structures, jewelry and flowers, lace and ribbons.[50] To the sentimental mind such flagrant costuming could only be seen as a form of hypocrisy, part of the larger fashionable masquerade that was court life. "The nineteenth century," one *Godey's* contributor wrote in 1849, "with its darker colors and more thoughtful energy, seems even now, when nearly half of its years are sped, to wear mourning for the criminal folly of its predecessors."[51]

For nineteenth-century sentimentalists the dangers presented by fashionable hypocrisy were incalculable. The life of fashion, in destroying personal sincerity, threatened to reduce middle-class "society," and by implication American society, to complete chaos. The evil potential of even the smallest act of parlor deceit was vividly illustrated by *Godey's* in a short story entitled "The Fatal Cosmetic," published in 1839. The hero of the story is Mr. Hall, who has been betrayed by a false lover and is now searching for a perfectly sincere woman. The efforts of this sentimental Diogenes have, however, met with little success, for the life of fashion has transformed all men and women into lying hypocrites. Says Hall, "I cannot enjoy an artificial state of society. I consider *truth* as the corner stone of the great social fabric, and where this is wanting, I am constantly looking for ruin and desolation." Truth he finds finally in the heroine Margaret Howard, who first reveals her sincerity by quietly observing in formal company that the young lady who has just played the piano has no musical talent. In Margaret the admiring Hall finds "a young, beautiful, and accomplished woman, surrounded by the artifices and embellishments of fashionable life, keeping the truth, in all simplicity and godly sincerity as commanded by the holy men of old."[52]

Margaret's fashionable foil is Mary Ellis, who immediately establishes her hypocrisy by politely flattering the bad pianist. In defense of Mary's etiquette, her lover Charles argues with Mr. Hall that "she has remarkably popular manners and if she *is* guilty of a few little innocent deceptions, such, for instance, as the present, I see no possible harm in them to herself, and they certainly give great pleasure to others." Charles goes on to warn Hall that, "if you look upon the necessary dissimulations practised in society as falsehoods, and brand them as such, I can only say, that you have created a standard of morality more exalted and pure than human nature can ever reach."[53] From the opening scene of "The Fatal Cosmetic," Margaret and Mr. Hall represent one view of social intercourse, while Mary and Charles represent the opposing view. The sentimental couple assert the view that sincerity and perfect truthfulness must pervade every social exchange, and the fashionable couple insist that some dissimulation is necessary to keep the wheels of sociability well oiled. The sympathy of the reader is, of course, enlisted on the side of the sentimentalists.

As the plot of "The Fatal Cosmetic" unfolds, the fashionable dissimulations of Mary begin to escalate. Soon after she flatters the bad pianist, she falsely denies that she has broken a costly mirror in the home of her hostess. The angry Mrs. Astor blames her black servant and has her whipped. Finally, on the evening before her marriage to Charles, Mary purchases a poisonous cosmetic to treat an ugly eruption of her complexion. When Margaret anxiously asks whether Mary has carefully disposed of the deadly poison, the hypocrite replies that she has. In fact, she has misplaced it, and the chambermaid ignorantly puts it away in the medicine chest. On the next day Mr. Hall's false lover, Mrs. St. Henry, arrives at the wedding reception, catches sight of him, and falls to the floor in a faint. A doctor is called, he prescribes calomel, the fatal cosmetic is accidentally administered, and the beautiful Mrs. St. Henry dies in agony. For those few readers who may have missed the heavy moral of this tale, the authoress spells it out clearly: "Let those who consider a *white lie* a venial offence, who look upon deception as necessary to the happiness and harmony of society, reflect on the consequences of Mary Ellis's moral delinquency and tremble at the view."[54]

"The Fatal Cosmetic" is a classic expression of the sentimental view of fashionable hypocrisy. Ridiculous though it may seem to modern readers, it must have had a chilling effect on the sentimental audience of *Godey's Lady's Book*. "The Fatal Cosmetic" is the story of a thoughtless young woman of fashion who moves steadily from a polite insincerity through a series of larger lies until one of her deceptions results in unintentional homicide. Significantly, Mrs. St. Henry dies from a dose of a poisonous cosmetic. Just as she is literally poisoned by a cosmetic that was purchased to disguise a blemish on the face of a fashionable young woman, parlor society was figuratively poisoned by fashionable hypocrisy. The message of the story was quite clear: when sincere social intercourse was replaced by the masquerade that was fashion—when even the smallest social lie was told in the interests of polite sociability—then the sentimental ties that bound society together snapped and chaos ensued. She who dared to flatter a bad pianist would live to see her lies become deadly and would spend the rest of her days regretting her error.

The fashionable hypocrite who dominates "The Fatal Cosmetic" is not a confidence man but a painted woman. The hypocrisy practiced by Mary is far more dangerous than that of her lover Charles: while his pursuit of fashion was merely frivolous, hers was deadly. As a woman, she exercised an incalculable influence over the manners of an entire age: "The prevailing manners of an age depend, more than we are aware of, or are willing to allow, on the conduct of the women: this is one of the principal things on which the great machine of human society turns."[55] Sarah Josepha Hale, who edited *Godey's Lady's Book* from 1837 to 1877, was one of the most outspoken champions of the sentimental ideal of woman's influence.[56] She and many other contributors to *Godey's* during this period feared above all fashion's power to transform women into hypocrites and thus to undermine their moral influence over the larger society.

Even as the sentimentalists at *Godey's* hammered out their critique of fashion, however, they had to recognize that fashion was becoming an active force in middle-class social life. "We are still rocked in fashionable cradles, and buried in fashionable coffins—and in all the intermediate scenes of our existence, we feel the influence, and acknowledge the supremacy of the grand enchantress."[57] In this modern era, *Godey's* was coming to acknowledge, fashion governed change in the social world just as technology determined change in the material world: "Do you expect, in these days of telegraph and locomotives, Fashion is going to stand still, with folded hands, and allow her empire to fall from under her feet?"[58] Realistically, a number of columns in *Godey's* admitted that the laws of fashion were here to stay. Even more realistically, *Godey's* began to advise readers to observe these inescapable laws of middle-class social life: since fashion "has existed, and continues to exist, and, in fact, to become a part and parcel of the laws of society, an observance of its laws becomes indispensable: nor indeed is it *alone* indispensable, it is *advisable.*"[59]

The ephemeral laws of fashion, according to *Godey's Lady's Book*, were coming to exert an irresistible force over the dress styles worn by American women. How was this growing power of fashion to be reconciled with woman's great responsibility to exert moral influence over the manners of the age? In confronting this problem, *Godey's* began to retreat from an attack on the fashion principle per se and to stress the evils of particular fashions. In attacking the theatrical styles of the eighteenth-century European aristocracy, *Godey's Lady's Book* developed a moral rationale for a new kind of fashion: republican fashion. Eighteenth-century fashions were ridiculous, *Godey's* explained, because they were set by the arbitrary rules of an artificial society. Republican fashion was different: "But here, in our Republic, on each man and woman rests the responsibility which free citizenship imposes."[60] Wherever the people were free to exert their own sense of taste, the resulting fashions would be sensible and moral: "Here we have the opportunity of consulting individual taste, with out reference to any arbitrary standard of high rank to sanction the adoption of extravagant, inconvenient, or immodest modes, and we should be careful that our fashions are not inconsistent with good sense and pure morals."[61] Under European despotism, women were particularly oppressed. But wherever women were free to choose their own dress, as in enlightened Christian America, there "purity of heart, and correctness of mind, as well as elegance of taste, may be shown in the external appearance."[62] When republican women took over from aristocrats the task of guiding fashion, according to *Godey's Lady's Book,* no conflict would arise between the power of fashion and woman's moral influence, because "the fashions of dress may be made auxiliary to that moral and mental progress which the Lady's Book has so steadily advocated."[63]

What, according to *Godey's,* was the connection between fashions in dress and moral progress in the American republic? A woman's personal beauty exercised a "regulating, refining power" over man: "The impression which beauty makes upon the heart, refines mere sensuality, and elevates it to a level with that which is celestial."[64] An attractive woman, in other words, sheds an uplifting moral influence over a man simply through the beauty of her appearance. *Godey's* hastened to say, of course, that such beauty was not "a mere physical formation" but an offshoot of a woman's sensibility, "made up of thought, sensation, feeling, hope, memory, regret, happiness."[65] True womanly beauty was not an accident of form; it was the outward expression of a virtuous mind and heart. A woman's beauty thus resided in her transparency: "But it is only when the *mind* and the *heart* shine through the dark lustre of the eye, or leave a legible and beautiful language upon the cheek—or lend a deeper music to the rich voice, that the outward impress of beauty can be deeply and lastingly felt. Unillumined by the spirit, the most perfect form is but a cold and desolate temple."[66] *Godey's Lady's Book* repeatedly informed readers that any woman might become beautiful through moral self-improvement, and might then use her beauty to enhance her moral influence over others. Every woman in the American republic had a social responsibility to cultivate her own beauty.

The concept of personal beauty set forth in *Godey's Lady's Book* was the sentimental ideal of transparency. In a woman of true beauty, "the body charms because the soul is seen."[67] Within this concept of beauty as transparency, however, dress presented a potential problem. Beauty rested on the body's power to express inner sentiment: "The body is as much a part of the human creature as the mind; by its outward expression, we convey to others a sense of our opinions, hopes, fears, and affections."[68] The sentimental arbiters of fashion were firm believers in the doctrine of physiognomist Johann Lavater that "physical beauty and moral excellence" were firmly connected.[69] The problem with dress was that it threatened to obscure this connection between character and physiology by covering the body. Man, according to *Godey's,* was the only animal vain and hypocritical enough to disguise himself with clothing:

> He is the only being who is coxcomb enough not to go out of the world naked as he came into it; that is ashamed of what he really is, and proud of what he is not; and that tries to pass off an artificial disguise as himself. . . . Man, in short, is the only creature in the known world, with whom appearances pass for realities, words for things; or that has the wit to find out his own defects, and the impudence and hypocrisy, by merely concealing them, to persuade himself and others that he has them not.[70]

Men and women wore clothing, according to this extremist adherent to the cult of sincerity, in a hypocritical effort to conceal their true natures behind a disguise.

Cultural revolutionaries of the 1960s, in an effort to fulfill their radical vision of personal authenticity, sometimes practiced nudity. For middle-class Americans in the early Victorian period, however, an abandonment of all clothing could not be seriously considered as a solution to the problem of the hypocrisy of dress. Sincerity was their major concern: "To practice sincerity, is to speak as we think; to do as we profess; to perform what we promise; and, really to be what we would seem and appear to be."[71] But sincerity would have to be practiced by respectably clothed men and women. The problem confronting the sentimental arbiters of fashion was this: how could a woman's dress be made to enhance her transparency rather than to disguise her inner qualities? "Fashion," in the pejorative sense of the term, forced upon women "an outward seeming wholly at variance with the inward reality."[72] But the sentimental woman was to choose only those forms of dress that would not hide or distort her "inward reality." How, then, was she to dress? Sentimentalists had decided opinions about what dress styles were to be worn by the woman anxious to enhance her transparency and which styles should be shunned for disguising her soul. An understanding of sentimental dress must begin with a brief look at the history of Western dress from the classical period, 1800 to 1822, through the romantic period, 1822 to 1836, to the sentimental period, 1836 to 1856. By the turn of the nineteenth century, women's fashion had become largely an international phenomenon. Western European women looked to Paris for the latest fashions, and American women looked to London as well, for English modesty often dictated modifications of the styles acceptable to the more daring French, and American women inclined toward the Anglicized versions.[73] But the basic outline of each major style—the classical, the romantic, and the sentimental—was accepted by women in all three nations. Only by examining these three phases can we place sentimental dress in historical context and attempt to understand the meaning assigned to this style by the American sentimentalists, who embraced it as a fulfillment of the sincere ideal.

The dominant dress style for women at the turn of the nineteenth century was classical. The French Revolution had sharply accelerated the eighteenth-century transformation of fashion from a court-based, aristocratic phenomenon into an urban, bourgeois concern. In the decades following the Revolution, the middle classes, though eager to practice fashion-based exclusiveness, revolted against aristocratic fashion content. A popular fascination with the ancient Greek democracies and the Roman republic led the middle classes to adopt their own idealized notion of classical dress. Ironically, the classical style succeeded less in resembling the dress of the ancients than in capturing the appearance of classical statuary. Women dressed in sandals and classically draped white gowns and wore their hair in short curls. The classical gown was drawn in at a high "empire" waist, usually just below the bosom. The skirt was long and disproportionately narrow and hung either in loose folds or in a stiff tubular form. Short, puffed sleeves left most of the wearer's arms bare, and low necklines and backs exposed a great deal more of her. The central concept of classical dress was that the beauty of the body should be revealed. Classical gowns were usually made of thin, semitransparent materials such as muslin, batiste, lawn, tulle, gauze, and taffeta, that clung to the form; and the classical woman usually wore a minimum of underclothing. The more daring women of Paris enhanced this clinging effect by keeping their dresses damp. The primary effect of classical dress was, as fashion historian C. Willett Cunnington has observed, exhibitionistic.[74] The classical woman was bold and theatrical: she applied rouge freely, wore curly wigs over short-cropped hair, used "bosom friends" of wax or cotton, and, between 1815 and 1819, assumed a fashion stance called the Grecian bend by wearing a bustle just below the waist, stooping forward, and walking with short, hasty steps. English moralists of the Regency period complained that she was too bold, too sexually knowing, and far too scantily clad. At her nudest, however, she was French, not English or American.[75]

In its purest form classical dress displayed plain surfaces and clean, vertical lines with a minimum of distracting ornamentation. But this purity was short-lived, and the transformation of the classical style into the romantic style began first in the area of ornament. By 1803, frills began to appear at the neckline, wrists, and hem of the gown. From 1803 to 1817, the classical dress was modified first by Egyptian and Etruscan, and then by Spanish, ornamentation. Flounces, vandyked borders, gores, puffed and frilled hems, and increasingly elaborate decorations of the bodice— all foreshadowed the romantic style after 1811. Evening dresses came to be trimmed with artificial flowers and leaves of silk, satin, or velvet; a wider use of color, especially in stripes and floral designs, became evident. By 1817, the basic classical tube form began to disappear: skirts grew wider, waists grew narrower, and the large, sausagelike bustle used in the Grecian bend was introduced. Most important, tightly laced corsets came into fashion again, and the physical freedom that had been permitted the classical woman was no more.[76]

By 1822, the full transformation of classical dress into romantic dress was completed. The shift involved a reorientation of dress lines from the vertical to the horizontal. Romantic dress instituted a revival of sixteenth-century notions for the upper part of the costume, such as an expanded breadth of shoulder line, enhanced by wider sleeves, and this development in turn demanded that the bottom of the skirt grow wider to balance off the top of the costume. By the early 1820s, hems were wadded and skirts were often ornamented up to the knee level. Then, in 1824, the waist plunged downward to its normal position, and the skirt ballooned out; lacing grew tighter and petticoats were assumed for greater fullness; increased goring and then pleating were introduced at the waist to cope with an increasing mass of skirt material. If the outline of the classical woman was tubelike, the romantic woman was shaped like a capital X. In 1828, the hem of the romantic skirt rose from shoe level to ankle-length. By 1829, the romantic gown was a profusion of flounces, flowers, ruching, thick piping, and colored ribbons, and was further ornamented with plenty of jewelry, including lockets, crosses, chains, drop earrings, bracelets and gold armlets, chatelaines dangling from the waist, and brooches worn at the throat. The most striking and imaginative feature of romantic dress was the immense sleeves that began to appear by the mid-1820s. Demi-gigot and gigot, or "leg-of-mutton," sleeves, Donna Maria and Marmeluke sleeves, and "imbecile" sleeves (inspired by the straitjacket of the lunatic)—though different in detail of form, all were immense and balloon-like. By 1829, the apparent size of the upper arm was double that of the waist, and many sleeves required down-stuffed pads, linings of stiff book-muslin or buckram, or even whalebone hoops to maintain their shape.[77]

Whereas classical dress had focused attention on the body of the wearer, romantic dress disguised the body with tight lacing, padding, and whalebone supports, and called attention largely to the costume itself. The romantic woman was a distracting profusion of ribbons, froth, and superfluous movement: with her tiny waist and shortened skirt, her enormous sleeves and nodding plumes, she gave "a general air of great activity and constant skipping motion." Because her clothes seemed too large for her tiny figure and because she bounced rather than glided, she seemed like "a small girl wearing her mother's dress."[78] Like a little girl playing dress-up, the romantic woman was fussy, busy, and excessively ornamented. And like a little girl imitating her mother, she gave off an air of perfect self-assurance. The style of the romantic woman was exuberant and "carelessly rapturous."[79]

The transition from romantic dress to sentimental dress occurred very abruptly in 1836, when the enormous sleeves of the romantic style suddenly collapsed, and skirt lengths descended four or five inches to the floor. In general, the horizontal lines of romantic costume gave way to the new vertical orientation of sentimental dress. The sentimental form was long and willowy, with narrow, sloping shoulders and a slender, lengthening waist. The entire upper half of the costume shrank in size; sleeves became tight and fitted and were set into the dress just below the shoulder, making it virtually impossible for the wearer to raise her arms above a right angle to her body. Necklines became quite simple; for daytime dress, a simple neat collar hugged the throat; evening décolletage was extremely low, often extending in a straight line that entirely exposed the shoulders. The romantic profusions of ribbons and lace at the neckline were abandoned. The bodice grew tighter, and descended to a low, slim, pointed waist; it fitted closely over corsets laced to the utmost. Below the bodice, the sentimental skirt was full and bell-like, with its shape reinforced by petticoats and sometimes by padding placed just over the back of each hip. The primary

WALKING DRESS   EVENING DRESS

Published for the LADY'S BOOK for April 1831. by L. A. GODEY & CO. 112 Chesnut Street.

PHILADELPHIA.

Romantic women, 1831. Note the broad shoulder line and immense sleeves, the ankle-length skirt, the elaborate ornamentation, and the general air of fussy affectation.

Sentimental women, 1848. Note the vertical lines, the simple sleeves and
necklines, and the low, tight bodices of these gowns.

Sentimental women, 1850. The sincere ideal is captured here in the women's drooping posture, their expressions of yearning, and the sentimental caption "Will he never come."

colors so popular with the romantics were considered vulgar by sentimentalists, who inclined toward secondary and tertiary tints. Delicate grayed tones, such as lavender and lilac, tan, silver gray, gray green, and silver blue, came into vogue; and especially popular were the "shot silks" that combined two or more delicate tints in harmony. In the sentimental period, rouge became unfashionable; heeled shoes went out of style; elbow-length gloves grew shorter; parasols, muffs, and folding fans all shrank in size; and unmarried women began to wear very little jewelry.[80]

The overall effect generated by sentimental dress was one of demure self-effacement. Whereas classical dress had focused attention on the body, sentimental dress effaced it; the sentimental woman's form was sleek and slender, her arms were severely constrained, her legs and ankles were invisible, and her face was, theoretically at least, pale and rouge-free. Whereas romantic dress had called attention to the costume itself, sentimental dress was relatively inconspicuous: it was simple in line and ornament, and quietly harmonious in hue; accessories were small and few, and jewelry was kept to a minimum. In general, sentimental dress abandoned the fussy activity and busyness of the romantic style. The sentimental woman did not bounce, but glided, in an attitude of "drooping restraint."[81] Physically, the sentimental woman was "less active than at any period in the century; she was absorbed in acquiring the art of expressing emotions by graceful attitudes rather than by movement."[82] By effacing the body and the costume itself, sentimental dress was designed to enhance woman's sincerity.

The historical effort to assign a certain frame of mind to a particular style of fashion must be made with great caution. Some historians of costume argue that changes in dress styles tell us little about anything except the internal laws governing the periodic oscillations of fashion. In the history of women's dress, for example, only three distinctive outlines have been assumed by the skirt: the back-fullness shape, in which the skirt bulges out at the back; the tube shape, in which the diameter of the garment is relatively constant from top to bottom; and the bell shape, in which the uniformly full skirt assumes the contour of a bell. According to Agnes Brooks Young, women's fashions regularly move through all three of these options approximately once every century: the back-fullness shape dominated women's dress from 1760 to 1795; the tube shape, from 1795 to 1829, and the bell shape, from 1830 to 1867.[83] But such an analysis, although accurate, ignores an important dimension: it fails to explore the question of what certain fashions meant to those who wore them. The same style of dress could mean very different things within different historical contexts. For example, the tube style of the early twentieth-century fashion may have resembled the tube style of the classical period a century earlier, but the more recent tube was assigned an entirely new meaning by the flappers who wore it. The cultural historian must move beyond the mere mechanics of dress styles to the meaning of those styles to the people who wore them. As Anne Hollander has argued in *Seeing Through Clothes*, "Learning exactly how clothing was *made* in the past does not yield much knowledge about how it looked or felt. These qualities would have depended on how clothes were inwardly believed to look at the time when they looked outwardly natural."[84] The historian of sentimental fashion is presented with an excellent opportunity for studying the meaning of a particular dress style for those who wore it, because the arbiters of sentimental fashion self-consciously asserted the meaning of the sentimental form. The key to this form of dress was the sentimental typology of conduct, the belief that "your dress is a sort of index to your character."[85] To understand how this belief shaped the meaning attributed to the sentimental style, it is necessary to examine the early sentimentalist rejection of the romantic style.

In the 1820s and 1830s, the influence of literary romanticism had made it fashionable for women to be ostentatiously emotional, and tears and sighs, shrieks and starts, melancholy attitudes and fainting spells all came into fashion. The romantic woman "gushed."[86] By the mid-1830s, budding sentimentalists were beginning to attack this style of womanhood for its emotional theatricality. Although the sentimentalists, like the romantics, valued sensibility above all else, they regarded romantic emotionalism as affectation, a dangerous form of social hypocrisy. Emotional affectation, *Godey's* warned its readers, soon poisoned the inner heart with deceit:

Affectation, like the poisonous *Upas*, defiles all it touches. From her approach, nature recoils, and simplicity shrinks affrighted! At first, affectation is content to wind her fanciful wreaths around the *exterior* of her victim; but the *poison* therein concealed soon penetrates the inner temple of the heart. The most sacred affections are violated and made to attest her baneful influence. Truth and love—even religion herself—but issue thence in the garb of mockery![87]

Story after story in *Godey's* contrasts the hypocritical gushing of fashionable young ladies with the true sentimentalism of unfashionable country girls. In "Henrietta Harrison; or, the Blue Cotton Umbrella," written in 1838, the underlying falseness of the fashionable Rosabelle is immediately revealed by her first words to honest Henrietta, whom she has just met: "Ah! my beloved Miss Harrison . . . or rather my sweet Henrietta. . . . I feel that we are destined to tread the thorny path together, and that the friendship commenced this day, will endure till the wing of time shall sever us."[88] Such gushing immediately reveals Rosabelle's underlying hypocrisy: her professions prove to have no basis in true sentiment.

The romantic woman, according to her sentimentalist critics, used dress as a vehicle for the expression of her sham sentiments. Before saying good-bye to her father, for whom she cares but little, Rosabelle theatrically "prepared for a melancholy parting . . . by drawing her veil over her face, and unfolding a handkerchief which she took from her reticule."[89] In trying to substitute the outward forms of dress for the inner sensibility of grief, Rosabelle was guilty of hypocrisy. For sentimentalists, the busyness of the romantic style easily lent itself to such forms of emotional affectation and hypocrisy. In a story called "The History of a Hat," published in *Godey's* in 1834, the insubstantial quality of a woman's romantic hat style is viewed as a symbol of the insubstantiality of her "romantic" sentiments.

> It was certainly the prettiest hat in the world—the most elegant, the most graceful, the most coquettish!—It was a hat of lilac gauze, with trimmings of straw round the brim, and a bunch of wild poppies and corn flowers mingled with bows of riband, slightly inclining towards the right, and resting upon the brim!—
>
> And it was, also, the frailest and least profound love possible!—a light sentiment of a light woman—a sentiment of fantasy, with capricious favours and artificial tenderness!—[90]

To sentimentalists, the romantic woman, with all her ribbons and gauze and artificial flowers, seemed incapable of any but artificial feelings.

In reaction to the "artificial" quality of romantic fussiness, *Godey's Lady's Book* set forth the sentimental ideal of simplicity in dress. "The charm of Nature is simplicity. . . . Why do we not fashion our own tastes by this standard of nature, and prefer simplicity to pomp?"[91] True beauty, according to the sentimentalists, came from within, and the woman of good character needed no fashionable trappings to set off her charms: "There is an elevation of soul imparted by superior virtue, intelligence, and piety, which requires no trappings to invest its possessor with a dignity, grace and loveliness which will never fail of securing the esteem and affection of the really worthy."[92] The sentimental woman would be "more anxious to wear a diamond in the *heart*, than in the ears, or upon the fingers; and more ambitious of intellectual than of personal or mere physical superiority."[93] The central concept behind the sentimental style was that the woman who dressed with simplicity was more sincere than the woman who loaded her person with ornamentation. In "Art and Nature," a story by Harriet Beecher Stowe, the attractive and wealthy George Somers passes over two showy older sisters to propose marriage to simple little Fanny and explains his decision to her by saying, "I like you for being a real, sincere, natural girl—for being simple in your tastes, and simple in your appearance." Fanny is described as "a fair, slender girl, with a purity and simplicity of appearance, which if it be not in itself beauty, had all the best effect of beauty, in interesting and engaging the heart." Her chief charm lies in her faithful adherence to the sentimental typology of conduct: "Her character was in precise correspondence with her appearance—its first and chief element was feeling."[94] The sentimental view of dress condemned elaborate decoration for interfering with any effort of the wearer to commune with a kindred spirit:

> Now, as the goal of all real feeling is truth and sympathy, urging the mind to track its fellow, the soul to claim its kindred—elaborate dress being a thing of artifice and ostentation, seems to *put off* confidence and intimacy, to postpone true communion, and keep the external condition of society constantly in memory.[95]

The bonds of sentimental affection, in other words, could not extend to a heart buried under ostentatious display.

The styles of dress worn by self-proclaimed sentimentalists were not, however, entirely consistent with the sentimental ideal of dress. Throughout the 1840s, for example, *Godey's Lady's Book* insisted repeatedly that dress should not serve as a disguise that cloaked the body, but as an unobtrusive cover that followed the body's natural lines and thus freed its powers of emotional self-expression. Sentimentalists attacked tight lacing, not just for its harmful effects on women's health, but for its distortion of the natural lines of the body. Margaret Howard, sentimental heroine of "The Fatal Cosmetic," is far too sincere to wear a corset, as Mr. Hall notes upon first sight of her: "There was evidently no artificial compression about the waist, no binding ligatures to prevent the elastic motions of the limbs, the pliable and graceful movements of nature."[96] But the fictional Margaret Howard's example did not noticeably alter the course of fashion history in the 1840s and 1850s. Women laced themselves tightly into corsets that emphasized the long, slender waist of the sentimental style; they used cotton wool padding in their bodices and over the backs of their hips; they wore layers of petticoats to obscure the shape of their legs. Nevertheless, sentimentalists continued to insist that this style conformed to the natural lines of the body. Ultimately, their insistence that slender vertical lines were more natural, more sincere than the wide horizontal lines of romantic dress is more significant than the fact that sentimental dress distorted the human figure. C. Willett Cunnington, in labeling sentimental dress "Gothic" because it disguised the body, has failed to recognize the central intent behind this fashion.[97] The sentimental style did distort the human figure, but it represented an effort to reveal the feelings of its wearer. This conflict between avowed intent and actual result is a remarkable testimony to the Victorian ability to confuse the natural with the ideal: "People too often forget that [the Natural and the Ideal] are profoundly compatible; that, in a beautiful work of imagination, the Natural should be ideal, and the Ideal natural."[98] Despite its success in disguising woman's body, the sentimental style of dress must be recognized as an effort to reveal her soul.

In one major area of dress the sentimental ideal of simplicity and sincerity did shape American styles between 1836 and 1856: the area around the face. Within the sentimental concept of sensibility, the face was the most transparent part of the body. A woman's feelings were revealed in her smile, in her complexion, and especially in her eyes: "There is the timid glance of modesty, the bold stare of insolence, the warm glow of passion, the glassy look of indifference, the light of intellect and genius, the leaden gaze of stupidity, the calm serenity of innocence, the open frankness of candor, the furtive look of hypocrisy."[99] Even the shape of her nose revealed her character: *Godey's Lady's Book* quoted Lavater's physiognomic law that a nose equal in length to the forehead, with a top that nearly joined the arch of the orbit of the eye, a nose that was neither hard nor muscular, pointed nor broad, always indicated an excellent character.[100] In "The Fatal Cosmetic," the description of Margaret Howard stated first the simplicity of her gown and then moved immediately to her hairstyle, her facial features, and her complexion:

> Her hair of pale, yet shining brown, was plainly parted over a brow somewhat too lofty for mere feminine beauty, but white and smooth as Parian marble. Her features, altogether, bore more resemblance to a Pallas than a Venus. They were calm and pure, but somewhat cold and passionless—and under that pale, transparent skin, there seemed no under current, ebbing and flowing with the crimson tide of the heart.[101]

This description of Margaret Howard illustrates a fundamental concept behind sentimental dress: that "female costume, regarded as a matter of feeling, resolves itself chiefly into the arraying of the head and neck."[102] As the voluminous sleeves and busy necklines of romantic dress yielded to the tight sleeves and simple necklines of sentimental dress, the focus of attention shifted toward the face. To ensure sincerity, sentimentalists developed decided opinions on hairstyles, headwear, and the complexion.

The romantic hairstyles of the 1820s were very high and elaborate, and they drew the viewer's attention away from the countenance to the fantastic structures at the top and back of the head. Over the course of the decade, the topknot gradually spread upward and outward, becoming an elaborate arrangement of bows, loops, and braids requiring skillful dressing with wire frames and special pins. As hair arrangements became more complicated, ornaments were added, including feathers, pearls, ribbons, tortoise-shell combs, ears of wheat, and flowers wired to stand erect. In the late 1820s, styles descended briefly, but then soared to new heights in the early 1830s as women began to wear high flying bows of hair, wired to hold their shape. By 1830, the most fantastic example of the romantic style had achieved popularity: it was called à la girafe. Not since the fashionable creations of Marie-Antoinette's reign had hairstyles been so elaborate.[103]

In the 1830s, the sentimentalist attack on the fussy distractions of romantic excess caused hairstyles to descend. The topknot shrank, often to a mere knot, twist, or small bow, and moved to the back of the head, usually below the crown; and the artificial structures of

Romantic women, 1835. Note the busy ornamentation of the hairstyles and
bonnets and the simpering expressions on the women's faces.

wire and ornamentation disappeared. The enormous clusters of side curls began to droop into long spiral curls or braids, or even disappeared altogether. In the sentimental style the body of the hair was sleek and flat, usually parted in the middle (like Margaret Howard's) in a style called *à la Madonna*. In the 1840s, curls and braids, although still worn in the evening, were replaced for daytime by sleek bands of hair brought over the ears and carried to the back of the head. The effect of this hairstyle was to "preserve or assist the oval form of the face," and women were advised to choose a style with careful attention to their own individual physiognomy.[104] The arrangement of the hair around the forehead was of great importance, *Godey's* told its readers, but the arrangement of the back hair mattered little: "As it interferes but little with the countenance, it may be referred to the dictates of fashion, although in this, as in everything else, simplicity in the arrangement, and grace in the direction of the lines, are the chief points to be considered."[105] Since the back of the head provided few or no clues to the woman's character—except perhaps to a phrenologist—fashion might there have free rein.[106]

As hairstyles changed, hats and bonnets necessarily changed too. From 1824 to 1831, both hats and bonnets were popular. Like the hairstyles they covered, they were immense, and lavishly trimmed with flowers, feathers, and bows or loops of ribbon, often wired to stand erect. But from 1831, the bonnet began to gain in popularity over the hat, and within a few years the hat had virtually disappeared. An article published in 1847, entitled "Old and New Fashions," explained why. The hat, it said, was "at best an unmeaning thing, without any character of its own, and never becoming to any face that has much."[107] But the bonnet focused attention on the face by framing it with a simple oval line, and it rapidly became the most popular sentimental headgear. Throughout the 1830s, bonnet brims became smaller and more circular, and their high, distracting crowns, once needed to accommodate elaborate hairstyles, gradually descended. Most popular among sentimentalists was the cottage or poke bonnet, which closed around the face like a narrow inverted U; its distinguishing feature was the continuous straight line from front to back, formed by the crown and brim. A variation on the poke bonnet was the Pamela bonnet: named after Samuel Richardson's heroine, it was a small straw bonnet, trimmed with ribbons and sometimes flowers, with a narrow brim that was open around the face. As the bonnet grew in popularity, the brocaded

Sentimental women, 1841. These women's bonnets frame their faces with a simple oval line, and their hairstyles are sleek and flat as they enjoy a significantly "natural" setting.

gauze veil that was widely worn in the 1830s was replaced by a shorter veil of net or lace that often covered just the bonnet itself. The sentimental woman was not to veil her face.[108]

More important than the sentimental woman's hair or her bonnet was the quality of her complexion. For in the woman of sensibility, *"the skin's power of expression"* was greater than that of any other aspect of her personal appearance.[109] The blush of honesty and purity, the sudden glow of love, the hues of sorrow and despair—all spoke through "the transparent surface of a clear skin."[110] A woman's complexion was said to give spirit to her appearance, "as if her very body thought."[111] Within the sentimental ideal of dress, therefore, the use of face paint represented a flagrant violation of the cult of sincerity. The use of paint, *Godey's* admonished, did not enhance true beauty but buried it beyond hope of discovery:

—He that will undergo
To make a judgment of a woman's beauty,
And see through all her plasterings and paintings,
Had need of Lyceneus' eyes, and with more ease,
May look, like him, through nine mud walls, than make
A true discovery of her.[112]

The brief histories of fashion often published in *Godey's* never tired of condemning the eighteenth-century usage of white paints and enameling, lip coloring, eyebrow pencil, and beauty patches, and the romantic woman was blamed as well for her use of rouge. The woman who used cosmetics, like Mary Ellis of "The Fatal Cosmetic," proclaimed to the world the hypocrisy of her manners and her heart.

The sentimental woman was to cultivate a beautiful complexion not through the use of cosmetics, but through a rigorous program of ablution, exercise, and temperance in food and drink. Beyond these simple rules, aspiring beauties were advised to improve their minds and their hearts, so their beautiful thoughts and sentiments might shine forth through their skin. Above all, the sentimental woman was instructed to exercise moral self-control. Passions, especially envy and anger, were believed to be injurious to the skin: "I must not indulge in envy or ill temper, for these are moral jaundice, injurious to the blood and the complexion. I hope I should want to avoid these evil passions for higher motives, but now I am thinking of complexion."[113] Bad-tempered women left the permanent marks of their indulgence engraved on their countenances. But women who exercised "ingenuous candour, and unaffected good humour, will give an openness to their countenance that will make them universally agreeable."[114] Finally, readers were warned, early retiring preserved a woman's vivacity; her refusal to play cards warded off wrinkles; and her avoidance of novel-reading by candlelight preserved her eyes and the warm hue of her complexion. "Moral cosmetics," as *Godey's* called this beauty program of moral self-improvement, was based on the idea that true beauty was the transparency of a beautiful soul.[115] Within the sentimental ideal of transparency, the condemnation of face paint drew power from a much-used Puritan metaphor for hypocrisy: that of the painted sepulchre. "Beauty without virtue," according to *Godey's*, "is like a painted sepulchre, fair without, but within full of corruption."[116]

The concept of moral cosmetics encapsulated the sentimental ideal of personal appearance. The practitioner of moral cosmetics focused her beauty ritual not on her person but on her soul. Shunning the cosmetic arts of that feminine version of the confidence man, the painted woman, she cultivated physical beauty through moral self-improvement. Her beauty was not the deceitful product of surface work, but the transparent outward reflection of her inner mind and heart; she was beautiful because she was sincere. The woman whose dress was simple and natural, whose hairstyle was plain and sleek, whose bonnet framed and accentuated the lines of her countenance, and whose very skin shone forth the sentiments at work within practiced a perfect candor whose moral influence over others, the sentimentalists believed, was incalculable.

The 1840s have been called the "dullest decade in the history of feminine dress," a period of "insipid mediocrity" and "slender seriousness."[117] What this analysis fails to recognize is the meaning that was attributed to the quiet simplicity of women's dress during the sentimental years. Sentimental dress, for those who wore it, was not dull: it was lit from within by the power of sentiment. Richard Sennett, in *The Fall of Public Man*, has argued that mid-nineteenth-century dress was dull because middle-class men and women feared to reveal the innermost secrets of their hearts through the forms of their dress.[118] But Sennett has failed to explain why, if the middle classes so feared self-revelation, they did not simply abandon their view that dress was an index of character and return to an eighteenth-century use of dress as disguise. Sentimental dress was simple and unobtrusive precisely because its central aim was to translate purely the inner character into outward forms that could be read by any one who glanced upon the wearer's person. Self-revelation, the transparent shining through the clothing of the inner mind and heart, was the sentimentalists' answer to the problem of hypocrisy in the modern world.

Ironically, the sentimental ideal of dress, which initially sprang from a middle-class American suspicion of the power of fashion, ultimately encouraged a middle-class acceptance of fashion. The sentimentalists at *Godey's Lady's Book* first assured their readers that personal beauty, when it was the transparent outward reflection of a woman's character, enhanced her moral influence over others, and then advised their readers concerning those dress styles that would assist the wearer's sincerity. The most important unintended consequence of the sentimental ideal of dress was to transform the pursuit of fashion—that is, of sentimental fashion—into a form of moral self-improvement. Increasingly in the 1830s and 1840s, sentimental transparency was becoming a matter of style. The irony of this development is perhaps best captured in the so-called Pamela bonnet. Samuel Richardson's *Pamela,* the eighteenth-century classic of sentimental literature, was an extended hymn to the sanctity of private experience and personal emotions. But the popular Pamela bonnet of nineteenth-century sentimental fashion was ultimately a form of public display, a formulaic, almost ritualistic way of participating in the ideal of transparent sincerity. In the Pamela bonnet, and in all forms of dress that made up the sentimental style, the sincere ideal was formalized and made a matter of fashion.

The sentimental style of dress had barely achieved its fullest expression when the sentimentalists themselves began to recognize that any false-hearted woman of fashion could now assume the trappings of transparency to disguise an evil heart. By the mid-1840s, *Godey's Lady's Book* was printing stories of men and women who champion the sentimental ideal of sincerity in dress in order to disguise their own selfishness and hypocrisy. One such story is "Conformity to the World," written by Timothy S. Arthur and published in 1845. A merchant, Mr. Gravesman, who is scrupulously plain in dress and active in church, attacks the innocent young daughter of a fellow merchant, Mr. Shaw, for wearing ribbons and flowers in wicked conformity to the ways of the world. But soon after his sanctimonious attack, Graveman privately learns that the price of flour has risen; he immediately purchases Shaw's entire stock and thus cheats his honest competitor out of two hundred dollars. Miss Shaw, along with the magazine's readers, thus learns that simplicity in dress is no certain index of a virtuous character.[119] In a similar story published in 1850 and entitled "The Spring Bonnet," pious Martha attacks Caroline for her evil conformity to the world in wearing a gay dress. But Martha overworks her seamstress in order to have a simple new bonnet completed in time to wear to church on Sunday, while Caroline benevolently withdraws her own order to give the woman, who has fallen ill, a needed rest. "Wicked and worldly-minded as I am, Martha," says Caroline, "I had too much religion to do what you have done." In "The Spring Bonnet," it is the young woman outwardly conforming to the sincere ideal who turns out to be a hypocrite.[120]

By the late 1840s, some sentimentalists were beginning to suspect that simplicity of dress would not resolve the problem of hypocrisy in American life. The woman who assumed the fashionable styles of simplicity and alleged transparency was still a woman of fashion, who wore what she wore not because she was sincere but because she wished to be à la mode. In the 1850s, the arbiters of middle-class conduct would begin to grow less anxious about the hypocrisy of formal social conduct in the Victorian parlor and more sophisticated about the role of fashion in bourgeois society. Before they could fully accept fashion as the most significant force at work in their social lives, however, they had to confront another form of fashionable hypocrisy: etiquette. In etiquette, as in dress, early Victorians detected the poison of social hypocrisy contaminating their parlor intercourse. Once again, this threat of hypocrisy had to be defeated within the sentimental ideal of personal conduct.

Sentimental Culture
and the Problem of Etiquette

In the decades after 1830, etiquette, like fashionable dress, was becoming a powerful force shaping the social life of the American middle-class parlor. The social stamp of success was that elusive quality of gentility which aspiring middle-class men and especially women sought to achieve by studying the art of politeness. Between 1830 and 1860, approximately seventy American etiquette manuals were published, many of which went through several editions; and European visitors such as Francis Grund and Harriet Martineau observed that the urban middle classes were inordinately conscious of polite social usage.[1] But the encroachments of formal etiquette in parlor society, like those of fashionable dress, did not proceed unresisted. During the years when *Godey's Lady's Book* was delivering its attack on the hypocrisy of fashionable dress, the many guides to polite conduct were setting forth a similar critique of fashion. For the bourgeois "civilizing process," as Norbert Elias has pointed out, demanded of the would-be genteel a virtually flawless physical and emotional self-restraint, and that self-restraint was at odds with the sentimental ideal of transparently sincere self-expression.[2] To the sentimental mind, a gentleman's or a lady's perfect outward command of the laws of polite self-control could be the disguise behind which lurked an evil heart. Those archetypal parlor hypocrites, the confidence man and the painted woman, were masters of the false art of etiquette: their artificial manners were assumed merely to dazzle and deceive an ingenuous audience. Sentimental critics of middle-class culture feared that etiquette, like fashion, was poisoning American society with hypocrisy.

In response to this new threat, many arbiters of parlor conduct set forth the sentimental ideal of politeness. True courtesy, they insisted, was not a matter of outward rules and ceremonies; it was simply the outpouring of right feelings from a right heart. Sentimental courtesy, like sentimental dress, was to serve as the transparent revelation of the soul and thus was to help restore truth and social confidence to American society by putting an end to the parlor confidence game of false etiquette. But how was this ideal of transparent courtesy to be reconciled with the rigorous demands of the civilizing process? The conflict between sentimental sincerity and genteel self-restraint was resolved in what I have called the genteel performance, a system of polite conduct that demanded a flawless self-discipline practiced within an apparently easy, natural, sincere manner. At the center of the genteel performance was an important contradiction: the contents of polite social intercourse, as perceived by sentimentalists, were natural and sincere feelings; but the forms of polite conduct, as evidenced in the detailed complexity of the laws of etiquette, were deliberate and restrained. The sentimental proponents of true courtesy did not recognize this inconsistency within their system of polite conduct. In fact, they unconsciously structured the genteel performance to shore up the polite fiction that the courtesy of those ladies and gentlemen who adhered to the hundreds of rules governing parlor conduct sprang from right feelings and not out of the painstaking study of etiquette manuals. Ironically, the ultimate effect of the genteel performance was to formalize the sentimental ideal of sincerity in the accepted norms of polite conduct. Just as the sentimental ideal of dress had encouraged the eventual middle-class acceptance of fashion, the sentimental ideal of courtesy permitted the American middle classes to practice the self-conscious and theatrical forms of bourgeois etiquette—in the avowed interest of transparent sincerity.

Colonial Americans before 1775 read etiquette books from the two major traditions of seventeenth-century English courtesy literature. Southern planters, striving to model their conduct on the English landed gentry, read works from the courtly tradition such as Henry Peacham's *The Compleat Gentleman* and Richard Allestree's *The Whole Duty of Man,* which emphasized the traditional ideals of Christian chivalry: nobility, valor, probity, piety. Northern merchants, professionals, and tradesmen, on the other hand, imported English courtesy manuals in the moralistic tradition of Erasmus of Rotterdam and Sir Walter Raleigh, books such as *The Friendly*

Instructor and Hester M. Chapone's *Letters on the Improvement of the Mind.*[3] The more substantial classes in both the South and the North generally approved of a graded social class system, but prevailing standards of gentility dictated that invidious class distinctions be softened with polite kindliness: "The gentleman's function was not so much to insist upon social distinctions as to humanize them, alleviating the harshness of rank by a gracious deference on the one hand and a kindly condescension on the other."[4] Both the courtly tradition of the South and the moralistic tradition of the North tended to equate manners with morals, and morals with religion.

By the late eighteenth century, the moral emphasis of American etiquette was yielding to the striking popularity of Chesterfield's *Letters to His Son,* first published in 1774. At a time when the polite world was expanding to include those who could buy privileges once reserved for noblemen by birth, Chesterfield adapted the older humanistic ideal of courtly behavior to the demands of the ambitious middle classes. Chesterfield's concept of good breeding was based on consideration not for others, but for oneself. Morality, while it might facilitate the display of good breeding, was not his main concern; self-interest demanded only the pleasing polish of manner. Dissimulation, according to Chesterfield, was essential to self-advancement, and he instructed his son to cultivate merely the outward appearances of good breeding. Unexpurgated, Chesterfield's *Letters* aroused the indignation of many Americans: Abigail Adams, for one, criticized him severely for "inculcateing the most immoral, pernicious and Libertine principals into the mind of a youth" while teaching him "to wear the outward garb of virtue."[5] But American publishers were soon editing their own versions of Chesterfield's work, which left out his greatest improprieties, especially those concerning women. By 1806, thirty-one editions of Chesterfield had been published in America; within the next decade, six new editions came out; and in 1827, *The American Chesterfield* "fully naturalized" the work of this eighteenth-century British Machiavelli.[6]

The growing popularity of Chesterfield's work reflected a significant change in the class basis of the courtesy ideal. The American Revolution and the rise of Jacksonian Democracy had helped undermine the hierarchical structure of the colonial social system and had thus transformed the American meaning of gentility. As Arthur M. Schlesinger has observed, the Jacksonian passion for equality was expressed not in the view that gentlemen should cease to be, but in the idea that now any man could become a gentleman.[7] As one manual proclaimed, "In this free land, there are no political distinctions, and the only social ones depend upon character and manners. We have no privileged classes, no titled nobility, and every man has the right, and should have the ambition to be a gentleman—certainly every woman should have the manners of a lady."[8] Proudly, Catharine Sedgwick, one of the most influential sentimental writers of her generation, contrasted republican society with aristocratic society: "It is not here, as in the old world, where one man is born with a silver spoon, and another with a pewter one, in his mouth. You may all handle silver spoons, if you will." "You have it in your power," she told her readers elsewhere, "to fit yourselves by the cultivation of your minds, and the refinement of your manners for intercourse, on equal terms, with the best society in the land."[9] The republican concept of etiquette that emerged after 1830 asserted that the "best society in the land" was middle-class: "It is, therefore, to the middle class, almost exclusively, that we must look for good society; to that class which has not its ideas contracted by laborious occupations, nor its mental powers annihilated by luxury."[10] After 1830, the American middle classes proudly proclaimed their usurpation of courtesy from the courts of the Old World. "I have never seen better models of manners," wrote Catharine Sedgwick, "than in the home of a New England farmer."[11] It was absurd according to one devoté of republican gentility, to suppose "that, because people are of high rank, they cannot be vulgar; or that, if people be in an obscure station, they cannot be well-bred."[12] Gentility in republican America was seen as the product not of fortunate birth but of middle-class effort.

The republican view of etiquette did not, however, assert that all men would become gentlemen. As one etiquette manual honestly admitted,

In remodelling the form of the administration, society remained unrepublican. . . . None are excluded from the highest councils of the nation, but it does not follow that all can enter into the highest ranks of society. In point of fact, we think that there is more exclusiveness in the society of this country, than there is in that even of England—far more than there is in France.[13]

The rules of polite society, as a function of the fashion principle, acted both as a standard and a barrier in the middle-class struggle for social advancement: the "thorny hedge of *etiquette*" closed behind the successful aspirant to good society, to prevent others "from coming in and diminishing the distinctiveness and separateness of his position."[14] Polite society in urban middle-class America, as many European travelers noted, was organized into many distinct "sets" graded according to the relative stringency of their admission requirements. By admitting some applicants and excluding others at various levels, polite society offered a way of establishing a clear social identity for placeless men and women in a fluid, middle-class society. As Leonore Davidoff has observed, "Sociologically, Society can be seen as a system of quasi-kinship relationships which was used to 'place' mobile individuals during the period of structural differentiation fostered by industrialisation and urbanisation. As such it can be understood as a feature of a community based on common claims to status honour which were in turn based on a certain life-style." The middle-class parlor was to provide "a haven of stability, of exact social classification in the threatening anonymity of the surrounding economic and political upheaval."[15] By offering to aspiring middle-class men and women a precise classification, polite society imposed some order on a society of placeless, liminal people, and by establishing a community of mutual social recognition, it offered a haven from the dangers of life in a world of strangers.

How did the aspiring middle-class man or woman lay claim to genteel social status? The most important influence on nineteenth-century etiquette in America as well as England was Chesterfield's *Letters to His Son,* which definitively marked the transformation of courtesy into a middle-class phenomenon. In Chesterfield's work, "the basic ethics of polite behavior" under the courtly ideal were "garnished over, almost beyond recognition, with the pretentious rules of etiquette."[16] Nineteenth-century American etiquette books were packed with hundreds of detailed rules covering not inner morals but outward conduct. Readers were taught the importance of proper dress, personal cleanliness, and good table manners; they learned how to behave at ceremonial visits, dinner parties, evening parties, and public balls; they were instructed in the arts of greetings and farewells, handshakes and bows; they learned the rules governing polite conversation and correspondence, courtship and marriage. Running throughout these rules was the primary law of middle-class politeness: gentility was the exercise of perfect physical and emotional self-restraint. "Propriety in the carriage of the body"[17] was essential, and detailed instructions were offered on the proper form of the walk, the bow, the gesture, the entrance and the exit, the wave of the hand and the tip of the hat, the proper carriage of the arms. As one manual spelled out, "The general positions for the arms are about the level of the waist, never hanging down or being quite stiff, but being gently bent, the elbow a little raised, the fingers not stretched out stiffly, but also a little bent, and partially separated, or the hands half crossed one over the other, or placed in each other, &c."[18] Excessive bodily activity was forbidden. Etiquette manuals warned readers not to snap their fingers, rub their hands, or "beat the Devil's tattoo," and even the expressive use of the hands was to be sparing: "if you use them at all, it should be very slightly and gracefully, never bringing down a fist upon the table, nor slapping one hand upon another, nor poking your fingers at your interlocutor."[19] Most important, certain bodily processes were to be repressed entirely: polite people were not to yawn, sigh, spit, scratch, cough and expectorate, or examine their handkerchiefs after blowing their noses. Finally, the demands of early Victorian gentility extended to the complete command of all facial expressions. "While every Christian should avoid habits of insensibility," one manual read, "he should obtain the entire command of his countenance. He who has not gained some power over his features, is not the peaceable possessor of his own thoughts."[20]

Why was such rigorous self-control demanded of the man or woman of gentility? The insistence of popular conduct codes on self-restraint has been analyzed by Norbert Elias in his brilliant history of Western manners, *The Civilizing Process*. In the civilizing process, Elias shows, a medieval disregard for self-control has gradually given way to modern demands for physical and emotional self-restraint, demands first met by a courtly ideal of conduct and then gradually, since the Renaissance, adopted by larger segments of society. The key to this broad expansion of the courtly code, Elias argues, is the bourgeois idea that outward conduct reflects inner virtue. The claim to bourgeois social status rests on virtue, and personal conduct has been shaped to demonstrate virtue in the form of the complete self-restraint of bodily processes. Over the last few centuries, the demands for self-control have grown greater. Early in the civilizing process, for example, conduct codes included injunctions against urinating in public and passing wind, but as the "shame threshold" for such activities gradually rose, these social failings were no longer mentioned. By the nineteenth century, it was considered hopelessly uncivilized or vulgar to refer at all to such lapses in bodily repression.[21]

Etiquette manuals instructed middle-class Americans anxious to rise on the social scale in how to demonstrate their gentility to others by practicing perfect physical and emotional self-restraint. But even as they articulated a large body of rules governing "propriety in the carriage of the body" and the regulation of facial expressions, many etiquette guides criticized all formal etiquette for its superficiality. The advice manuals for young men were most emphatic in their condemnation of that "hollow-hearted courtesy which has its place and its purpose in the fashionable world."[22] But more significant were the attacks on etiquette made within the etiquette books themselves. "In politeness, as in every thing else connected with the formation of character," lamented one anonymous writer, "we are too apt to begin on the outside, instead of the inside; instead of beginning with the heart, and trusting to that to form the manners, and leave the heart to chance and influences."[23] Such a superficial manipulation of what the advice manuals called the "mere surface of character" was condemned as "but a clumsy imitation" of true courtesy, an imitation "selfish in its object and superficial in its character"[24] This critique of the "mere ceremonies, forms of etiquette, and customs of society" was sentimental: it condemned as useless and selfish all acts of politeness performed with "no heart in the work."[25] At bottom, antebellum etiquette manuals were deploring what they considered to be the hypocrisy of "heartless" politeness: "The least tincture of [dissimulation] in the mind, tarnishes the simplicity of the manners, and diffuses a dark and mysterious hue over all the character."[26]

What was that true courtesy of which false etiquette was only a clumsy imitation? "All that is involved in the term manners," wrote H. T. Tuckerman in 1852, "is demonstrative, symbolic—the sign of exponent of what lies behind, and is taken for granted; and only when this outward manifestation springs from an inward source—only when it is a natural product, and not a graft—does it sustain any real significance."[27] Readers were urged to direct their efforts at the state of their hearts: "Let the young polish their manners, not by attending to mere artificial rules, but by the cultivation of right feeling."[28] Politeness, like evangelical Christian piety, was simply the social manifestation of "a *right heart.*"[29] In fact, antebellum etiquette manuals often invoked the term "Christian courtesy" to distinguish true politeness from false etiquette: "Christian courtesy is the becoming expression of love to God and man in every sphere of social intercourse."[30] The forms of true courtesy were compared by one writer to the sacraments, those "visible means of invisible grace": "True politeness is the outward visible sign of those inward spiritual graces called modesty, unselfishness, generosity."[31] But the view of Christianity that pervaded the etiquette manuals of this period was ultimately less sacramental than evangelical. Their repeated condemnations of the hollow ceremonial observances of false etiquette strongly resembled revivalistic attacks on the empty rituals of religious formalism. In the sentimental view of true courtesy, an Edwardsean theological concern for a religion of the affections was cast in a social framework. The smallest act of ceremonial politeness was to be not a mere form, but a "natural flowing forth of right feeling."[32] Implicit in this sentimental view of true courtesy was the importance of the perfect sincerity of every polite act: "Sincerity requires our words and acts not to misrepresent our thoughts and designs."[33] In etiquette, as in dress, sincerity meant transparency, "the unstudied manifestation in deportment of a soul at once luminous and pure."[34] "The manners of a gentleman are the index of his soul."[35]

The sentimental view of courtesy, if applied literally to polite society, would have rendered unnecessary a specific code of social conduct. For if true courtesy were simply the social expression of a right heart, then the cultivation of right feelings would have rendered all virtuous middle-class men and women truly polite, without benefit of etiquette manuals. But having set forth the sentimental ideal of courtesy, the manuals went on to instruct readers on minute matters of personal bearing and conduct, with the primary emphasis on physical and emotional self-control. That increasing demand for perfect self-restraint, however, was in apparent conflict with the sentimental ideal of transparent emotional self-expression. How were these two strains in American etiquette to be reconciled?

The answer lay in the sentimental insistence that all polite manners be completely natural: "The simpler and the more easy and unconstrained your manners, the more you will impress people of your good breeding."[36] The adherents to false etiquette were constantly ridiculed throughout the popular courtesy guides for being "precise and etiquettish to an intolerable degree."[37] They assumed a stiff and unnatural bearing and struck exaggerated attitudes of delicacy, indifference, or enthusiasm; they simpered and frowned, quirked their little fingers, and danced with ridiculous precision.

Sentimental parlor scene, 1847. Both male and female guests display the proper air of sincerity and "right feeling."

The reason for their awkwardness was clear: because their manners were fundamentally insincere, they never achieved the ease and grace of sentimental politeness. In contrast to their labored constraint, the true gentleman exhibited perfect ease in every move he made—his walk, his bow, his dancing, his manner at table, his facial expression—because all were simply the revelations of his true feelings. The sentimental ideal of unconstrained manners was exemplified in the republican concept of the *natural gentleman,* who possessed gentlemanly attributes without artifically cultivated refinements. The finest example of this type was James Fenimore Cooper's Leatherstocking, whose emergence from the Western woods distinguished his natural gentility from the etiquettish behavior of false gentlemen from the Eastern cities and, beyond, from the courts of the Old World. The frontier scout fulfilled the sentimental ideal of politeness by expressing his morals and feelings in every word and deed. His manners were easy and natural because they sprang from a right heart.[38]

In embracing the cultural symbol of a natural gentleman such as Leatherstocking, however, middle-class Americans were, in a sense, protesting too much. For the ease and unconstraint of sentimental gentility were merely apparent and did not alter the major thrust of the conduct code's demands for flawless physical and emotional self-restraint. The line between true gentility and false etiquette was perilously thin: the true lady or gentleman walked with quiet dignity but not primness, gestured precisely but not woodenly, wore a smile just below the surface but did not smirk. How was the aspiring lady or gentlemen to practice economy and precision of movement and still obey the sentimental injunction that there be "no *stage effect*"?[39] How was she or he to obey the many laws of self-restraint and still appear to be expressing the innermost sentiments of the heart? The genteel performance was made possible by the hundreds of specific rules laid out in the etiquette manuals of antebellum America, rules which may be divided into three areas: the laws of polite social geography, the laws of tact, and the laws of acquaintanceship. These laws made possible the genteel performance by serving two major functions: they constructed the necessary theatrical framework for the performance, and at the same time they legislated the ways in which the theatricality of the performance was to be politely denied. In spite of all sentimental protestations to the contrary, the middle-class parlor was a stage setting for the genteel performance. But proper ladies and gentlemen were studiously oblivious to the theatricality of their parlor conduct, for the part they played was that of sincerity.

The central function of the laws of polite social geography was to establish the parlor as the stage upon which the genteel performance was enacted. Rules governed every aspect of conduct from the visitor's entrance upon that stage until his or her exit. Upon arriving at the house, the polite visitor handed a calling card to the servant who answered the door, and waited to be announced; or, if no servant were present, knocked gently and waited momentarily before entering. If an appointment had been made, the visitor was to stand at the door as the clock chimed the hour: "If you make an appointment to meet anywhere, your body must be in a right line with the frame of the door at the instant the first stroke of the great clock sounds. If you are a moment later, your character is gone."[40] These conventions served as preliminaries to the moment when the visitor made his or her formal entrance and the performance began. The moment when a caller first entered the parlor was a critical point of the genteel performance: "Coming into a room and presenting yourself to a company should be also attended to, as this always gives the first impression, which is often indelible."[41] Upon entering the parlor, the visitor was to proceed immediately to the mistress of the house and greet her first. The polite visitor's physical carriage and facial expression conformed perfectly to bourgeois demands for self-restraint:

> Her face should wear a smile; she should not rush in head-foremost; a graceful bearing, a light step, an elegant bend to common acquaintance, a cordial pressure, *not shaking,* of the hand extended to her, are all requisite to a lady. Let her sink gently into a chair, and, on formal occasions, retain her upright position; neither lounge nor sit timorously on the edge of her seat. Her feet should scarcely be shown, and not crossed.

Such careful self-control was never to betray, however, any stiltedness: "She must avoid sitting stiffly, as if a ramrod were introduced within the dress behind, or stooping."[42] After successfully accomplishing her entrance, the polite visitor remained in the parlor for the proper interval—ten to twenty minutes for ceremonial calls. A well-bred lady signaled her intention to leave soon by leaving her parasol in the hall, and wearing her bonnet and shawl throughout the visit; a gentleman carried his hat and cane into the parlor for the same purpose. At the end of the call, the visitor made some final comments, bowed gracefully, and maneuvered out of the parlor without turning his or her back on the hostess. The hostess rang the bell for the servant, who concluded the ceremony by escorting the visitor through the hall and letting him or her out the front door.

Although the demands of gentility on personal conduct were high, they were clearly circumscribed by the walls of the parlor. The polite hostess did not meet her guests at the front door or even gaze at them through the window as they approached the house. The laws of polite social geography offered visitors every opportunity to prepare for the moment of their entrance into the parlor. At formal evening parties dressing rooms were provided for ladies and gentlemen to tidy up and compose themselves after their arrival. In these second-floor areas, visitors removed their outer garments and washed their faces and hands; ladies even washed their feet as they changed from their boots into their evening slippers, while gentlemen simply brushed their own boots; and ladies and gentlemen both arranged and combed their hair. Before leaving the room, etiquette manuals advised, they should consult a mirror and finally ask a friend or a servant to double-check their appearance. "Through defect of this," one manual impressed upon its readers, "a gentleman once entered a ball-room, attired with scrupulous elegance, but with one of his suspenders curling in graceful festoons about his feet."[43] Without the dressing room, visitors would doubtless have found it difficult to enter the parlor in a state of genteel self-discipline. Without first stopping in the dressing room, for example, a lady might commit the blunder of "breathing hard, or coming in very hot, or even looking very blue and shivery."[44] On the assumption that even a well-bred lady or gentleman might enter the house breathing hard or shivering, or simply looking a bit dusty and unkempt, it was considered rude to address anyone before the formal entrance into the parlor: "When you arrive at your friend's house, do not speak to any one in the hall, or upon the stairs, but go immediately to the dressing room."[45]

Once a visitor entered the parlor, the genteel performance was begun, and any further adjustment of personal appearance was considered a dreadful faux pas. Nothing was regarded with greater contempt than the intrusion of dressing-room activities into the parlor: "Remember that every part of your person and dress should be in perfect order before you leave the dressing-room, and avoid all such tricks as smoothing your hair with your hand, arranging your curls, pulling the waist of your dress down, or setting your collar or sleeves."[46] Even to draw on gloves outside the dressing room, or to remove them, except at supper, was considered highly ill-bred; if a man's gloves became soiled during the evening, he was to leave the room to change them. The evils of public nail paring, teeth picking, and hair combing were strenuously condemned. "Some people have a habit of running their fingers through their hair when at table [and] this is truly indecent; they might as well bring in their whole paraphanalia [sic] of the toilet and exhibit before their friends the interesting performance."[47] Once the entrance had been made, even an apparent preoccupation with personal appearance was forbidden: "In large parties do not exhibit any remarkable anxiety for the care of your dress, nor, if any accident should happen thereto, exhibit peculiar or violent emotion."[48]

The many ceremonial rules governing parlor entrances and exits were designed to reinforce the crucial social distinction between that region of the house—the parlor and its environs—where the laws of gentility were in force, and those regions—the hall, the stairway, and the dressing rooms—where those laws were relaxed. Why did the many rules of polite social geography dictate such a clear distinction? In *The Presentation of Self in Everyday Life,* a study in the theatricality of daily social intercourse, sociologist Erving Goffman has suggested an answer. In societies built on the promise of social mobility, high demands for control over bodily and facial expressiveness made necessary a division of living space into front regions and back regions. In the front regions, firm social discipline holds in place a mask of manner and expressive control is maintained. In the back regions, the mask can be lowered and expressive control relaxed. In theatrical terms, the front regions are where the performance is given, where the social actor is onstage or "in character." The back regions are where the performance is prepared, repaired, and relaxed, where the social actor is offstage or "out of character." Without recourse to the back regions, Goffman believes, no one could maintain the perfect expressive control demanded in the front regions.[49] This analysis is particularly applicable to the polite social conduct of middle-class Americans in the decades before the Civil War. For them, gentility meant the ability to exercise complete command over physical carriage and facial expressions in a manner of perfect ease and grace. Any lapse in self-discipline, or even any betrayal of the effect required to maintain that self-discipline, undermined the genteel performance of the aspiring lady or gentleman. All such interruptions in the demonstration of "natural" self-restraint were thus banished to the back regions of the house, where the genteel performance could be prepared, repaired, or momentarily relaxed. Without those back regions, many middle-class social climbers could never have met the high demands of bourgeois gentility.

The genteel role of the polite guest was simply to maintain proper self-control without betraying any stage effect—without revealing, that is, the preparation and effort required to sustain the genteel performance. The role of polite hostess was far more difficult. She was responsible not only for her own person, but for the setting of the collective genteel performance: "Perfect order, exquisite neatness and elegance, which easily dispense with being sumptuous, ought to mark the entrance of the house, the furniture, and the dress of the lady."[50] The polite hostess had to select and arrange her furniture for the maximum social advantage of all assembled in her parlor: "how greatly the style and arrangement of furniture contribute to make a party go off well, and those engaged in it look well."[51] The right furniture was thought to ease social intercourse by helping visitors look their best, and, when correctly arranged, by encouraging circulation. Similarly, the hostess who tastefully arranged potted shrubs, plants, and flowers throughout the room helped "brighten" and "enliven" the company by placing them in "almost a fairy-like scene."[52] In addition, she selected and displayed the "curiosities, handsome books, photographs, engravings, stereoscopes, medallions, any works of art you may own," which were the stage properties of polite social intercourse. Such conversation pieces, according to one etiquette manual, were the good hostess's "armor against stupidity."[53] The polite Victorian hostess was not simply an actress in the genteel performance; she was also the stage manager, who exercised great responsibility for the performances of everyone who entered her parlor.

The good hostess, like her guests, was to exclude all forms of back-region behavior from polite social intercourse. But again, her responsibilities were far greater than those of her guests, for while they were responsible only for concealing the activities of the dressing room, she had to work to keep all private domestic arrangements from intruding upon the genteel performance. In an unusually explicit statement of the theatrical nature of her task, one manual stated that "the internal machinery of a household, like that portion of the theatre 'behind the scenes,' should . . . be studiously kept out of view."[54] Implicit in this concern was the conviction that domestic activities were not genteel. When a visitor entered the parlor, the good hostess quietly laid aside her sewing or needle-work. When giving a dinner party, she closed the shutters and lit the lamps before her guests arrived rather than fumbling through these duties in the middle of dinner; when having someone for tea, she never covered her furniture or shut up the house for the night before her guest's departure. Above all, the polite hostess never introduced domestic matters into the parlor by telling guests of her household affairs or discussing with them her own experiences with "the servant problem." "In a well-ordered household the machinery is always in order, and always works out of sight."[55]

While a hostess entertained her visitors, the machinery of her household was being run by her servants, and thus her own gentility rested in part on their ability to remain inconspicuous. A good servant was to be "well trained, silent, observant, scrupulously dressed, and free from *gaucherie*. A good servant is never awkward. His boots never creak; he never breathes hard, has a cold, is obliged to cough, treads on a lady's dress, or breaks a dish."[56] During afternoon visits, the major role of the servant was to assist the commencement and the termination of the genteel performance by answering the door, carrying in visitors' cards, ushering and sometimes announcing guests into the parlor, and taking care of refreshments. But the crucial test of a well-ordered household was the dinner party. The polite hostess gave her orders before dinner and never had to speak to the servants during the meal, for "with well-trained waiters, you need give yourself no uneasiness about the arrangements outside of the parlors."[57] The servants were responsible for all details of preparing and serving the meal, since these activities were deemed too vulgar for the attention of the genteel. In the 1840s, in fact, all food platters were banished from the table to the sideboard in the new vogue called dinner *à la Russe*. At the sideboard servants alone faced "that unwieldy barbarism—the joint" and freed the host from "the misery of carving."[58] Good servants contributed to their employers' claims to gentility by leaving the host and hostess free to devote themselves entirely to their guests: "Dish after dish comes round, as if by magic; and nothing remains but to eat and be happy."[59]

Within the reigning conventions of bourgeois politeness, everything happened as if by magic: guests entered the parlor composed, combed, and free from the dust of the street; their hostess received them without a care in the world for the complex domestic arrangements of her household; refreshments were prepared and served by invisible hands. In reality, of course, guests were entering the parlor only after tidying themselves in the second-floor dressing rooms; their hostess might well be calculating whether the leftover mutton was fresh enough for another dinner and when the baby would awaken; and servants were busy in the rear of the house anticipating, it was devoutly to be hoped, the needs of their mistress in the parlor. But the most important law of polite social geography was that no one shatter the magic of the genteel performance by acknowledging the existence of the back regions that alone made the performance possible. The hostess knew, of course, about the dressing rooms and her visitors' use of them; the guests knew something about the complex domestic arrangements of a middle-class household; and even the best-trained servants could not make themselves literally invisible to genteel observers. But within the bounds of the parlor, guests and hostess were to remain unconscious of all behind-the-scenes preparations and repairs that made possible their genteel performance.

The genteel refusal to acknowledge the uses of polite social geography was legislated by a second body of etiquette: the laws of tact. These laws governed not the genteel performance itself, but its reception by those who witnessed it. For polite ladies and gentlemen were not simply performers on the social stage of the parlor; they were members of an audience watching the genteel performances of one another. The function of the laws of tact was to ensure that members of the polite audience would assist, encourage, and honor a genteel performer's claims to gentility. By tactfully honoring the genteel performance of another lady or gentleman, the social aspirant was demonstrating his or her own gentility. More to the point, the tactful lady or gentleman was ensuring that her or his own claims to gentility would be reciprocally honored, within a kind of golden rule of politeness: "You may set it down as a rule, that as you treat the world, so the world will treat you."[60]

One of the most important laws of tact was to honor the sanctity of the back regions. The polite visitor never intruded into the back regions of the house unless specifically invited, lest he or she surprise those who were relaxing or repairing their own gentility. The caller who entered the house, went straight to her friend's chamber, and entered without knocking, etiquette manuals warned, was in danger of finding her hostess in a state of personal or domestic disarray: "You may find her washing, or dressing, or in bed, or even engaged in repairing clothes,—or the room may be in great disorder, or the chambermaid in the act of cleaning it."[61] Unless invited upstairs, the polite caller sent up her card and waited in the parlor. Even upon invitation, the well-bred lady gave due ceremonial warning by knocking at the door and waiting for an invitation to enter. Once admitted to a private chamber, she exercised tact by not appearing curious about its contents. Eliza Leslie's portrait of an inquisitive intruder was expressed as a stern warning to her readers: "Nay, we have known one who prided herself upon the gentility of her forefathers and foremothers, rise from her seat when her hostess opened a bureau-drawer, or a closet-door, and cross the room, to stand by and inspect the contents of said bureau or closet, while open."[62] Even the intimate friend who had been granted the entrée of the house—the privilege of entering areas usually forbidden to visitors and of calling at all hours—was warned to use her privilege sparingly. The laws of tact condemned those who ran in and out at all hours, seeking out the lady of the house in all her domestic employments, entering by basement or back entrance if the front door were locked, and following the lady of the house upstairs and down, into attic and cellar, kitchen and storeroom. The indiscriminate use of an entrée increased the possibility that a tactless visitor would stumble upon a friend who was momentarily "out of character" or "offstage" and thus undermine her claims to gentility.

The problem posed by the back regions was particularly important to house guests, who could not be expected to confine their presence to the parlor. Thus, the laws regulating the conduct of house guests were devoted almost entirely to enforcing a tactful avoidance of back regions. To begin with, no well-bred person invited herself to stay in a friend's house or accepted a general invitation ("You are always welcome to come and stay with us"), or extended her own invitation to include someone else. As a house guest she did not "make herself at home" even though urged to do so by her hostess. She confined herself mainly to her chamber and to the parlor and avoided the nursery and the kitchen unless specifically invited. She received her own guests only in the parlor, and she avoided the parlor while her hostess received guests unless invited to join the company. In turn, the polite hostess avoided those back regions used by her guest: she granted her completely private use of the spare room, knocked always before entering, and kept her children away. The most tactless blunder a house guest could commit was to carry tales of her hostess's household:

Another class of tattlers are those who visit their friends and take note of all the habits and customs of the family, the conversations at table, the government of children, treatment of servants, family expenditures, employments and dress of the mistress, and even the late hours of the male members, should there be any who stay out late. These are told in detail at the next visiting place.[63]

Not only was she never to tattle; she was to avoid acquiring any knowledge of domestic problems by tactfully taking her leave if sickness or trouble broke out during her visit. This rule of tact applied to the morning caller as well as the house guest: "Your friend may not appear to notice the screams of a child, a noise in the kitchen, or the cry from the nursery that the fire board has caught fire, but you may be sure she does hear it, and though too well-bred to speak of it, will heartily rejoice to say good-bye."[64]

Norbert Elias has suggested that the bourgeois family was an institutional outgrowth of the civilizing process. As demands for civilized self-restraint increased, Elias shows, bourgeois privacy became necessary as a shield for those least civilized members of the family, the children, while they underwent an increasingly lengthy period of socialization. Within the polite social geography of nineteenth-century American etiquette, the laws of tact that ensured bourgeois privacy also shielded essentially "civilized" adults relaxing their genteel performance in the back regions of the house. "The right of privacy," etiquette manuals intoned repeatedly, "is sacred, and should always be respected."[65] The manuals condemned specifically the social crimes of opening boxes, packets, and papers; reading papers that lay open to view; eavesdropping through open windows and keyholes and cracks in doors; and even watching the neighbors from the attic window. One imaginative manual enjoined readers not to hide in the parlor before the lamps were lighted in order to listen to a private conversation. Another rule forbade polite visitors to examine the books in a closed book case or the calling cards in the basket on the parlor table. The polite visitor did not even walk about the parlor while awaiting the hostess or examine the ornaments and pictures placed there for display. These laws of privacy represented an extreme example of the tactful unwillingness to uncover any failings in the genteel performance of another: "Avoid, if you can, seeing the skeleton in your friend's closet, but if it is paraded for your special benefit, regard it as a sacred confidence, and never betray your knowledge to a third party."[66]

Within the polite social geography of the genteel performance, all intrusions into the back regions, where demands for genteel self-restraint were not in effect, had to be forbidden by the laws of tact. But tact was demanded as well in response to any momentary failures of gentility that took place in the front regions of polite society. Within nineteenth-century etiquette, it was assumed that even well-bred ladies and gentlemen would experience certain lapses in gentility, and the laws of tact demanded that no one else take notice of them. When any domestic trouble intruded into a hostess's parlor, for example, the polite caller appeared not to notice. When a guest spilled his wine or broke a dish at dinner, the other guests ignored his error, unless the hostess responded with the most tactful move of legendary Victorian politeness by duplicating her guest's faux pas—by dumping her own wine, for example, so he might feel easy again. The polite guest never refused the last portion on the platter, lest he imply his host had no more in the kitchen; nor did he apologize profusely for breaking a plate, lest he suggest the importance of the financial loss to his host. Excessive apologies only made everyone uneasy and interrupted the genteel performance of the party as a whole; the polite guest showed his regret in his face and quietly resumed his own self-control. When dinner was late, all guests, of course, appeared unaware of the delay. By ignoring disruptions in the genteel performance of another, the well-bred lady or gentleman attempted to assist him or her in regaining the appearance of natural and easy self-restraint demanded of true gentility.

The laws of tact also governed polite conversation. The polite social aspirant did not dominate conversation or even talk too well himself: the aim of his conversation was to draw out others, by leading them to their favorite topics and encouraging them with appropriate responses. He always listened carefully and, more important, always *seemed* to listen: "Be, therefore, not only really, but seemingly and manifestly, attentive to whoever speaks to you." Only vulgar people, warned this manual, "fix their eyes upon the ceiling or some other part of the room, look out of the window, play with a dog, or twirl their snuff-box," while being addressed by another.[67] True gentility demanded laughter at others' jokes but not at one's own. Ladies and gentlemen avoided asking questions, lest they stumble upon any personal embarrassment: "A lady inquired of what branch of medical practice a certain gentleman was a professor. He held the chair of *midwifery!*"[68] Furthermore, the well-bred gentleman never insisted on hearing someone who had suddenly checked his conversation: "If a person in conversation has begun to say something, and has checked himself, you should avoid the tactless error so often committed, of insisting on hearing him."[69] The rules of polite conversation forbade scandal, whispering, speaking in hints or innuendos, and speaking of anything that might cause embarrassment or remind another of his troubles. Above all, the well-bred conversationalist never gave the slightest indication that he did not believe what he heard: "To show by word or sign any token of incredulity, is to give the lie to the narrator, and that is an unpardonable insult."[70] The well-bred lady or gentleman honored the conversational performances of others in polite society by responding with deep attention, interest, sympathy, and credulity. In so doing, they evinced acceptance of the conversationalist's claim to gentility.

The detailed complexity of the rules enjoining polite middle-class men and women to practice tact suggests above all the difficulty of sustaining flawlessly the genteel performance. Antebellum American etiquette manuals assumed that well-bred men and women would occasionally drop plates, serve dinner late, bore their companions in conversation, and suffer their hair to go uncombed and their beds unmade. When such lapses in gentility occurred, however, the performance was sustained by the tact of the genteel audience, who looked interested when they were bored, who looked away when a plate was smashed, who never looked into rooms where the beds were not made. Middle-class claims to gentility could thus be sustained only in the company of those sufficiently well-bred to recognize the successful aspects of a genteel performance and to overlook its failures. The laws of tact thus rested on the third major category of etiquette—the laws of acquaintanceship. Only the great demands of the genteel performance for tact can fully explain the intense middle-class concern over social acquaintanceship. Since any ill-bred person who entered rooms without knocking or turned to stare when someone spilled his wine threatened to undermine everyone else's claims to gentility, such rudeness had to be banned from polite social intercourse. As one manual bluntly stated,

Etiquette is the barrier which society draws around itself as a protection against offences the "law" cannot touch; it is a shield against the intrusion of the impertinent, the improper, and the vulgar,—a guard against those obtuse persons who, having neither talent nor delicacy, would be continually thrusting themselves into the society of men to whom their presence might (from the difference of feeling and habit) be offensive, and even insupportable.[71]

This barrier against the vulgar consisted of the laws of social acquaintanceship.

Because the genteel performance demanded that all tactless, ill-bred people be barred from the parlor, the mechanisms for excluding social undesirables were many and elaborate. Prominent among them was the calling card, which was used in the ceremonial morning visits through which ambitious ladies and gentlemen laid claim to genteel society. When a lady reached a certain social position, she set an "at-home" day when she settled into her parlor at ten or eleven in the morning and received callers. When acceptable visitors sent in their cards, the hostess instructed her servant to usher them into the parlor. When unacceptable visitors dared come to her door, on the other hand, the hostess sent her servant back to say that she was not at home. Visitors turned away with this significant message were expected not to call again without first receiving a visit or a card from the lady who had spurned them. Ironically, etiquette demanded that the rejected social applicant exercise genteel tact in honoring the hostess's preferences—which were based on her poor opinion of the applicant's gentility.

The laws governing social introductions were another important mechanism for regulating social acquaintanceship, for well-bred people were not to intrude themselves upon anyone without a formal introduction. At evening parties introductions were not deemed necessary, because all guests were presumed genteel by virtue of their having been invited to attend; all were regarded, for the time, as social equals. But elsewhere, the rules regulating social introductions were rigorously enforced, because introductions permitted both parties to make social claims upon each other, claims which might prove undesirable to one or the other. Etiquette manuals repeatedly warned readers not to make an introduction unless the mutual desirability of the acquaintance was beyond doubt. This rule applied not only to face-to-face introductions but also to letters of introduction, which were viewed as "certificates of good social position."[72] A gentleman never introduced a friend into the home of another without explicit prior consent; he never introduced anyone to a lady without her consent; and he never introduced a tradesman to anyone under any circumstances. But certain kinds of meetings did not have to be honored as formal introductions; these included traveling acquaintanceships, meetings during morning calls, and any presentation to a lady for dancing. Similarly, letters of introduction incurred only a limited social obligation: the recipient of such a letter was obliged to leave a calling card with the bearer, but not necessarily to extend an invitation to the stranger thus introduced.

Although proper introductions imposed certain social obligations, well-bred people did have recourse to polite ways of terminating an undesirable acquaintanceship. By treating an acquaintance with increasing social formality, by failing to return a formal call, or, more subtly, by returning a personal visit with a card, a lady or gentleman could politely indicate a desire to sever the connection. The system of ceremonial morning calls provided certain specific opportunities to weed out some acquaintances and to reaffirm the desire to continue seeing others. After a long trip or mourning period, for example, a family signified its renewed willingness to receive visitors by sending out calling cards; those acquaintances who failed to receive a card were thus notified that they were being trimmed. And following a wedding, no bachelor friend of the bridegroom was to call upon the couple unless he received a card: "When a man is about to be married, he usually gives a dinner to his bachelor friends; which is understood to be their *congé*, unless he chooses to renew their acquaintance."[73] The ruling assumption here was that the companions of a man's bachelorhood might prove unfit associates for his wife. Once again, ironically, middle-class gentility depended on the tact of all participants, including those whose gentility was being called into question. The well-bred lady or gentleman, warned the etiquette manuals, was always to be on the alert for any cooling of a social acquaintance or any lapses in the punctilious give-and-take of ceremonial calling: "Keep a strict account of your ceremonial visits . . . and take note how soon your calls are returned. You will thus be able, in most cases, to form an opinion whether or nor your frequent visits are desired."[74]

Once admitted to a given social circle, etiquette manuals advised, polite men and women took care not to jeopardize their position by being obtrusively familiar. Gentlemen did not freely touch or slap others, stare at them, or "buttonhole" them in conversation. Within the rules of polite parlor conduct, not only body contact but also body warmth was considered offensive: no gentleman offered his seat to a lady, or removed a glove to shake someone's hand if his own hand were clammy. Finally, aspirants to good society were instructed to keep teeth, hands, feet, linen, and boots clean and free from odor at all times. Gentlemen, the manual advised, should not smoke tobacco, drink spirits, or eat onions before entering polite company.

The laws against excessive familiarity and physical offensiveness, like the laws of tact, were directed at those genteel men and women who had passed the "cardboard barrier"[75] and been admitted into the polite parlor. Undesirable intruders into that region—those who jeopardized the gentility of others by staring at their errors, following them into kitchen and nursery, slapping them on the back, and breathing tobacco in their faces—had to be barred from polite society or, it was feared, they would destroy it. What happened, then, to the genteel performance when it was taken out into the public street, where the lower classes were free to mix with polite company? After 1860, improvements in urban transportation would enable the middle classes to segregate themselves into suburban neighborhoods, in order to escape the company of the tactless mob milling around the city streets. But until then, the socially ambitious middle classes had to learn to sustain the genteel performance before a vulgar and even hostile audience and to keep social upstarts at a proper distance. Consequently, etiquette manuals devoted careful attention to the problem of polite behavior on the street.

The crucial law of polite street behavior was that the genteel performance must be flawless when exposed to the inspection of strangers:

A lady's conduct is never so entirely at the mercy of critics, because never so public, as when she is in the street. Her dress, carriage, walk, will all be exposed to notice; every passer-by will look at her, if it is only for one glance; every unlady-like action will be marked; and in no position will a dignified, lady-like deportment be more certain to command respect.[76]

All the rules enforcing physical self-restraint, so important in the parlor, were doubly important in the street, and chapters on street etiquette repeated injunctions against picking the nose or blowing it with the fingers, scratching the head, staring, swearing or talking loudly, and losing the temper. All dressing-room activities forbidden in the parlor were also forbidden on the street: to pick the teeth, draw on the gloves, or even adjust the collar after passing out the front door was considered the height of ill breeding. Ladies were, of course, considered dangerously susceptible to the improper remarks or advances of common people on the streets: the polite lady did not walk the streets unaccompanied, and even on her brief passage from the house to a waiting carriage she was to be escorted by a gentleman or a servant.

One important concern of street etiquette was how to avoid physical contact with strangers. To avoid jostling and being jostled, polite pedestrians passed on the right and turned sideways; the social superior or the lady walked next to the wall and was always accorded the right of way. In the crowded and mixed assembly of the public street, the genteel constantly attempted to circumvent all physical contact: "By having your wits about you, you can win your way through a thronged street without touching even the extreme circumference of a balloon sleeve; and, if each one strove to avoid all contact, it would be easily accomplished."[77] Although the common herd was considered too vulgar to exercise any care in maneuvering through the streets, ladies and gentlemen were expected to ensure that no physical contact with strangers could take place.

The main problem confronting the genteel when they ventured out into the public domain was that no thorny hedge of etiquette kept rude people at a proper distance, either physically or socially. In the public street, calling cards, invitations, and introductions were all useless in protecting the boundaries of polite society. On the street, therefore, the genteel performance was threatened not just by the rude clown who jostled a lady's arm, but by the upstart who boldly addressed by name a gentleman who did not care to recognize him socially. For this reason polite men and women did not address each other audibly by name or make introductions while in the street. But the most important rules of street etiquette were the detailed instructions on how to keep the people one met at the proper social distance. A welcome social acquaintance was to be greeted with a cordial bow or a graceful wave of the hand; a more distant acquaintance, with a brief touch of the hat; an unwelcome acquaintance, with a cold bow or, in extreme cases, a cold stare of nonrecognition: "do not recognize the salute, but pass on, and leave him to suppose that you imagined it was intended for another."[78] Ladies were to be greeted with great deference, but only when they first registered recognition; no true gentleman was to greet a lady who appeared unconscious of him. The best way to express the degree of intimacy desired in a particular relationship, according to etiquette manuals, was through the facial expression, "which can indicate familiarity by a smile or look of conscious recognition, and reserve by a composed aspect and an indifferent glance."[79] With endless detail and occasional humor, etiquette manuals instructed readers on the subtle art of the "cut." Some advised their readers to avoid cutting outright. But even in recognizing an undesirable acquaintance on the street, the gentleman might make clear his views of the man's claim to his company: "If you meet a rich *parvenu,* whose consequence you wish to reprove, you may salute him in a very patronizing manner: or else, in acknowledging his bow, look somewhat surprised and say 'Mister—eh—eh?' "[80]

When Francis Grund scornfully observed that in America, "in order to be 'genteel,' it is necessary, in the first place, to know nobody that is *not* so," he was recognizing the importance of the many laws of acquaintanceship among the socially ambitious middle classes.[81] But Grund failed to understand why Americans were so anxious to patrol the boundaries of their social acquaintanceship. Only by ensuring through the laws of acquaintanceship the tact of all admitted into their society could members of the middle classes ensure that their own claims to gentility would be honored. For the genteel performance by which the rising classes endeavored to secure a higher social status could be sustained only in the presence of tactful men and women who were willing to avoid those back regions where the laws of bourgeois self-restraint were not in effect and to look the other way in the front regions whenever any lapse of self-restraint occurred. Concern about the virtual impossibility of sustaining the genteel performance in the presence of the vulgar pervaded all three major areas of etiquette—the laws of polite social geography, the laws of tact, and the laws of social acquaintanceship.

What emerges from the hundreds of laws governing the polite conduct of middle-class Americans during the decades before the Civil War is a deep conviction of the vulnerability of the genteel performance. Any vulgar boor, it was feared, could at any moment rip the fragile mask of manner from the genteel performer and expose the would-be social climber in all his or her own underlying vulgarity. For this reason social aspirants were advised that "a well-bred lady or gentleman will sustain their characters as such at all times, and in all places—at home as well as abroad."[82] Those who relaxed their performance ran the risk of being discovered in their vulgar "undress": "It is a folly," warned one manual, "to sit by the fire in a slovenly state, consoling oneself with the remark, 'Nobody will call today. Should somebody call we are in no plight to see them.'"[83] Should somebody call, that is, the genteel performance of the private sloven would be exposed for just that—a theatrical performance, played only for effect. This powerful middle-class fascination with the sudden intrusions that could expose the genteel performer's underlying vulgarity was revealed in a stock plot of sentimental literature. A lover calls unexpectedly on his fiancée, who is known for her great beauty and fine manners. But she is not yet prepared to receive visitors, and he finds her untidy and yawning over a late breakfast. Relieved to discover her true vulgarity before it is too late, he breaks off the engagement and eventually weds a young lady whose appearance and conduct never vary with the hour or the company. Though she creates less of a sensation at formal social occasions than the former object of his affections, she alone is truly genteel.[84] So great were middle-class anxieties about the possibility of one's exposure as a secret slob that in one short story published in *Godey's* the scenario took shape as a nightmare:

> I once dreamed, when I was a girl, of finding myself, by some unaccountable agency, at a ball, with my hair in curl-papers, my person in a *robe de chambre,* and my feet without shoes—not in a small room, so packed that nobody could see his or her next neighbour, but one so large that it could scarcely have been crowded, and affording space for each one to have a full view of hundred.[85]

This powerful middle-class concern about the vulnerability of the genteel performance goes a long way toward explaining the sentimental insistence on the sincerity of true courtesy. "An attempt to pass for more than you really are," one manual warned, "will not only make you offensive, but unpopular. We never love to see people strutting in a borrowed dress."[86] In reality, however, many middle-class Americans were attempting to pass for more than what they really were, in the sense that they were trying to rise in society, to assume a new and better social identity. As marginal men and women, they were all engaged in the activity that in sociological terms is called *passing*.[87] To lend credence to their claims to higher social status, they thus had to reaffirm continually the sincerity of every genteel act they performed. But many must have been plagued with the secret conviction that, like the jackdaw in Aesop's fable, they were simply strutting around in borrowed peacock feathers. Beneath the middle-class concern about the vulnerability of the genteel performance lurked the antirepublican conviction that gentlemen were not in fact made but born. In a revealing Calvinist metaphor, one anonymous etiquette writer compared the social graces to that divine grace which was bestowed only upon the elect: "It is true, there is a class of mortals, upon whose mental birth the Graces have not smiled; and who seem to be hopeless subjects of this art. They are the non-elect of courtliness. After every effort they must at last be abandoned to a reprobate manner."[88] If gentility was, like divine election, predestined for only a few, then the claims of most middle-class men and women to gentility were fraudulent, and the eventual unmasking of their secret vulgarity or "grace-lessness" was inevitable. The social reprobate—the non-elect of courtesy—was, like the spiritual reprobate of Puritan theology, a hypocrite. Vulgar to the core, the parlor confidence man had "to be *always* acting a part, to torture and tutor every thought, word, and action in common life and daily intercourse, so as to produce a factitious result."[89]

How were socially ambitious middle-class men and women to demonstrate the sincerity of their gentility? As discussed earlier, they were to cultivate, first of all, an easy, graceful manner—proof of the naturalness or sincerity of their bourgeois self-restraint. They were also to ignore and implicitly deny the theatricality of the laws of polite social geography—the division of social space into on-stage areas and off-stage areas—for theatricality, to sentimentalists, was a dangerous form of insincerity. But the essence of the sentimental ideal of true courtesy was the sincere expression of right feelings, the standard of courtesy met, for example, by Margaret Howard of "The Fatal Cosmetic," who invariably revealed in words and appear-ance her innermost sentiments. The formal etiquette manuals of the antebellum period set forth very few laws of conversation that fulfilled the ideal of sentimental transparency practiced by a Marga-ret Howard. But they did offer very clear guidelines for sincere expression in a different form of social intercourse: writing letters. The fullest statement of the sentimental ideal of courtesy was made in the numerous guides to epistolary etiquette published during the decades before the Civil War. Letter-writing manuals instructed by example and offered hundreds of sample letters to be emulated in polite correspondence. These samples were overwhelmingly statements of sincere and heart-felt sentiment: they included marriage proposals, acceptances, and rejections; accusations of romantic infidelity and their responses; avowals of friendship, sympathy, and familial affection. The feelings discussed in the sample letters of the letter-writing manuals were the stock emotions of sentimental culture. Love, regard, attachment, affection, friendship, sympathy, fidelity—all were invoked with monotonous regularity and often used interchangeably. The greatest challenge of polite correspondence was to express these feelings with a warmth and sincerity that brought the written words to life. All attempts to produce an effect through fine words, the manuals warned, should be abandoned for the simple art of expressing true feeling: any letter-writer who "went to a dead sepulchre of words instead of speaking from his living heart,"[90] especially in writing a marriage proposal, deserved rejection. Sample letters thus dwelt less on the precise nature of the sentiment expressed than on its deep sincerity. To a sick guardian, for example, a young person was advised to write, "Accept, my dear sir, my sincere assurances of the sympathy which I feel for your sufferings"; to a newly married man, a friend was to write, "I offer you my most sincere and heartfelt congratulations"; to his father, a young man might write of his courtship of a young lady, "We love each other sincerely."[91] Time after time, letters closed with "Your sincere friend," "Believe me to be, Yours, sincerely attached," and "Believe me to be sir, Your truly attached and sincere well-wisher."[92] Sincerity was not, however, merely the emotional state conveyed by polite openings and closings; many letters were devoted entirely to singing the praises of candor. A father might write to his daughters in this vein: "Dear Daughters, The luxury and dissipation which prevail in genteel life, as it corrupts the heart in many respects, so it renders it incapable of warm, sincere, and steady friendship."[93] To the mother of his beloved, similarly, a young lover might write, "I have always been of opinion that nothing deserves censure which is truly honorable and undisguised."[94] One sample letter may be read as a concise statement of the sentimental ideal of courtesy: a young lady praised her suitor by saying, "His behavior here was polite without affectation, and an air of sincerity appeared in all he said."[95] Finally, a young man apologizing to his lover discussed the superior grace of a written apology to a personal one, saying "Such a letter should bear the stamp of candor, sincerity, and earnestness": he thus sang the praises of the sincere letter within an avowedly sincere letter.[96] The letter-writing manuals of mid-nineteenth-century America were not merely guides to the epistolary art; they were brief treatises on the importance of sincerity in emotional self-expression.

Although all letters between friends and relatives adhered to the rhetoric of polite sincerity, many samples dwelt specifically on sincere romantic love. Young lovers protested their sincerity at every turn and often devoted the substance of their discussion to the abstract importance of sincerity in matters of love. A young gentleman courting a lady of superior fortune was advised to appeal to her good judgment of character to recognize his own sincerity: "You have judgment enough both of your own good qualities, and the characters of those with whom you converse, to make a proper estimate of my sincerity on this occasion."[97] A young lady responding to a marriage proposal might begin her letter, at great and circuitous length, with an expression of fear that she has concealed her "real sentiments" too long; apologetically, she might explain that "hypocrisy is the same, under whatever character it appears; and the person who is guilty of it in the smallest matters, will be equally so in the greatest," and finally accept his proposal.[98] In contrast, another young lady might plead her sincerity in rejecting a suitor whom she has received under duress by her parents: "This is a confession made perhaps with an offensive sincerity; but that conduct is much to be preferred to a covered dislike, which could not but pall all the sweets of life, by imposing on you a companion that languishes for another."[99] Finally, letter-writing manuals invariably included sample correspondence between lovers discussing their fidelity: accusations of infidelity abounded, and their standard replies usually protested the continuing sincerity of the offended party. In some sample letters the young lady delicately refused to name the gentleman's offense and laid it to his conscience to enlighten him. But other examples spoke bluntly to the point: "Do not equivocate; I have too convincing proofs of your insincerity; I saw you yesterday walking with Miss Benson, and am informed that you have proposed marriage to her."[100] In courtship, mutual sincerity was regarded as the substance of the romantic contract, and if one party failed in sincerity, the contract was broken. A lady breaking off a young man's addresses or their marriage plans explained, "It is true that many protestations of a sincere attachment have passed between us; but, sir, those protestations were made under the supposition that neither party would descend to deception."[101]

For the sentimentalists who instructed the American middle classes on epistolary etiquette, writing a letter was an act of emotional self-expression. At the same time, letters, like manners, were a critical aspect of the genteel performance. Just as personal appearance reflected character in face-to-face social relations, the appearance of a letter reflected character at a distance. Polite men and women were thus advised to use good paper and fine wafers to seal their letters and to keep their handwriting neat: "As all persons are more or less governed by first impressions and externals, the whole affair should be as neat and elegant as possible."[102] In fact, because "letters travel farther than the sound of the voice, or the sight of the countenance can follow," they "should convey no incorrect or unfavorable impression."[103] In sending a letter, readers were warned, they left "written evidence either of your good sense or your folly, your industry or carelessness, your self-control or impatience."[104] Fortunately, however, letters, in contrast to personal interviews, allowed a careful selection of words to convey an exact meaning. Before beginning a letter, proper ladies and gentlemen were advised to "weigh well in your own mind the design and purport of it; and consider very attentively what sentiments are most proper for you to express, and your correspondents to read."[105] The genteel art of letter-writing demanded above all a *controlled* communication of *proper* sentiments. The propriety of a given sentiment, in polite correspondence as in parlor conduct, was governed by the social geography of the genteel performance: "To write a business letter, and to write a familiar one, require as different qualifications as to enter a drawing-room and to knock at one's own street-door."[106] Different sentiments, in other words, were appropriate to different situations.

In many guides to polite letter-writing, as in all American etiquette manuals of the period, sentimental demands for sincere self-expression lay side by side with bourgeois demands for civilized emotional self-restraint. Although the avowed content of the polite letter was heart-felt sentiment, its form was rigorously self-restrained, stylized, and most significant, standardized. Even as the letter-writing manuals warned their readers that no dead sepulchre of words could convey the true feelings of the living heart, they offered hundreds of standard forms for the expression of the deepest sentiments of middle-class Americans. Romantic love, familial affection, friendship, jealousy, sympathy, gratitude—all found their way into standard forms that varied little from one guide to the next. (One canny guide did, however, advise the young gentleman reader not to send an exact copy of its standard marriage proposal to his beloved, because she might have read the same manual and thus reject his offer out of literary scorn.) The sentimental demand for sincerity shaped the specific conventions governing genteel correspondence: the polite letter opened with a statement of sincerity, went on to discuss the abstract importance of sincerity, and closed with a formal reminder of sincerity. But the more formalized the polite expression of sentiment became, the more it resembled that dead sepulchre of words that threatened to destroy the sincerity of emotional self-expression. In the standard forms of polite letter-writing, the problem of hypocrisy created a vicious circle. The sentimental demand for sincerity generated social forms labeled as sincere, but once these conventions were established—once they became fashionable—they could be condemned as forms of hypocrisy.

This vicious circle characterized the larger pattern of social conduct that I have called the genteel performance. The central irony of sentimental courtesy was simply this: the sentimental demand for a true courtesy that would betray no stage effect ultimately contributed to the theatricality of social life in the parlor. Even as sentimentalists condemned all superficial forms of etiquette as hollow-hearted and hypocritical, they advocated a system of polite conduct that was loaded with "etiquettish" social forms. In fact, sentimental efforts to establish sincerity as the guiding norm of polite conduct actually assisted the ritualization of parlor society by the mid-nineteenth century. The increasingly theatrical conduct of middle-class men and women in the parlor testified once again to the futility of sentimental efforts to embody sincerity in cultural forms. Just as the sentimental critique of fashion inadvertently enhanced the power of fashion over American dress, the sentimental critique of etiquette ultimately expanded the power of etiquette over polite social conduct. By the 1850s, in their discussions of courtesy as well as dress, the sentimental arbiters of middle-class culture were beginning to recognize the vicious circle in which they were caught and to admit the futility of establishing sincere forms of daily conduct. As they entered what John Higham has called the "age of consolidation," they grew increasingly willing to ridicule all efforts to formalize sincerity as the highest norm governing the lives of middle-class Americans.[107] This dawning recognition affected their views not just of dress and etiquette, but of a powerful social ritual that dominated middle-class culture by mid-century: mourning the dead.

Mourning the Dead:
A Study in Sentimental Ritual

One of the most significant expressions of sentimental culture was the cult of mourning. Beginning in the eighteenth century, the sentimentalization of death in America had gradually shifted the focus of popular attitudes away from the objective, physical fact of death toward the subjective response to death by those who mourned. By the mid-nineteenth century, death had come to preoccupy sentimentalists, who cherished it as the occasion for two of the deepest "right feelings" in human experience: bereavement, or direct mourning for the dead, and sympathy, or mournful condolence for the bereaved. Within the sentimental cult of mourning, bereavement and sympathy were regarded as visible signs of a mourner's Christian piety, social benevolence, and sincere sensibility. Mourning, the natural human response to the greatest human affliction, was held sacred by sentimentalists as the purest, the most transparent, and thus the most genteel of all sentiments. In mourning, a middle-class man or woman was believed to establish very clearly the legitimacy of his or her claims to genteel social status.

Because mourning offered middle-class men and women an opportunity to demonstrate true gentility, the social expression of mourning became very significant in sentimental culture. By conforming to the explicitly defined rules of mourning dress and etiquette, the bereaved and their sympathetic acquaintances enacted publicly a genteel performance of their deep sensibility. In other words, mourning was subject to the same civilizing process shaping other aspects of bourgeois conduct. But once again, middle-class efforts to embody private feelings in established cultural forms aroused deep anxieties about the conflict between social form and sentimental content and gave rise to a sentimentalist attack on the hypocrisies of middle-class life. Sentimentalists feared that the struggle for bourgeois gentility was poisoning even mourning with calculated self-interest and transforming mourning ritual into a masquerade of affected sensibility. Any confidence man or woman, it was feared, could easily assume the proper mourning dress and etiquette, stage a deceptive performance of deep grief, and thus establish a false claim to genteel social status. But the sentimental critique of the hypocrisies of formal mourning did not halt the ritualization of bereavement. Just as the sentimental attack on fashion and etiquette ultimately provided for their acceptance by the American middle classes, the sentimental critique of mourning ritual merely increased the complexity of the sentimental typology of grief and made mourning ritual the most elaborate expression of a dominant middle-class culture by the mid-nineteenth century.

For seventeenth-century New England Puritans, death had been a grim and terrifying reality. The morphology of conversion that shaped their efforts to achieve sainthood offered no assurance of salvation; those who claimed to know definitively that they were of the elect merely revealed that they were probably damned. While the elect soul faced the prospect of eternal life, the damned soul confronted eternal death, and the iconography of Puritan death dwelt on the darker probability. The physical terrors of death had firm hold on the Puritan imagination, as evidenced by the death's head or winged skull that appeared on most seventeenth-century gravestones, as well as on funeral elegies, broadsides, and mourning rings. And the common epitaph "Prepare for death and follow me" ceaselessly reminded all who strayed past the graveyard of their own mortality.[1]

Throughout the course of the eighteenth century, however, this stark Puritan image of death was gradually modified and softened. The Great Awakening, the most significant theological revolution of the century, introduced the belief that men might anticipate their own salvation without fear of godless pride. Under this new doctrine of assurance, the death of a Christian came to be regarded as an occasion for great joy. By the mid-eighteenth century, death as described in poetry, sermons, journals, and sepulchral art was an object of longing and not of dread. Gradually the death's head that had dominated gravestone design until 1740 evolved into a smiling cherub's face, suggesting eternal spiritual life rather than eternal physical death. Seventeenth-century epitaphs which had gloomily reminded readers of their own mortality and imminent judgment gave way to eighteenth-century epitaphs which cheerfully stressed the temporary nature of physical death: "Farewell my wife and children dear / I leave you for a while." By the nineteenth century, death had come to be viewed as a sweet deliverance from life, a promise of salvation for virtually all.[2]

In their sentimentalism, popular nineteenth-century effusions about the beauty and joy of death far surpassed all eighteenth-century discussions. But time had wrought greater changes than those of degree, for nineteenth-century views of death focused not on the event itself but on the mourning of those left behind. As Philippe Ariès has argued, the sentimentalization of death meant a shift from the medieval concern with "la mort de soi" to a romantic interest in "la mort de toi." This growing interest in "thy death" carried with it an intense concentration on "my grief." Tombstone design revealed most dramatically this crucial shift in the American view of death. Pre-nineteenth-century tombstones depicted the dead: the grim seventeenth-century representation was a skeleton; the more hopeful eighteenth-century design was an angel; and one eighteenth-century variant offered a medallion portrait of the deceased, with wings often added or suggested by an abstract design. By the late eighteenth and early nineteenth centuries, however, these representations of the deceased were yielding in popularity to the classical urn-and-willow design. This design featured a central funeral urn over which hung the branches of a willow tree, with the willow's drooping posture and enormous need for watering suggesting mourning. During this same period, roughly from 1780 to 1840, school girls were turning out mourning pictures based on the same design, but with a significant addition: a woman who wept over the urn, the lines of her drooping figure conforming to those of the willow. By about 1835, mourning pictures were being mass-produced by lithographers such as Nathaniel Currier; these prints offered blank tombstones on which purchasers might inscribe the name, age, and date of death of their lost loved ones. By the 1840s, the mourning figure had become part of sepulchral art itself: life-sized statues, sometimes actual representations of living mourners, leaned and wept over stone-carved urns, crosses, and caskets. Later in the century mourners would cluster around open caskets for mourning photographs and sometimes pose alone, gazing sadly upon locket photographs of the deceased.

In the nineteenth century, the dead vied with those who mourned them for iconographic attention, and often lost the contest.[3] The full emergence of the cult of mourning that distinguished nineteenth-century views of death occurred in the rural cemetery movement of the 1830s. Colonial graveyards, not surprisingly, were regarded as unpleasant places to be avoided by the living. By the late eighteenth century, even as the first urn-and-willow tombstones began to suggest the growing significance of mourning, burial grounds were deteriorating into weedy fields filled with fallen tombstones and the offensive odor of decay. Not until the early decades of the nineteenth century did critics begin to attack these messy places of death and to suggest that new rural cemeteries be established and carefully attended. One important concern of the rural cemetery movement was the health hazards created by the crowded old burial grounds, often located in the centers of rapidly growing cities. More important, however, reformers planned the rural cemeteries as beautifully landscaped gardens to encourage mourners to visit the graves of their lost loved ones—to encourage the living actively to mourn the dead. With the rural cemetery movement the transformation of Puritan death into Victorian death was complete. As one sentimentalist wrote,

> Formerly it was the practice to locate the "burying ground" in the most lone, desolate and barren spot that could be found; as if the very space the dead occupied was grudged them. Every thing about it was disagreeable and calculated to repel. What inscriptions and epitaphs on the gravestones! What emblems— ghastly skulls, cross-bones; and grim skeletons! all eminently fitted to fill the mind, and particularly the young mind, with dismal thoughts, and to make death and the grave subjects most unwelcome, and to be shunned as gloomy and terrifying intruders on the joys of life. But now all this is passing away.[4]

By 1831, when Mt. Auburn Cemetery was established on the outskirts of Cambridge, Massachusetts, the mourner had almost entirely upstaged the dearly departed for the lead role in the sentimental drama of death. What was the significance of this intense concern with mourning? The answer lies in the vast literature of mourning that became available to the middle-class reading public after 1830: death poetry, funeral sermons, consolatory essays and letters, and mourning manuals, which were anthologies of all these. Ann Douglas has recently categorized this literature as "contemporary consolation literature."[5] But just as the popular American literature on personal health reflects less a national concern with health than a national obsession with sickness, nineteenth-century consolation literature reveals more about the impulse to mourn than about the quest for solace.[6] Because these manuals offered extensive instruction on how and why to mourn, they may be read as the advice books of bereavement and sympathy, and a close examination of their content reveals much about the meaning of mourning in sentimental America.

Mourning manuals, like sepulchral art, provide evidence of an extraordinary self-consciousness about the act of mourning. In a poem entitled "Dirge for a Young Girl," for example, the poet dwelt at length not on the dead girl but on those who mourned her, and verbally copied the weeping figures captured in stone by sepulchral sculptors: "Yes, they're ever bending o'er her, / Eyes that weep, / Forms that to the cold grave bore her, / Vigils keep."[7] In *Agnes and the Little Key: Or, Bereaved Parents Instructed and Comforted*, a popular mourning manual of the 1850s, the writer provided for his readers' edification an extensively detailed discussion of his and his wife's bereavement over their daughter Agnes, dead at age one. He recorded, for example, every minute emotional response to the central problem of the book, where they should keep the key to Agnes's coffin. With the intensity of a sentimental surgeon he dissected their every feeling: he carefully recorded their response to seeing the empty high chair for the first time; he probed the question whether he or his wife suffered more; he compared his feeling on the day of the burial to his feelings on seeing the grave for the first time after the burial. Finally, he suggested to his wife this method for organizing their thoughts and feelings:

> I should love to join with you, some evening, and put down in a little book our thoughts and feelings in connection with [the key]. We shall read it, hereafter, with great satisfaction. . . . I will name some use, or reflection, or purpose, suggested by the little thing; and, when we have discussed it, I will write it down here. Then it shall be your turn to propose a sentiment.[8]

For middle-class sentimentalists, mourning the dead was an intensely self-conscious experience, to be probed and examined in the Puritan tradition of spiritual self-examination.

One of the first tasks of popular mourning literature was to assure readers that mourning was not forbidden. For New England

Puritans intense bereavement had been viewed as a rebellion against the will of God: the good Puritan strived to use the occasion of death as a reminder of his own mortality and then to cease his mourning as soon as possible. In contrast, nineteenth-century Americans were encouraged to weep over the dead. Grief, they were assured, was a fitting response to death: "Ye weep, and it is well; / For tears befit earth's partings."[9] The natural workings of the human body in response to death gave evidence that mourning was not meant to be denied: "The smitten heart will bleed; the workings of nature must have vent. It is right. Tears were not made that they should never be shed: nor the passion of grief implanted only to be stifled."[10] Jesus himself, the manuals repeatedly pointed out, had wept at the grave of Lazarus, so "surely, he allows you to weep; surely, there is a 'needs be' that you feel a heaviness under such a trial."[11]

In fact, mourning was believed to be a peculiarly Christian response to death. "The religion of Christ," the mourning manuals reminded their readers, "is eminently the religion of the heart."[12] In weeping over the dead, the mourner was thus performing an act of Christian piety: "The heart of the true saint quivers at pain, and his eyes are filled with tears."[13] The death of a loved one was clearly part of God's plan to bring the mourners to pious sensibility, for, as one mourning manual exclaimed in 1836, "How naturally does affliction make us Christians!"[14] The working of affliction upon the immortal souls of mourners, as described in sentimental mourning literature, resembled the crude morphology of conversion that characterized nineteenth-century evangelical revivalism. In the first stage of the mourner's conversion, the death of a loved one induced in him a strong sense of his own spiritual insufficiency: "When the hand of God lies heavy upon us, we plainly discern our own insufficiency and weakness, and yet see nothing about or near us that can afford us any real relief."[15] Out of the mourner's grief came a deep sense of the vanity of earthly happiness: "Consider, pensive mourner, that which stole your heart from God, is gone. That which engrossed your time and thoughts, and left no room for Christ and eternal realities, is gone."[16] God visited death upon the spiritually careless to remind them that their day too would come: "[Death] compels us to feel most sensibly because there is uniformly something peculiarly affecting and solemn in mortality, and because we are necessitated to anticipate the period when we shall grapple with 'the last enemy.' "[17] The mourner thus came to realize that men must not "have a dependence on ourselves," but must "come out of ourselves to be able to resign ourselves to God."[18] God had designed the affliction of death "to melt and soften our hearts to such degree as he finds necessary, in order to the good purposes of his grace."[19] Convicted of his insufficiency, deprived of his earthly happiness, reminded of his own mortality, his heart softened by affliction, the mourner finally fled "to *Him* who only can [afford us any real relief], who is rich in mercies and mighty to save; both able and willing to stretch himself out to all our wants, and to fill our emptiness."[20] God was the one "True Consoler" and Christianity the "religion of consolations."[21] Christian mourning, the sentimentalists assured their bereaved readers, was a vital religious experience, a kind of personal revivalism in which the death of a loved one convinced the mourner of his utter worthlessness and softened his hardened and reprobate heart. By weeping freely the mourner was believed to assist God in preparing his heart to receive divine grace.

In the sentimental cult of mourning, the story of Jesus weeping at the tomb of Lazarus was frequently cited to illustrate the Christian piety of the mourning experience. This story also established the significance of mourning as a form of sentimental social bonding, for in weeping over his friend's grave, Jesus was said to have shed dignity on "the most sacred of our social feelings."[22] In mourning, the bereaved proved that they had not forgotten the dead: "Then forget not the dead, who are evermore nigh us, / Still floating sometimes to our dream-haunted bed."[23] Specifically, mourning over lost loved ones was believed to demonstrate the enduring strength of family ties. Within the sentimental view, death was not powerful enough to sever the bonds of domestic love. The departed loved one acted as a guardian angel who shed continued influence over the heart of the mourner:

> The memory of the sainted dead hovers, a blessed and purifying influence, over the hearts of men. At the grave of the good, so far from losing heart, the spiritually minded find new strength. They weep, but as they weep they look down into the sepulchre, and behold angels sitting, and the dead come nearer, and are united to them by a fellowship more intimate than that of blood.[24]

The bonds of love that stretched across the great divide of death were thus believed stronger than those ties that bound families together in life. Furthermore, the death of one family member united the living family in greater love: "The chain of family love on earth becomes much more strong and enduring, when some of its precious links are in heaven."[25] Finally, mourning ensured that family love would be perfected in the domestic heaven pictured by sentimentalists: "I love to think," mused the father of Agnes, "that our separations, griefs, and our improvement under them, will make us love each other intensely when we meet again."[26]

This sacred social feeling of mourning was not limited, however, to the close-knit family circle. When affliction melted the ice around the hardened heart of a mourner, he felt a rush of benevolence toward all men: affliction "has a direct tendency to soften the character, and call forth and improve all the benevolent affections."[27] The flow of love toward a now departed friend was necessarily diverted into new channels of benevolence:

> When a river of love is suddenly checked in the heart by the death of a friend, it needs various channels to drain off the waters that otherwise must drown it in the suffocating agonies of repression . . . after the heart has given one great throb of pain, it may turn for relief to immediate acts of benevolence to human beings who may not know from what depths of pain such love is wrung, nor how the poor, crushed, bleeding heart seeks to still its own throbbings by·blessing others.[28]

The death of a loved one, by reminding mourners of every unkindness they had committed against the departed, encouraged them to check their passions and to meet one another in kindness and peace, in a heightened awareness that "our social ties are golden links of uncertain tenure, and, one by one, they drop away."[29] When mourners learned from their affliction to practice kindness toward all, then "gentleness diffuses itself over society" and displaces "suspicion and distrust, those cankerworms that sap the life and purity of communities where they exist, while it restores and strengthens confidence between men."[30] When men and women learned this great lesson of mourning—to love one another—they helped establish on earth the social harmony they would one day enjoy in the sentimentalist heaven, where "universal love expels all selfish passions, prompts every heart to seek the general good, and diffuses serenity over the scene, and contentment among the myriads of the blessed."[31]

Mourning was regarded as the most sacred of social feelings because the heart softened by affliction turned with greater love not only to the departed loved one, but to all living members of the family, and finally to all mankind. But although mourning was seen as a social feeling, it was not depicted in sentimental mourning literature as a social practice. The mother of little Agnes wept alone in a darkened room, with a Bible in her lap, despite the fact that her conscientiously grief-stricken husband sat in the next room; and the bereaved parent of "The Little Boy that Died" wrote, "I am all alone in my chamber now, / And the midnight hour is near."[32] In mourning pictures the bereaved invariably wept with face averted, or partly concealed by a hand, a handkerchief, or a drooping sleeve. "Why should we make a parade of grief, and blazon it as it were upon the housetops?" apologized one mourner before speaking of the death of his son.[33] Solitude was such a crucial element of sentimental mourning because "those who grieve unseen are sincere."[34] Solitary mourning was sincere mourning, and public displays of grief, in the sentimental view, were regarded with distaste.

True mourning, the sentimentalists believed, was not intended for the eyes of the unsympathetic: "[Tears] are not for the gaze / Of the cold, scornful eye; / No mocking look shall rest, / None know,— but purity."[35] And most eyes, it was assumed, were in fact shockingly unsympathetic. All the world outside the small circle of mourners was regarded as a "tearless crowd," a "thoughtless throng," who gave to "the hearse, the coffin, and the shroud, a passing glance" and then carelessly hurried on.[36] This conviction that mourning was too sacred to be witnessed by the cold and careless generated a sentimental hostility to death iconography. In sentimental literature, graves were often lonely, unmarked, and even hidden from the gaze of a heartless world: "For thickets heavy all around should screen it / From careless gazer that might wander near, / Nor even to him who by some chance had seen it, / Would I have ought to catch his eye, appear."[37] Not in erecting elaborate gravestones did the sentimental mourner memorialize the dead, but in faithfully grieving over their departure and thus carving their memory on the heart: "There is no stone raised there to tell / My sister's name and age, / For that dear name in every heart / Is carved on memory's page."[38] One story told of a young mountain girl whose entire family had died, leaving her lonely and mourning her loss. She did erect a stone over the grave of her brother, but could only write an epitaph in pencil, and a passing stranger commented on the faithfulness of her grief:

Gracious heaven! said I within myself, what mausoleum could preserve the memory of the dead so faithfully as this tearful mountain-girl does that of her brother, coming night and morning as she does, to reengrave his memory upon her heart, by writing over again upon this poor chip of granite the heart-melting inscription, MY BROTHER'S GRAVE![39]

Public iconography was condemned and replaced by a sentimental reverence for the personal tokens or keepsakes left by the deceased: "In every home there is an enshrined memory, a sacred relic, a ring, a lock of shining hair, a broken plaything, a book, a picture, something sacredly kept and guarded, which speaks of death, which tells as plainly as words, of some one long since gone."[40] Rings, pictures, and locks of hair were cherished in the sentimental cult of mourning because they could be handled and wept over in domestic privacy.

The lonely woman weeping over an unmarked grave, the solitary man gazing sadly at a locket he wore over his heart—both gave sure evidence, within the sentimental conventions of mourning, that they sincerely grieved over their loss. In hiding their tears from careless passersby, in scorning to erect tombstones over their dead, in retreating to closed rooms and drenching their pillows with tears at midnight, these mourners proved their grief a matter of the heart. In the privacy of their grief, they practiced a heartfelt sensibility that demonstrated their alienation from "this blighted orb," this "living tomb" of earth, "Where all are strange, and none are kind; / Kind to the worn, the wearied soul."[41] One poetic mourner not only wept privately but hid his grief under the guise of happiness upon his return from his loved one's grave: "The vows are paid my spirit sought to pay; / The thoughtless throng must see me weep no more; / Back to the busy world I take my way, / To seem as happy as I was before."[42] To ensure the higher sincerity of his bereavement, this mourner deliberately practiced the hypocrisy of hiding his grief.

Sentimental mourning, as exhaustively described in the mourning literature, was an act of Christian piety, of deep social feeling, and of sincere sensibility. The true mourner was a Christian whose grief confirmed and strengthened his piety, a devoted family member and a benevolent member of all human society, and a person of true sensibility whose sincerity was evinced by the solitude of his grief and by his alienation from a heartless and unfeeling world. "By the sadness of our countenances," many manuals informed their bereaved readers, "our hearts are made better."[43] Death assumed such importance in the sentimental culture of nineteenth-century America because mourning provided the greatest opportunity to experience deep and lasting sentiment.

In praising the uses of affliction, however, the sentimentalists did not depart from the genteel demand for propriety of emotional self-expression. Although middle-class men and women were encouraged to indulge "the luxury of grief"[44] as a mark of their sentimental sensibilities, they were instructed never to grieve excessively. The rationale given for this repeated warning was religious: the heathen and the Jew howled in impious anguish over their departed loved ones because they had no hope of resurrection, but the Christian "gives way to the feelings of nature, which prompt the bursting tear and sad regret; but at the same time, his sorrow is not without hope."[45] The Christian did not wail with despair over the death of a loved one. Mourning was to be instead an occasion for discipline in emotional self-expression, for genteel self-improvement: the proper mourner strived to cultivate "finer sensibilities" and a "high moral culture," "a better taste" and "a more Christian feeling."[46] Even in mourning for the dead—in fact, especially in mourning for the dead—the bourgeois quest for genteel propriety was not to be abandoned.

The view that proper mourning was a mark of respectability was well expressed by Rev. F. R. Anspach in *The Sepulchres of Our Departed*, published in 1854, in which the writer urged upon his readers the "propriety of caring for the dead." "The condition of a grave-yard," he wrote, "is, generally speaking, a very good index of the character of the community in which it is located." Anspach warned his readers to "have a care about your confidence, and interest, and reputation among a people where you witness an air of negligence and desolation overspreading the sacred enclosure where the departed repose." Those who properly mourned the dead maintained beautiful cemeteries, which stood as a testimony to their respectability. Those who failed to mourn their dead and let their graveyards fall into ruin could not be trusted to practice the lofty principles they professed; they were confidence men. "They may affect to love you, and profess a high esteem, as long as caprice and policy may dictate; but they will cast you off as they would a worthless garment, when their own selfish ends can no longer be subserved by your presence."[47] Mourning the dead, like proper dress and polite social conduct, stamped the middle-class American with the mark of good character. Mourning was also viewed as a means to form good character and thus to establish bourgeois respectability. In *Agnes and the Little Key*, Nehemiah Adams described at some length the transformation of an uncouth laborer into a genteel merchant through the powers of bereavement. In their newfound sympathy for other bereaved parents, Agnes's parents attended the funeral of another small child. Agnes's genteel father described this other father as follows:

> The father was a drover. He was a stout, coarse-looking man, with a very large head, which he leaned back against the ceiling where he sat, rolling it to and fro, with his mouth open, the tears running down with no effort to conceal them or wipe them away, and every now and then he would beat with his head against the wall.

Here, clearly, was a heathen mourner who mourned without hope, and an uncouth mourner who mourned without any of the physical or emotional self-control that stamped the man of gentility. Enter Agnes's parents. Having made sure that the grass was dry and "the ground was safe to kneel upon," they persuaded the lubberly drover and his meek Christian wife to pray at the gravesite. With this act they launched a long and patient effort to convince this impious heathen that his only hope to see his wife and child in heaven lay in religion. The drover's eventual conversion to Christianity and gentility deserves to be quoted at length:

> He became a consistent Christian, joined the church, took a seat in the choir, he having a splendid baritone voice; and sometimes, when I have listened, I could not be mistaken in the feeling that the subduing influence of affliction had raised him in the scale of being, and had opened susceptibilities in him which made him tenfold more of a man than he was before, besides enduing him, through grace, with that which made him a new creature, and had changed his prospects for eternity.
> Several months after that, he called, with his wife, at my house, very respectably dressed, being now the owner of a provision stall in a large market, and in profitable business. His countenance was changed. It was refined, urbane, full of feeling; he was gentle and affectionate; he was a happy man.[48]

Affliction had brought to this once coarse and lowly man not only a new heart and a new countenance but a new job and a new suit of clothes. In his mourning, he had been raised in the social scale and ushered into the ranks of the sentimental genteel.

Because of the social imperative to mourn, sentimental bereavement sought outward expression in the middle-class observance of the many social regulations governing mourning dress and mourning conduct. To mourn was to grieve inwardly over a lost loved one; but to be "in mourning" was to wear black, to assume a demeanor of bereavement, to limit one's social activities for the appropriate period following the death. The social forms of mourning were regarded by sentimentalists as simply the outward signs of inward grief: "Why is that mother robed in mourning? It is the outward token of a mourning which the heart alone can feel."[49] But the primary purpose of these social forms was to establish the mourner's claim to his or her due status as one of the sentimental genteel. And it was this social function of mourning forms that would arouse deep middle-class concerns about the hypocrisy of genteel bereavement.

"The chief use of mourning attire," an etiquette manual of 1852 explained, "is to express our grief and humiliation."[50] Mourning dress was to be "an appropriate emblem" of inward bereavement.[51] In the Western European mourning tradition, nineteenth-century Americans generally accepted the color black as "the best suited to the sombre tone of the spirits when one has met with a recent loss,"[52] and in this outward emblem of grief the proper mourner dressed from head to foot. Although styles of women's mourning varied as fashions changed, "close plain" or "full" or "deep" mourning dresses were usually made of black bombazine—a silk and wool mixture with a sooty, lustreless look—and trimmed with black crape or braid. In choosing mourning fabrics, consumers were cautioned to select "a dead, solid color" of black that gave no hint of blue or rust.[53] Collars, sleeves, cuffs, and bonnets were all made of crape—a silk treated to assume a dull, matte surface—and mourning bonnets were covered with a long, thick, black crape veil. For outerwear, black cloth cloaks, black Thibet cloth shawls, and black furs were worn. Black silk was considered inappropriate for deep mourning because of its shine, and gloves were of plain black cotton or of "shammy" leather, which had a dull, suedelike surface. Mourning handkerchiefs were of sheer cambric, unembroidered, with a broad plain hem or a black border that grew narrower throughout the mourning period. Ornaments worn during mourning were to be few and plain. Mourning rings, brooches, lockets, pins, necklaces, and earrings of jet, set in gold, could be worn; but an oval brooch surrounded by rings of jets and pearls and containing a lock of hair from the deceased was often the sole ornament donned by the mourner. Finally, mourning fans, parasols, umbrellas, aprons, pincushions, and walking sticks were made of black and trimmed with crape. Throughout most of the period from 1830 to 1860, the genteel woman in deep mourning wore no white.[54]

The degree of mourning reflected in dress varied according to the mourner's relationship to the deceased, and the time that had elapsed since the death. Strictly speaking, a widow was expected to wear mourning for two years and to remain in deep mourning, as described above, for the entire first year. After the first year she assumed half mourning, also known as "second" or "lighter" mourning. "The first outward token of lighter mourning is laying aside the veil."[55] Gradually, the widow replaced the black crape sleeves and collars of deep mourning with white tarleton and French cambric; black crape trim gave way to black lace. The woman in second mourning often wore shiny black silk in place of sooty bombazine and varied her sombre wardrobe with some garments of gray, violet, and white. In general, full mourning was worn for parents, grandparents, spouses, and siblings, while half mourning could be assumed from the beginning for uncles and aunts, cousins, and intimate friends and acquaintances. A woman who had lost a parent or a child mourned for one year; for a grandparent, a brother or sister, or a friend leaving her an inheritance, she mourned for six months; for an aunt or uncle, nephew or niece, she mourned for three months and was allowed to wear white trim. Mourning children under the age of twelve wore white in summer and gray in winter; their suits were trimmed with black buttons, ruffles, belts, and bonnet ribbons.[56] In donning mourning apparel, men and women were warned to avoid the extremes of extravagance and of total neglect. "The custom is ancient—it is useful, to the bereaved, and to the community."[57]

The man or woman who donned proper mourning attire assumed with it a properly bereaved social demeanor. One purpose of wearing mourning, in fact, was "to remind us of our bereavement on those occasions, when we are liable to be gay and thoughtless."[58] In other words, mourning dress not only expressed grief, it enforced a social manner of grief that was to be maintained at all times during the mourning period. Mourning attire also signaled to others the proper demeanor to be assumed in the mourner's presence: "It is also a caution to others, not to converse on light or mirthful topics in our presence; yet we should not speak of death to one who wears a weed."[59] In the genteel performance of mourning, the bereaved expressed grief in dress and manner, and social acquaintances of the bereaved responded with appropriate gravity.

Upon first assuming mourning, the bereaved man or woman was to assume an air of quietly controlled grief. "We should be calm, humble, and discharge every duty. Excessive grief will do no good—the event has occurred—the departed cannot be recalled."[60] Lest the mourner be guilty of grieving too violently—or, perhaps, too complacently—mourning dress assisted the proper bereavement by placing certain well-defined restrictions upon the mourner's social activity. In the dramaturgical context of nineteenth-century etiquette, the mourner's semiseclusion expanded the back regions in which the genteel performance could be relaxed. For the first month after the funeral, mourning women were not supposed to leave home except to attend church and arrange business matters; for the first six weeks, they were expected not to make visits or to dine away from home. For the entire deep mourning period, women were forbidden to attend weddings or festive parties.[61] A mourner who received a social invitation sent her regrets with a reference to her proper social seclusion: "When I tell you that my dear———is no more, you will at once sympathise with me, and feel the impossibility of anything like mixing in society. Believe me, amidst my own griefs, Your ever sincere friend, . . ."[62] And in an emblematic statement of the grief that incapacitated her for social activity, the mourner used black-edged stationery. In letters, as in face-to-face social intercourse, the properly sensible mourner used the mourning token as a reminder never to slip into any inappropriate sentiments or activities.

The mourning dress and mourning etiquette of the middle class pointed to an enormous concern for sustaining the proper demeanor of bereavement by assuming the proper forms for expressing genteel grief. Within sentimental mourning literature the feeling of grief itself was all that mattered, and the privacy of its expression was the test of its sincerity and depth. But in social practice middle-class attention shifted from the sentiment to its forms of expression, and the ideal of private feeling yielded to bourgeois demands for its public performance. The rules curtailing the social activities of mourners did enforce upon them, to a degree, the solitude demanded by the sentimental ideal. But the rules of proper mourning attire directly violated the sentimental conventions of heartfelt, private grief. In donning proper mourning attire, the mourner wore her heart on her sleeve and expressed her grief not privately but publicly. The sentimental image of the handkerchief drenched with tears by night became a black-edged handkerchief carried by day; the poetic image of the private keepsake of the lost loved one became a lock of hair displayed under the glass front of a jeweled brooch backed in gold. Genteel mourning ultimately subordinated the sentiment of bereavement to the respectable performance of bereavement, but not without generating sentimental resistance. The problem was simply stated by the Reverend Orville Dewey: "The truth is, these trappings of grief seem to me indifferent and childish where there *is* real grief; and where there is not, they are a mockery."[63] Once again, the middle-class attempt to formalize sentiment in the interests of bourgeois gentility was arousing anxiety about the problem of hypocrisy in middle-class culture.

The best statement of the perceived conflict between private sentiment and its public expression was Timothy S. Arthur's short story, "Going Into Mourning," published in October 1841. The story opens with the funeral of Willie, youngest child of the respectable Condy family. A group of less respectable neighbors are cynically commenting on the haste with which the Condys have assumed proper mourning, and one says, "These bombazine dresses and long black veils are truly enough called mourning— they are an excellent counterfeit, and deceive half of the world." In supposing the Condys insensible of their loss, these local gossips prove mistaken, for the family's grief runs deep. But Mrs. Condy is very concerned about their mourning apparel and is anxious to replace the dresses she and her two oldest daughters have borrowed for the funeral with her own. Her husband tries to dissuade her, saying, "Sarah, black dresses, and an outside imposing show of mourning, cannot make us any the more sorry for the loss of our dear little one. . . . We know our grief to be real, and need no artificial incitement to keep it alive." But Mrs. Condy refuses to ignore the dictates of proper society and orders the family seamstress, Ellen Maynard, to make up three mourning dresses in time for church on Sunday. Ellen tries to refuse the job because her sister Margaret is dying of consumption. But the Condys insist, and the

poor seamstress leaves her sister to work day and night in the
Condy home, where she herself falls ill. Finally, escorted by kind
Mr. Condy, Ellen arrives at her own garret apartment late Saturday
night to find Margaret near death. Mr. Condy sends for a physician
and for his own family, who arrive in time to realize what they have
done. As Mary Condy sits with the dying girl, she thinks of her dead
brother and realizes that "since her thoughts had become interested
in the getting and making up of her mourning dress, she had felt
but little of the keen sorrow that had at first overwhelmed her, and
that now came back upon her mind like a flood." She admits that
she has desired less "to commemorate the death of her brother, in
putting on mourning, than to appear before others to be deeply
affected with grief," and in a sudden burst of repentance she
resolves not to attend church the following day "for the too vain
purpose of displaying her mourning apparel."[64]

In "Going Into Mourning," Arthur, one of the most popular
writers of his generation, expressed the peculiarly Victorian concern that the social forms of bereavement were at war with the
sincere sentiment of grief. Even though the Condys are not hypocrites of bereavement, they do allow their anxious concern for social
approval to blunt their sincere feelings of grief. In fact, in their
haste to fulfill genteel social expectations, the Condys fail to exercise
the most important sentiment of middle-class gentility—
disinterested benevolence. They work Ellen until she feels ill, and
ensure the miserable loneliness, if not the premature death, of
Ellen's sister Margaret. In repentance for their sins of selfishness,
the Condy family pay Margaret's funeral expenses and invite Ellen
to come live with them. As Ellen sits in her new home, working on
mourning dresses for the younger children, Mrs. Condy extends to
her one more offer of charity—a piece of bombazine for her own
mourning. But Ellen quietly refuses it and thus completes the
lesson in sentiment she is teaching the Condy women, who now
respect her for shunning "all exterior manifestation of the real
sorrow that they knew oppressed her spirits. And never did they
array themselves in their sombre weeds, that the thought of Ellen's
unobtrusive grief did not come up and chide them."[65]

"Going Into Mourning" presented clearly the critique of empty
social forms that lay at the heart of sentimental anxieties about
hypocrisy. But Arthur's short story did not entirely condemn the
custom of wearing mourning attire. Significantly, the Condy family,
after performing penance by absenting themselves from church on

the first Sunday of their bereavement, did not cast aside their mourning dresses. Even as they admired the unobtrusive grief of their seamstress, they themselves did not abandon the genteel social custom. A poor seamstress, Arthur thus suggested, might ignore social forms that middle-class people could not avoid and still maintain respectability. In retaining quiet respect for Ellen's purer, private grief, while obeying the dictates of genteel custom, the Condys struck the proper balance between pure sentiment and its outward social expression, the balance that represented the genteel mourning ideal.

Even *Godey's Lady's Book*, whose fashion columns regularly included advice on mourning attire, delivered periodic sentimental apologies for its contributions to the formalization of bereavement. Its critique focused, of course, on the fashion of assuming mourning apparel. Because the afflicted human heart "craves this outward type of loss," the writers at *Godey's* explained, they chose to "quarrel with the *fashion,* but not the *custom,* of mourning."[66] Fashionable mourning involved an extremely literal equation of inner sentiment with precise outward forms:

> We quarrel with the *fashion,* which judges of grief by the depth of a fold, that brings remark or censure upon a widow as to whether she wears her veil up or down . . . that modifies shades according to weeks or months, instead of softened feeling.[67]

Those who confused form with feeling, *Godey's* warned, lost sight of the true purpose of mourning attire: to signify bereavement, not to substitute for it. Those who dressed in mourning for the sake of personal vanity rather than as the outward expression of inner grief were guilty of hypocrisy:

> We quarrel with the *fashion* . . . that puts on black for a third cousin, because becoming, and lays it aside at Newport for a fancy ball; or counterfeits it by a mockery of white tarleton, with violet streamers, and marabout feathers tipped with the same shade; or goes glistening in bugles and jet to the gayest entertainments.[68]

The magazine's columns condemned excessive mourning jewelry, fabrics with checks and bars and stripes, bonnets decorated with streamers and bouquets, and dresses covered with bugles and artificial flowers of white and black crape. Such fashionable atrocities were not sincere emblems of bereavement but the mere "mockeries of grief" that made up what was contemptuously called "dressy" mourning. Whenever mourning became "a study of an ornament," *Godey's* warned, "it loses its significance."[69]

The best expression of the magazine's avowed contempt for the excesses of "fashionable tribulation" appeared in a satirical farce entitled "The House of Mourning," published in May 1844. The story is of a country squire and his lady on their first visit to a large, modern London mourning establishment. This "house of mourning" is divided into various departments for the different degrees of mourning, and each department is staffed by a salesperson who delivers his or her sales pitch while affecting the precise attire and demeanor of bereavement appropriate to that department. In the deep mourning department a solemn young man dressed in black greets the Lady Hamper lugubriously, "May I have the melancholy pleasure of serving you, madam?" He shows the rustic couple dresses with names such as the "Inconsolable," a watered silk— "watered, as you perceive, to match the sentiment"—and the "Luxury of Woe," made of expensive velvet. When Lady Hamper asks the solemn youth about half mourning, he tells her that they sell "Full, and half, and quarter, and half-quarter mourning, shaded off, if I may say so, like an India ink drawing, from a grief prononcé to the slightest nuance of regret." In the "intermediate sorrow department," a young man in gray, "who affects the pensive rather than the solemn," shows the lady a dress called "Settled Grief" and a warmly tinted black fabric called "a gleam of comfort." In the coiffure department, a saleswoman in deep mourning shows the couple a fancy cap called "the sympathizer" and a handkerchief called "The Larmoyante—with a fringe of artificial tears, you perceive, in mock pearl." Meanwhile, Squire Hamper delivers a constant series of asides concerning the hypocrisy of this fashionable mourning. When the solemn salesman excuses the flimsiness of a fabric by saying, "But mourning ought not to last for ever, sir," the squire replies, "No, it seldom does; especially the violent sorts." When the pensive salesman proclaims one fabric as "the happiest [i.e., the finest] pattern of the season," the Squire replies, "Yes, some people are very happy in it, no doubt." Finally, the Squire closes the farce with a flash of country simplicity and sincerity:

> Well, if it's all the same to you, ma'am, I'd rather die in the country, and be universally lamented, after the old fashion— for, as to London, what with the new French modes of mourn-

ing, and the "Try Warren" style of blacking the premises, it does seem to me that, before long, all sorrow will be sham Abram, and the House of Mourning a regular Farce![70]

Squire Hamper's attack on the hypocrisy of urban mourning customs was clearly not limited to the fashionable excesses of proper mourning attire. In a broader sense, the good Squire was condemning the commercialization of mourning. In the 1840s and 1850s, as formal mourning became widely accepted as a mark of middle-class gentility, *maisons de deuil* such as Besson and Son of Philadelphia began to spring up in the largest American cities, and mourning departments appeared in the new large department stores. These mourning establishments encouraged a wide range of distinctions in the degrees of bereavement expressed in proper mourning attire, and thus contributed to the extreme literalness of middle-class views concerning the relationship between inner senti-ment and its outer social expression. By 1854, *Godey's Lady's Book* was announcing that because mourning attire had "become the subject of so much conventional formality and abuse," many people were refusing to assume it, "their sorrow being of the heart, and their mourning not meant for the eyes of the world."[71]

The genteel imperative of formal mourning was not, however, to die so easily, and it is clear from their continued advice on mourn-ing fashions that *Godey's* did not expect all women to abandon the custom entirely. Instead *Godey's* advised their readers that in mourning, as in all dress, plainness and simplicity were recom-mended as the purest and most sincere form of emotional self-expression. In the 1850s, *Godey's* began to suggest ways in which mourning attire might express more accurately the precise senti-ments of the mourner. For example, it became proper for mourn-ing mothers to wear dresses in quiet colors, white dresses with dark ribbons, or black silk dresses with a white crape or straw bonnet. These modifications of stark traditional mourning were viewed as better expressions of "the sadness with which we see a child taken from us, yet from the cares and anxieties of life as well."[72] At the same time, mourners anxious to avoid the hypocrisy of fashionable mourning were encouraged to abandon the rigidly codified time periods for the various levels of mourning, since "this code of fashion, which many families follow in our more stylish city circles, would seem to indicate the day and hour when grief terminates, and the dead are forgotten."[73] The mourner who set aside her formal mourning whenever her bereavement faded thus demonstrated the sincerity of the social expression of her grief.

In the sentimental ideal of mourning, bereavement was a sacred sentiment that was best and purest when most private. In the social practice of mourning, however, the bereavement of the heart sought outward, public expression in the highly and precisely symbolic trappings of mourning dress. True sentiment, ideally a matter of the private heart, was also the outward sign of middle-class gentility, and therefore open to the threat of hypocrisy. The act of death itself was admired by sentimentalists because the dying seldom dared to cling to the hypocrisies of earthly existence: "Seldom has any one sufficient strength of motive or of nerve to act a part when the stern realities of another world begin to press upon him. Hypocrisy dare not look the king of terrors in the face."[74] Mourning the dead was a different matter entirely, for any confidence man or woman aspiring to higher social status might assume the outward trappings of bereavement to lay claim to bourgeois gentility: "Man finds his account in dissembling, not only to the living whose good opinion he would propitiate, but also over the unconscious remains of the dead, that he may keep up a reputation for sensibility and friendship among the living."[75] But since sentiment was the stamp of gentility, the social forms of sentimental expression could not be cast aside: genteel Americans, like the Condy family, had to condemn the fashion of mourning without abandoning the custom of mourning. The sentimental typology of grief was repeatedly defended and apologetically shaped anew into "truer" expressions of bereavement. But it was not abandoned by middle-class men and women seeking to establish their respectability by demonstrating in outward social forms the deep sensibility of their private hearts.

Mid-nineteenth-century middle-class Americans were obsessed with mourning their dead because, in their sentimental scheme of social status, the capacity to experience deep grief demonstrated true gentility. For the same sentimental reasons, they were almost equally obsessed with the act of offering sympathy to those who mourned. The sentimental duty of consolation expanded the genteel opportunities presented by a single death far beyond the family and intimate friends of the deceased to all who knew or barely knew the mourners themselves. Little Agnes's father noted, for example, that men who had scarcely bowed to him before his daughter's death now noticed the mourning weed in his hat and the sorrow in his face and saluted him respectfully on the street. The grateful man wrote, "It made me love my fellow-men more than ever; it made me resolve to be kind to people in trouble."[76] Sympathy, as well as bereavement, brought men and women closer together in the sentimental bonds of disinterested benevolence. The mourner was said to be unusually open to the influence of others: his mind was "sensitive and alive to whatever affects it; and is often powerfully touched by the slightest action or word." No office of friendship, therefore, demanded "greater discernment and delicacy of mind" than consolation.[77] And no office of friendship demanded "a more calm and tender piety. . . . 'Pure religion and undefiled' is to visit the widow and fatherless, the childless and bereaved 'in their affliction,' to stretch out a helping hand to our suffering brethren, 'to bear each other's burdens,' 'to weep with those who weep, to comfort those who mourn.' "[78] Sympathy, as well as bereavement, was cherished by Victorian Americans and cultivated as a mark of sensibility.

Within the cult of mourning, moreover, sympathy was believed to be quite rare, for bereavement wrapped the mourner in "a grief, the depth of which another / May never know."[79] "The stranger knows not of it. The acquaintance cannot intermeddle with it; and even in the confidence of tender friendship, it may not be wise often to intrude it."[80] Sentimental mourning literature held to a convention that only those who had been mourners themselves could truly sympathize with the bereaved. At the same time, however, none knew better than they the uselessness of merely formal sympathy:

> Young mother! what can feeble friendship say,
> To soothe the anguish of this mournful day?
> They, they alone, whose hearts like thine have bled,
> Know how the living sorrow for the dead;
> Each tutored voice, that seeks such grief to cheer,
> Strikes cold upon the weeping parent's ear;
> I've felt it all,—alas! too well I know
> How vain all earthly power to hush thy woe!
> GOD cheer thee, childless mother! 'tis not given
> For man to ward the blow that falls from heaven.[81]

The most deeply sympathetic friend could only address the mourner with a delicate apology: "How to offer you consolation in your present grief, I know not."[82] And even such painful but well-intentioned professions of sympathetic incompetence were believed to be unusual, for all the world outside the family circle was seen as callously unconcerned about the mourner's grief: "Mid laughing crowds I stood alone, / Unutterably desolate."[83] Even the funeral attendants were labeled "a numerous unconcerned company, who are discoursing to one another about the news of the day, or the ordinary affairs of life."[84]

Why did sentimental mourning literature return again and again to this idea that even the well-intentioned could offer little or no consolation to the bereaved and that most of the world failed to share or even to notice the mourner's deep grief? By the nineteenth century, death in America was losing the communal significance it had had in the colonial period. Although seventeenth-century views of death had been grimly terrifying, the major shock of separation from the dead had been confronted and absorbed by the entire community. In the small colonial towns a tight network of mutual dependencies and primary relationships bound all men and women together, and the death of a single individual was viewed as an immediate loss to the entire community. In expression of their collective loss, members of the community helped lay out and attend the body before the burial, construct the coffin, bear the body to the burial site, and dig and cover the grave. The funeral was both a social function and a public event, to which all were summoned by the tolling of the meetinghouse bell. And in recognition of a bereavement that extended beyond the immediate family of the deceased, funeral attendants wore mourning rings, scarves, and gloves.[85]

As American society grew increasingly complex in the early nineteenth century, the death of a single individual gradually lost its communal significance. The nineteenth-century view of death had been sentimentalized, but the shock of separation now had to be borne almost entirely by the immediate family of the deceased. Death had become a private matter, and the older concern with the dead person's place in the community yielded to an interest in his or her place in the personal lives of family and friends. The most important sign of this shift was the early nineteenth-century professionalization of duties performed for the dead. Church sextons, who gradually had taken over the tasks of tolling the bell and digging the grave, now began to lay out and attend the body and direct the funeral procession; gradually, professional undertakers began to set up business. The funeral ceased to be a public function for the entire community and became a limited social occasion for which personal invitations were issued; mourning dress and jewelry came to be worn only by the family and closest friends of the deceased. By the mid-nineteenth century, mourning had become a private anguish experienced with little community support, and popular mourning literature bewailed the callous indifference of the "tearless throng."[86]

Despite the strong sentimental insistence on the ultimate inconsolability of the mourner, genteel mourning ritual nonetheless demanded that acquaintances of the bereaved express sympathy in certain prescribed ways. The one mourning rule specified in nearly every etiquette manual was that social acquaintances of a mourning family pay a visit of condolence within a week after the death. Relatives and intimate friends of the family were to pay a personal visit; more distant acquaintances were simply to stop by the house and send in a card with the servant. Polite condolence was to be expressed in formal tokens of sympathy: "It is courteous to send up a mourning card; and for ladies to make their calls in black silk or plain-colored apparel. It denoted that they sympathize with the afflictions of the family; and such attentions are always pleasing."[87] Just as mourning attire assisted the mourner in maintaining the proper demeanor of bereavement, sympathetic attire helped the visitor paying a condolence call to "let your manners and conversation be in harmony with the character of your visit."[88] Men and women paying polite visits of condolence maintained a quiet gravity of manner and avoided both gaiety and unnecessary references to the deceased. After paying one formal visit, they avoided calling on the bereaved family until they received cards signaling the family's emergence from the mourning period.

The formal visit of condolence was the subject of much controversy within popular mourning literature. Once again, the sentimentalists who guided middle-class conduct raised the problem of the conflict between social forms and true sentiment, between politeness and sincerity. The mother of Agnes explained her distaste for the visit of condolence:

Calls on a bereaved person are, for the most part, agonizing, unless there be great intimacy between the parties. ... I am resolved that, unless I am on very intimate terms, or in a peculiar relation to a bereaved person, I will express my sympathy merely by some message, or little gift, or act of remembrance, and not by being one of twenty or thirty people to make the poor sufferer go over the bitter tale again and again, or to make her sit and endure a stiff, ceremonious visit.[89]

Condolence offered as a matter of proper form by mere social acquaintances, Agnes's mother thus complained, could only be stiff and ceremonious, never warm and natural. "Each tutored voice" of polite sympathy was a source of pain, not comfort, to the sensitive nerves of the poor mourner: "And if there is ever a time when cold and formal phrases of piety, dealt out as words of course, are intolerable, it must be when they are addressed to a mind, that is alive with all the sensitiveness of grief."[90] Furthermore, formal condolence only intruded on the mourner's desired privacy: "Sorrow naturally seeks for quietude and privacy. . . . The afflicted, when they consult their natural feelings, do not wish to be in a crowd."[91] Heedless of the mourners' needs, however, the polite mob overwhelmed them with company:

> Into an afflicted soul the crowd thinks it has a right to enter; it is like a conquered city. The new comers overturn everything; carry off, bring in, derange, arrange;—protestations are of no avail; besides, they are so feeble, (mere sighs of pain,) that they are scarcely heard. . . . It is a grievous spectacle these barbarous invasions,—well intended, most of them; but very unseasonable, and very afflictive.[92]

An even more serious problem than the hypocrisy of polite condolence was the hypocrisy of funeral attendance. Victorian etiquette forbade anyone to refuse an invitation to a funeral, and then went on to instruct attendants on the proper demeanor of bereavement. In the funeral procession, for example, attendants were to "walk with the head uncovered, silently, and with such a mien as the occasion naturally suggests."[93] In offering detailed advice on how to act bereaved, however, such works clearly suggested that genuine grief might not be counted upon to carry the attendant through the ceremony with the proper gravity. And one unusually cynical manual openly admitted the necessary hypocrisy of the attendant's air of grief: "Your dress is black, and during the time of waiting, you compose your visage into a 'tristful 'haviour,' and lean in silent solemnity upon the top of your cane, thinking about—last night's party. This is a necessary hypocrisy, and assists marvellously the sadness of the ceremony."[94] As long as the funeral attendant assumed the properly sorrowful demeanor, he fulfilled social expectations of polite sympathy. In the funeral procession he might "walk with another, in seemly order, and converse in a low tone; first upon the property of the defunct, and next upon the politics of the day."[95] Consolation literature scornfully proclaimed that half "the mourners, so called" were "only nominally such," and attended the funeral "by custom rather than by their own feelings."[96] But etiquette manuals calmly accepted the inability of most funeral attendants to enact the genteel performance of mourning without specific instructions on the proper demeanor of bereavement.

Middle-class mourning ritual was caught, like dress and etiquette, in the vicious circle of sentimental form and feeling. In response to the relatively new isolation of the bereaved, polite middle-class society began to control the formal expression of condolence that replaced the emotional response of an earlier time. The new nineteenth-century focus on sympathy was itself of enormous significance: in colonial America, sympathy was not a major issue, for all who knew the deceased were themselves mourners; their own loss was not vicarious but direct. But by the mid-nineteenth century, only sympathy for those who mourned was demanded of those who had known the deceased; mere social acquaintances were not expected to grieve over one they scarcely knew or depended upon. And sympathy might be expressed simply through a polite visit of condolence, a mourning card, a black silk dress. But when the polite forms of condolence replaced communal bereavement, the Victorian spectre of hypocrisy reared its head and lent some credence to the sentimental lament that, beyond the circle of relatives and intimate friends of the deceased, none mourned, though many expressed polite sympathy.

How, then, were the aspiring genteel to express their sympathy? Within the conventions of sentimental mourning, the true mourner was inconsolable and any but the truest sympathizer was a cold and formal fraud who only intruded upon the mourner's privacy. But the genteel imperative of sympathy for the bereaved remained unaltered by all attacks on formal condolence; in fact, the difficulties of expressing sincere sympathy only made more precious any successful attempts to comfort the afflicted. After attacking the hypocrisies of formal condolence, therefore, mourning manuals went on to instruct their middle-class readers on how properly to offer sympathy. Although the "simplest expressions [of consolation], if only uttered in sincerity, will not fail of their intention; yet, for the most acceptable performance of it, something more is needed than mere zeal, or good feeling."[97] That something more was a "respectful regard for the afflicted; a certain reverence of sorrow, forbidding the intrusion of what is doubtful, or might be the occasion of pain."[98] The acceptable performance of consolation demanded, in short, the exercise of genteel tact. The duties of consolation, Rev. Orville Dewey explained at some length, demanded great discretion and delicacy: true sympathy was never rash or intrusive, never too sure of its powers to assuage grief, never convinced that it fully shared the mourner's feelings. True sympathy was respectful: silent and gentle, not noisy and bustling; slow to command the mourner's religious submission to affliction, and reluctant to rebuke the rebellious mourner.[99] The tactful sympathizer carefully confessed an inability to express formally his or her sympathy, an ignorance of the depth of the mourner's sorrow, and an impotence to assuage that grief; but finally offered his or her own deep sympathy as a possible source of consolation to the bereaved:

> I cannot say what I would in words. Would to heaven, I had power to say any thing to assuage that grief, which with the highest principles and the noblest views, must be poignant indeed. The greatness of this trial no one can fully know, that has not tested it. But I know enough to awaken all my sympathy. It is a poor gift; but if it will yield you any consolation, you may draw largely from this source.[100]

The most important task of the man or woman offering sympathy was to recognize the mourner's own deep grief. The tact of condolence, like all Victorian tact, involved a formal acceptance of the genteel performance of another—in this case, the mourner's performance of bereavement. The formal visit of condolence, the acceptance of the funeral invitation, the demeanor of sympathy— these polite forms were an expression of respect not for the dead but for the mourners themselves. Significantly, only mourners were required to attend the body to the gravesite; social acquaintances were required only to visit the home of the deceased and attend the church service, in an expression of tactful sympathy for the mourner.[101] In fulfilling the polite forms of condolence, the genteel Victorian was simply stating "I know you grieve deeply" to those who mourned and thus honoring their claims to gentility. And in avoiding them socially for the mourning period, the polite Victorian tactfully honored their genteel need for privacy. For the truly grief-stricken mourner, the high demands of gentility for physical and emotional self-control must have been difficult to meet for some time after the death of a loved one. And for the indifferent mourner, the demands of sentimental gentility for deep bereavement were equally difficult to fulfill. So the tactful acquaintance of the bereaved family honored their need for privacy by saying, "Though I should rejoice to meet you in the full enjoyment of your usual good spirits, yet I am aware that the grief which oppresses you, and which I regard as a credit to your feelings, must have its sway, and not till then can I hope for the pleasure of such a meeting." Having thus honored the mourner's grief as a credit to his or her feelings, this model letter-writer went on to lay his or her own claim to sentimental sincerity: "It is not, therefore, in the mere observance of a cold and formal custom, that I at present write, but in obedience to the dictates of the truest friendship. . . . Accept my condolence in your late bereavement, by the loss of ( ), and believe me to entertain the truest sympathy in your affliction." In the manner of proper Victorian correspondence, this letter thus disavowed all cold formalism and declared its own deeply sincere sympathy. And the polite response to such a letter was supposed to honor in turn the sincerity of this sympathy: "The perusal of your letter was indeed a solace to my grief, and convinced me that I have at least one friend who can sympathize in my afflictions."[102] Because the shadow of insincerity lay upon all attempts to offer condolence, the polite mourner expressly recognized the sincerity of all proper expressions of sympathy. The ritual was now completed: sentimental gentility had been claimed and mutually honored by both participants; the genteel performances of bereavement and of sympathy had been successfully enacted.

For the middle classes of mid-nineteenth-century America, mourning the dead was the most powerful sentiment of all and the most resistant to public expression through empty social forms. "There should be nothing in mourning but what is natural and spontaneous," wrote George Hervey, and "Besides, what is more absurd than weeping by rule, and wearing mourning according to a fashion."[103] Even as they articulated this sentimental view of mourning, however, the arbiters of middle-class conduct were erecting an elaborate framework of social forms that codified and regulated proper mourning dress and mourning etiquette as public expressions of bereavement and sympathy. In the many conventions of mourning, the most powerfully right feeling of sentimentalism was formalized in the most precisely detailed middle-class ritual. Once again, American sentimentalists confronted the problem of hypocrisy in middle-class culture. These fears of hypocrisy were rooted in the nagging awareness that mourning the dead was not solely a matter of indulging private grief but was a means of establishing a public claim to bourgeois gentility. In mourning the dead, middle-class social aspirants were enacting a genteel performance of bereavement and sympathy. Within the bourgeois equation of sentiment and social standing, sincerity was seen as the mark of authentic bourgeois gentility; but the pervasive middle-class desire to rise on the social scale was believed to taint all mourning sentiment with the hypocrisy of self-interest. Just as "the weeping of an heir, is laughter under a mask,"[104] the weeping of the would-be genteel was feared to be merely the public performance of skilled confidence men and women, anxious to rise in middle-class society. Throughout the 1830s, 1840s, and 1850s, American sentimentalists continued to express deep anxieties about the conflict between private, sincere sentiment and public, hypocritical social forms in the cult of mourning. But gradually, as mourning ritual grew more elaborate, middle-class anxieties about cultural hypocrisy began to wane. By the 1850s, the Victorian cult of mourning was becoming an important ritualistic expression of bourgeois pride and self-confidence. After mid-century, the American middle classes learned to embrace the art of social performance as a mark of cultural dominance in the age of consolidation.

Disguises, Masks, and Parlor Theatricals:
The Decline of Sentimental Culture
in the 1850s

On March 26, 1845, a play called *Fashion* began a long and successful run at the Park Theatre in New York. Written by popular sentimentalist Anna Cora Mowatt, it was a farce about the fashionable follies of the nouveau riche Tiffany family of New York. On the one hand, *Fashion* was a full-blown critique of the life of fashion, a critique grounded in sentimental middle-class hostility to the hypocrisy of "heartless" social ritual. Ironically, however, this attack on social theatricality was itself presented within a theatrical performance, and this critique of social ritual itself served as a ritual for its middle-class audiences. Many of the men and women who attended Mowatt's play went to laugh at the fashionable pretensions of their own class. What was new about Mowatt's sentimental critique was its broad sense of humor about social issues that had been the source of profound anxiety a few years earlier. Mowatt's *Fashion* provides a useful focal point for a discussion of the cultural transformation of the American middle classes at mid-nineteenth century. With the laughter that greeted the ridiculous pretensions of the fictional Tiffany family, sentimental culture in its purest form began to decline. In the late 1840s and the 1850s, the sentimental critique of fashionable dress, etiquette, and mourning ritual was giving way to a worldly acceptance of self-display, social formalism, and ceremonial ritual as appropriate expressions of middle-class position. Nowhere was the new direction of middle-class culture more evident than in the vogue of private theatricals that swept the parlors of America in the 1850s and 1860s. But this cultural transformation was already underway by 1845, when middle-class audiences began to gather at the Park Theatre to enjoy an evening of laughing at themselves and at each other for their increasingly fashionable social lives.[1]

For the entertainment of middle-class audiences, *Fashion* focused on the social pretensions and blunders of the newly rich. Mrs. Tiffany is, of course, the chief offender. She lavishes money on fine clothes for herself and her coquettish daughter, Seraphina; she hires a black flunkey named Zeke, changes his name to Adolph, and dresses him in gorgeous livery; she fills her drawing room with fashionable creatures such as Augustus Fogg, haughty young man about town, and T. Tennyson Twinkle, conceited lyrical poet; and she loudly ushers guests into her drawing room with the words "*Bung jure.*" Worst of all, Mrs. Tiffany shamelessly cultivates a titled Frenchman, Count Jolimaître, in an effort to lure him into marrying Seraphina. Jolimaître's fashionable credentials are early displayed in his disdainful comment, "Why at the very last dinner given at Lord—Lord Knowswho, would you believe it, Madam, there was an individual present who wore a *black* cravat and took *soup twice!*" Jolimaître is, of course, a fashionable confidence man who constantly reveals his true character to the audience in theatrical asides.[2]

The moral foils to Mrs. Tiffany and her drawing room lions are Adam Trueman, a wealthy upstate farmer who is an old friend of Mr. Tiffany, and Gertrude, a sweetly modest young woman, also from the country, who is companion to Seraphina. Trueman and Gertrude embody the virtues of simplicity and sincerity, in opposition to the hypocrisy of fashionable life. "This *fashion*-worship has made heathens and hypocrites of you all!" says Trueman. "*Deception* is your house-hold God! A man laughs as if he were crying, and cries as if he were laughing in his sleeve. Everything is something else from what it seems to be." To the sympathetic Gertrude, Trueman explains the sentimental ideal of transparency: "When you open your lips let your heart speak. Never tell a lie! Let your face be the looking-glass of your soul—your heart its clock—while your tongue rings the hours! But the glass must be clear, the clock true, and then there's no fear but the tongue will do its duty in a woman's head!" Mrs. Tiffany is, of course, a fashionable liar. When the rustic Trueman first rings her door bell, the snobbish social climber tells Zeke to dismiss him with that classic deception of middle-class etiquette, "not at home." Stupid Zeke tells Trueman, "Missus say she's not at home," and Trueman furiously strides past him into the drawing room saying, "Where's this woman that's not *at home* in her own house?" Fashion, he rages, is "an agreement between certain persons to live without using their souls! to substitute etiquette for virtue—decorum for purity—manners for morals!" In Trueman's demands for a candid countenance and a truthful tongue, he makes clear his sentimental view that social intercourse must rest on the transparency of the sincere soul.[3]

Like most antebellum American melodramas, *Fashion* moves to its conclusion through a series of character unmaskings. Trueman and Gertrude expose Count Jolimaître as an impostor, a former barber, cook, and valet named Gustave Treadmill who is already engaged to the French maid. Gertrude herself learns that she is Trueman's granddaughter, whom he had sent away as a child to prevent his great wealth from destroying her independence—to preserve her, that is, from enslavement to fashion. Finally, Mr. Tiffany is revealed as a forger by his evil clerk, Snobson. Because his wife's extravagances have driven him to the brink of bankruptcy, he has forged some checks, and Snobson has been blackmailing him, first for money and then for the hand of Seraphina. Through the laws of moral physiognomy, Trueman had instantly recognized Snobson for what he was: "Why he looks for all the world like a spy—the most inquisitorial, hang-dog face—ugh! the sight of it makes my blood run cold! . . . Antony, the next time you choose a confidential clerk, take one that carries his credentials in his face—those in his pocket are not worth much without!" In the closing scene, Trueman runs Snobson out of town and then offers financial assistance to Tiffany, on the condition that Mrs. Tiffany and Seraphina be sent to the country to learn the republican virtues of economy, independence, and domesticity. The play closes with Trueman's melodramatic tribute to nature's noblemen: "But we *have* kings, princes, and nobles in abundance—of *Nature's stamp,* if not of Fashion's,—we have honest men, warmhearted and brave, and we have women—gentle, fair, and true, to whom no *title* could add *nobility.*"[4]

Adam Trueman's appeal for a natural nobility of honest men and true women reveals one important historical source of sentimental antiritualism: eighteenth-century republican ideology. "Hurrah, for republican simplicity," Trueman shouts in a diatribe against Zeke's extravagant livery. In her introduction to the play, Anna Mowatt called it "a good-natured satire upon some of the follies incident to a new country, where foreign dross sometimes passes for gold, while native gold is cast aside as dross; where the vanities rather

than the virtues of other lands are too often imitated."⁵ For Mowatt
and her republican hero, fashionable American social forms were
the cultural remnants of a corrupt and decadent Old World aristocracy; all attempts to ape foreign manners undermined American
independence from Europe. From the time of the American Revolution, national self-confidence had rested on the Enlightenment
view of the New World's freedom from the corrupting refinement
of the Old World. What ultimately drove Americans to revolution,
argues Gordon Wood, was the fear that this precious social fabric
was being rent by luxurious living, that the cancerous corruption of
Europe was spreading to America.⁶ American republicans had long
raised the spectre of fashionable luxury and extravagance, and
these republican concerns lived on in the sentimental critique of
fashion in the 1830s and 1840s. Corrupt social formalism and
courtly self-display were believed to pose a serious threat to the
survival of the American republic.

A second source of sentimental antiritualism was Puritanism. The
sixteenth-century Puritan revolt against the Anglican Church was
established on the pulpit and the Bible against the altar and the
Eucharist—on the articulate power of the word as opposed to the
inarticulate power of symbol and ceremonial ritual.⁷ Like later
republican antiritualism, the Puritan antipathy for Catholic and
Anglican ritual was linked to a social critique of an extravagant
court life. Particularly offensive to the Puritan mentality were the
dramatic masques performed by the courts of Elizabeth and the
Stuarts. As Richard Slotkin has pointed out, the Puritans opposed
court masques and the Elizabethan drama not simply because of
theatrical associations with lewdness and impiety, but because such
dramas were "a kind of sophisticated pagan ritual."⁸ The English
Puritans were drawn largely from the rising middle classes, and
pagan rituals were the cultural earmarks of the English peasantry
and the urban lower classes. The Anglican Eucharist, the courtly
masque, and the Dionysian peasant revel were all linked together in
the Puritan mind. Through a pious opposition to ritual—to the May
Day festivities of a lower-class peasantry as well as the masques and
plays of a courtly aristocracy—seventeenth-century English Puritans set themselves off as distinctively middle-class.

The sentimental critique of fashion offered by Mowatt in her
popular farce was historically rooted in republican and Puritan
hostilities to ritual, but Mowatt's play did not assume a tone of high
seriousness. To the Puritan, the trappings of religious ritual se-

duced man from his quest for salvation, while the theatricality of masques and social rituals threatened to subject an entire nation to God's imminent wrath. To the republican, fashionable luxury and the extravagant excesses of court life threatened to destroy the virtues of the people and thus to undermine the very foundations of the republic. For both Puritan and republican, in short, the evils of a ritualistic social life were no laughing matter. Similarly, for early sentimentalists a ritualistic social life was not an appropriate subject for humor. In the view of Caroline Lee Hentz, who wrote "The Fatal Cosmetic" in 1839, polite flattery, the use of cosmetics, and the life of fashionable deceit could lead only to manslaughter and social chaos.[9] But for Anna Cora Mowatt in 1845, fashion was a problem to be confronted humorously, within "a good-natured satire." The middle-class audiences who flocked to see *Fashion* could laugh at fashionable pretension even as they may have congratulated themselves that their own minor follies did not begin to match those of the Tiffanys. They could laugh nervously or freely, but either way they could affirm the sentimental critique of fashion and still escape any implications it might hold for themselves.

The popularity of *Fashion* suggests a growing willingness to abandon the sentimental posture of moral earnestness toward matters of self-display and social ritual. In the late 1840s and the 1850s, this new worldliness became increasingly evident in prescriptive discussions of middle-class dress, etiquette, and mourning ritual. Articles in *Godey's Lady's Book* began to assume a lightly satirical attitude toward ostentatious display, and the sentimental concern for moral transparency in dress began to yield ground to a new interest in questions of style, taste, and elegance. Etiquette manuals evinced a new willingness to accept the structured formalities of polite social intercourse without challenging their sincerity, and a number of writers went so far as to acknowledge the larger value of polite social forms as masks and disguises for unpleasant personal qualities. Mourning ritual increasingly was coming to resemble a form of public theater, in which the performances not only of the mourners but of the corpse itself became the object of open and unabashedly theatrical concern. Gradually the sentimental demand for perfect sincerity was losing its tone of urgency and being replaced by a new acceptance of the theatricality of social relationships.

In *Godey's Lady's Book* a humorous new tone similar to that of Mowatt's *Fashion* provided the earliest evidence that an air of worldly cynicism about the middle-class pursuit of fashion was beginning to replace sentimental reservations about the morality of stylish dress. In February 1851, a *Godey's* fashion columnist followed up a brief moralization about fashion with a self-conscious, lightly humorous apology: "But, instead of chatting of the fashions, we have been betrayed into a homily upon 'vain apparel,' for which we beg your indulgence, dear ladies, and promise next month to be as entertaining as possible to atone for it."[10] This fashion column, not unlike Mowatt's play, managed to have its cake and eat it too: it did offer some words of caution against fashionable excess but then went on immediately to ridicule its own moralism. By 1857, the pseudonymous "Florence Fashionhunter" carried this new tone of ridicule even further in an article entitled "Rambles About the City":

> Come, reader, we will take a walk. Not that bonnet, if you please, my dear madam; that is a very pretty little affair—for some other occasion; but now you must don your most *recherche chapeau,* assume a thrilling mantle, "sport" your moire antique dress, draw on immaculate gaiter-boots and kid-gloves, raise a most fashionable parasol, and now, if you are as charmingly arrayed as your wardrobe will permit, we will start. Allons![11]

In such passages as these, the strongly moralistic critique of fashion that prevailed in the 1830s and 1840s had dwindled to a mild tone of sarcasm about fashionable excess. The sentimental attack on the hypocrisies of fashion had virtually disappeared from the pages of *Godey's.* In its stead there appeared occasional warnings against fashionable extravagance on the simple economic grounds that many husbands could not afford it.[12]

The sentimental view of dress that dominated *Godey's Lady's Book* in the 1830s and 1840s had rested on the concept of moral influence: the woman who dressed with simplicity and candor was believed to improve the moral condition of all who entered her sphere. But by 1853, a *Godey's* article was questioning the sentimental tenet that "one prescribed mode of dress is favorable to Christian improvement." More important, this writer raised the sarcastic question, "Is the poke bonnet a sure index of humility?"[13] By the 1850s, the sentimental view that a particular dress form could embody a particular feeling or moral quality was losing credence. And the sentimental belief that dress was a means of moral influence was gradually yielding to the aesthetic view of dress as the fine art of choosing clothing well suited to an individual woman's physical characteristics.[14] Once, the tyranny of fashion had been condemned for enslaving its votaries to the arts of hypocrisy and disguise. But by 1853, the tyrant Fashion was being criticized simply for dictating that all women should dress alike: "Like the bed of Procrustes, fashions are compelled to suit every one. The same fashion is adopted by the tall and the short, the stout and the slender, and the old and the young, with what effect we have daily opportunities of observing."[15] The art of dress, *Godey's* advised readers in the 1850s, was the art of selecting a wardrobe with an eye to one's height and weight, form and coloring, social position and age. This demanded serious self-scrutiny: "To know ourselves, even as far as our faces and figures go, is a knowledge which we can only acquire after some study. . . . *Fashion* can never of itself be a sufficient guide in matters of dress . . . its dictates must be modified to suit the characteristics of each individual."[16] Self-knowledge, once a moral imperative, had become a matter of the objective awareness of the strengths and weaknesses of one's physical appearance.

In the 1850s, the cult of sincerity was gradually yielding space in the pages of *Godey's Lady's Book* to a new cult of individual style. "The true secret of dress is to make it harmonize with the style of countenance and figure so as to identify it, as it were, with the character of the wearer."[17] Within the sentimental ideal, dress had been regarded as an index of character, a mirror of the soul, an outward revelation of inner moral qualities. But now, in the 1850s, the art of dress was the art of projecting a particular personal style, and this new concept of style was increasingly confused with character itself. To those young ladies "who are just commencing a self-forming process of character" one writer in 1852 announced that it was their "business to be beautiful."[18] Throughout the 1850s, it became clearer that this business demanded some efforts in the direction of personal disguise. Women were urged to study their own personal style so their dress might emphasize their good points and play down their bad ones: the forms of dress "should be so contrived as to enhance the natural charms of a well-made figure" and "to conceal imperfections where they exist."[19] A fascinating and revealing discussion of this newly acceptable art of concealing defects appeared in an article on "Modes of Wearing the Hair," published in 1855. The most important decisions concerning the arrangement of the hair, *Godey's* readers were informed, was where to locate the bulk of the hair when it was swept up on top of the head, and smart women made this decision through the science of phrenology. "Woman has very much the advantage over man in this respect. She can make her head show, phrenologically, for pretty much what she pleases." By using a bun to conceal a shallow spot on her skull, or to counterbalance a too-prominent bump, she "gives the head (the most common observer sees, without knowing why) a very different character."[20] By arranging her hair in a particular style, in other words, she might take on any character she wanted.

An important aspect of this growing acceptance of the art of disguise in the 1850s was the easing of the sentimental condemnations of cosmetics. Although warnings against excessive face paint still abounded, *Godey's Lady's Book* suggested in 1852 that some use of cosmetics was now permissible.[21] In 1855, a short story entitled "The Cosmetic: A Sketch of Southern Life" suggested by humorous indirection that cosmetics were no longer utterly forbidden. The heroine of the story, Harriet, decides for once in her life to use buttermilk to bleach the freckles on her face. But she accidentally applies varnish instead, and, as a result, misses her appointment to elope with her lover. He, however, turns out to be a romantic confidence man, who has all along been engaged to another woman. When his elopement with Harriet falls through, he marries his first fiancée and loses her entire fortune at the gaming table. The story concludes with Harriet's realization that her first use of a cosmetic brought her good fortune.[22] *Godey's Lady's Book* had come a long way since the publication of "The Fatal Cosmetic" in 1839. In "The Fatal Cosmetic," a fashionable confidence woman's use of a cosmetic results in the accidental death of another woman of fashion; in "The Cosmetic: A Sketch of Southern Life," the heroine's innocent decision to apply buttermilk to conceal her freckles results in the unmasking of a romantic confidence man and in her own well-deserved happiness.

In such stories as this and in the numerous articles on "Dress as a Fine Art," it was becoming evident in the 1850s that sentimental anxieties about the hypocrisy of fashion were on the wane. In discussions of dress, character was coming to be regarded as a matter of personal style, to be assumed as one donned a particular dress or cloak or hair style. Inner virtue was yielding to good taste as the touchstone of personal worth: "Taste is the discriminating talisman, enabling its owners to see at once the real merits of persons and things, to ascertain at a glance the value of individuals."[23] Most important, the sentimental dread of hypocrisy was yielding to a new appreciation for the aesthetic value of personal disguise. Sentimental views of dress lingered on in the 1850s in occasional discussions of the moral influence of simple dress and occasional attacks on the evils of tight lacing and heavy face paint. But the central thrust of *Godey's Lady's Book* in the 1850s was away from the sentimentalism of an earlier period toward a new worldliness about the fine art of personal appearance.

This new worldliness was reflected in the popular dress styles of the 1850s. During that decade the drooping slenderness of the sentimental outline was gradually replaced by a broad, inflated look. Skirts grew steadily wider and had to be supported by increasing numbers of petticoats, including some made of horsehair. By 1856, skirts had grown so wide—often to a circumference of twelve to fifteen feet—that the cage crinoline was introduced, a petticoatlike garment that had narrow steel hoops sewn into the hem. The horizontal lines of the fashionable figure were emphasized by flounces that covered the skirt from waist to hem—ruffled and pinked flounces, narrow and wide flounces, fringed and flower-bedecked and beribboned flounces—and by richly patterned borders. Bodices, too, were often elaborately trimmed with ribbon, lace, and artificial flowers; the effect was to accentuate the size of the bust. Sleeves grew wider with the introduction of the bell, bishop, Gabrielle, and pagoda styles; the pagoda sleeve, introduced in 1855, was actually a series of false sleeves narrowing at the shoulder. By the mid-1850s, the introduction of the sewing machine had initiated an orgy of braiding, pleating, puffing, and tucking that covered the fashionably dressed woman from head to foot. Richer fabrics such as gauze, tulle, wool, organdy, brocade, and velvet came into vogue, and the delicate pastel colors of sentimental dress were abandoned for dark and garish colors such as red, blue, crimson, maroon, brown, bright green, purple, plum, and magenta, often combined in violent contrasts. The transparent effect of the opalescent shot-silks that were popular during the sentimental period was cast aside for a bold opulence that often bordered on vulgarity. Whereas the sentimental woman had been slim, pale, and vaguely transparent, the fashionable woman of the 1850s was ample, brilliant, and decidedly opaque.[24]

As dress styles grew more opulent and ostentatious, hairstyles were also leaving the sentimental period behind. The hallmark of the sentimental hairstyle had been its focus of attention on the sincere countenance. Although hairstyles in the 1850s were still

Bourgeois women, 1859. The opulent style that replaced sentimental fashion after 1850 was bold and haughty, with broad horizontal lines and rich ornamentation.

parted in the middle and drawn smoothly over the ears, they acquired greater width as the hair was turned under or worn in plaits, and decorated with gems and flowers. Toward the end of the decade, emphasis shifted away from the face to the back of the head where the hair was drawn into a bun. To conceal the spaces in their braids or coils of hair, women wore a comb concealer or a *cache peigne*, a length of approximately three yards of velvet or taffeta ribbon, hanging in loops from a piece of stiff net and kept in place by ribbon wire that curved over the crown of the head. For evening wear the *cache peigne* was made of flowers and pearls, lace and ribbons, fancy combs and feathers. By the 1860s, the bun at the back of the head had grown into a large chignon, which usually required large quantities of false hair; and once the use of false hair had been accepted, women began to wear it all over their heads. More and more women began to dye or powder their hair. As hair arrangements moved to the back of the head, bonnets followed; and unlike the oval poke bonnet favored by sentimentalists, these new bonnets were often lined with frills of lace or ruchings of net, and with flowers and ribbons that marred the simple line framing the face. Hats, avoided by sentimentalists, also came back into style.[25]

All these developments point to a decline in sentimental concerns about simplicity and suggest that middle-class American women were more and more willing to accept dress as a form of disguise. Even more significant was the increasing use, after 1850, of cosmetics and especially of rouge. By the 1860s, painted faces and eyelids had become widely acceptable for middle-class women. Through the use of all these devices—comb concealers and ribbon wire, feathers and lace, false, powdered, dyed hair, and rouge—middle-class women were clearly leaving behind the sentimental insistence on the candid countenance. In their hairstyles, headgear, and use of cosmetics, as in the styles of their gowns, they were putting into practice their worldly new sense of dress as a fine art. That art was the art of disguise.[26]

As the sentimental demand for sincerity in dress gradually disappeared from the pages of *Godey's Lady's Book*, the sentimental demand for sincerity in etiquette was dropping out of American courtesy manuals. The etiquette guides written in the 1830s and 1840s had insisted that the only true politeness was the transparent outward reflection of inner right feelings—the sincere social workings of a benevolent heart. Within this sentimental view, any arbi-

Fashion as disguise, 1863. The women and children in this print are all in costume for a masquerade ball, a popular entertainment after mid-century.

trary social adherence that did not spring from a right heart was a kind of parlor confidence game, a dangerous form of social hypocrisy. Sentimental etiquette was thus based on the insistence that Christianity and politeness were one and the same. In the 1850s, however, the writers of American etiquette manuals were beginning to assert that Christian piety and social courtesy were entirely distinct. George W. Hervey's *Principles of Courtesy,* published in 1852, offered an avowedly evangelical code of etiquette which insisted that social courtesy must originate in divine grace, but even Hervey acknowledged that the mere imitation of Christian courtesy was, of all forms of hypocrisy, the least pernicious.[27] By 1857, Sarah J. Hale was openly stating that society, unlike Christianity, could demand only the appearance of virtue: "How can it ask more? How can it open your heart, and see if, with your bland smile and oily voice, you are a liar and a hypocrite?"[28] Society, according to Hale, did adapt the laws of Christian virtue to social intercourse. Christian meekness was required of polite people in the form of modesty, Christian peace was demanded as social harmony, Christian self-denial as a polite forgetfulness of self, and Christian trust was insisted upon as that "confidence in the good intentions of our neighbors" which "makes society possible."[29] But society, unlike Christianity, could not demand that these virtues stem from a changed heart.

This gradual acceptance of the distinction between courtesy and Christianity was perhaps most evident in the growing concern for church etiquette. Earlier etiquette writers had seldom instructed readers on proper church deportment: outward reverence was not deemed a courtesy problem, presumably because it would follow automatically from inner reverence. To the sentimentalists, any outward demeanor of reverence that did not spring from a pious heart would be hypocrisy of the deepest dye. But in the 1850s, American etiquette manuals began to offer directions on how to make church entrances and exits, how to sit and how to pray and how to listen properly while the choir sang.[30] Church etiquette demanded above all a demeanor of restrained piety, a genteel performance of religious reverence. In etiquette as in dress, character was being transformed into a matter of style: "Are we professedly religious? . . . The style of a religious person should be moderate, because moderation is in accordance with the whole tone of the Gospel."[31]

Once the arbiters of middle-class etiquette had articulated a distinction between courtesy and Christianity, they were but a short step away from accepting a view of etiquette as a useful form of social disguise. If courtesy demanded only an outward conformity to Christian virtues, a "seeming virtue" that was not to be condemned as relifious hypocrisy, then etiquette could serve as a way of masking personal defects for the collective benefit of polite society. In 1860, Florence Hartley admitted that manner did serve as "the cloak of the heart," but added that the heart's defects were better off hidden than paraded before all. "If politeness is but a mask," she wrote, "as many philosophers tell us, it is a mask which will win love and admiration, and is better worn than cast aside."[32] This growing acceptance of what sentimentalists had recently condemned as the mask of fashion rested on a growing cynicism about human nature. As one manual of 1869 expressed it,

> Manner, then, I am bound to confess, is the cloak of character, but if to bare the character be indecent, it is better it should wear a cloak than go about naked. Until we are all perfect, until there is a millennium on earth, it will always be indecent to wear our feelings in Adamite costume, and so long will a garment, like that of Manner, be necessary.[33]

Some etiquette writers of the 1850s and 1860s took the edge off this cynicism by assuring their readers that outward conformity to the rules of etiquette would actually nurture the inner growth of the virtues imitated: the mask of virtue would, they wrote, soon cease to be a mask, as virtue itself became natural and habitual to its polite imitator.[34] But this hasty apology for the concept of manner as a mask did not obscure the fact that etiquette was taking on an entirely new meaning. In the 1850s and 1860s, polite hypocrisy was achieving cultural legitimacy.

By 1870, the *Bazar Book of Decorum* was complaining, in a tone reminiscent of sentimentalism, that true hospitality had become virtually obsolete. "The ceremonious displays of fashion have usurped the place of the social entertainments of friendship." Heart-to-heart social intimacy had been replaced by formal ceremonies, performed by a coldly impersonal set of tradespeople: "the hired master of ceremonies, the upholsterers, the florist, the pastrycook and confectioner." Fashionable social intercourse, it seemed, had killed intimacy with formality: "It would seem to be the object of modern fashion to interpose as many formalities as possible between the members of society, in order to prevent intimacy of contact." But the *Bazar Book of Decorum,* having delivered this sentimental critique, went on to suggest why social formalism was necessary in a modern world. The use of calling cards, for example, was "a necessary result of the immense expansion of the great cities, and the consequent widening of the social relation." If every urban acquaintanceship were treated as an intimate friendship, social intercourse would become impossible; if all the acquaintances on a visiting list were to have the privilege of visiting whenever they pleased, the host or hostess would soon be incapacitated for all ordinary duties of daily life. Thus the calling card, which served as a symbol of the formal visit required on ceremonious occasions, freed both visitor and host from the excessive demands of urban social life.[35]

The *Bazar Book of Decorum* encapsulated the mid-nineteenth-century transition from a sentimental critique of social formalism to a worldly middle-class acceptance of the place of ritual in polite society. Heart-to-heart intimacy, the arbiters of social conduct were beginning to believe, had no place in a courtesy code designed for the smooth social intercourse of the urban middle classes. Sentimental sincerity could not govern face-to-face conduct among strangers and near strangers in an anonymous social world. Etiquette was no longer viewed as the polite social expression of evangelical Christianity but as a body of arbitrary rules necessary to ensure ease of social intercourse. And sincerity was no longer seen as the summum bonum of the polite world because, etiquette writers were increasingly convinced, "if every one acted according to his heart, the world would soon be turned upside-down."[36] The American middle classes after 1850 were beginning to accept the necessity and legitimacy of social forms they had once condemned as social hypocrisy and to accept a new view of character as a theatrical part to be played by respectable men and women.

As fashionable dress was gradually accepted as the art of personal disguise, and fashionable etiquette was increasingly defended as a necessary social mask, popular attitudes toward the middle-class ritual of mourning the dead were also undergoing change. In the sentimental cult of mourning, the death of a loved one had been viewed as the occasion for the deepest and most sincere human feeling. But as the social expression of mourning gradually took precedence over the private sentiment, mourning was increasingly viewed as a matter of elegance, good taste, and personal style. As early as 1848, *Godey's Lady's Book* informed readers that "a very

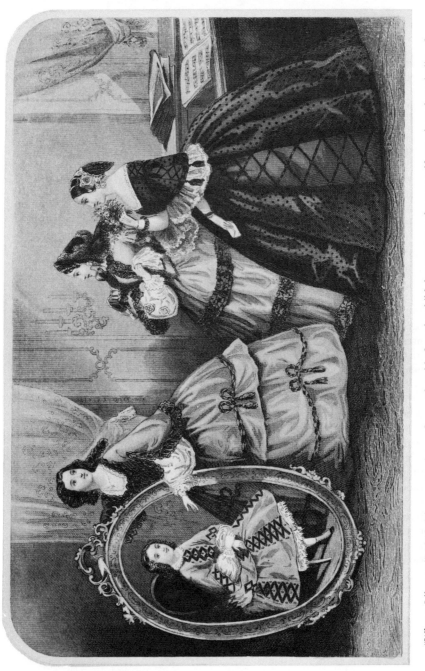

"What a Likeness!" 1859. The empty picture frame placed before the child demonstrates the new self-conscious theatricality of fashionable parlor society.

elegant evening dress" could be put together with the mourning accessories of jet ornaments, lavender gloves embroidered in black, and a handkerchief with a deep black border.[37] By 1857, the new criterion of elegance in mourning apparel was even more pronounced: "One of the most suitable and elegant mantles for second mourning, which we have seen, was noted at Genin's opening. . . . The effect was excellent."[38] The private sincerity of mourning demanded by sentimentalists thus yielded to a new interest in the public effect of mourning. Middle-class mourners once had been warned to dress simply for the sake of sincerity; now they were told to avoid excessive ornament in the interests of good taste and economy. More and more, fashionable mourning was being presented as a matter of personal taste. Mourning Philadelphians, *Godey's* complained, dressed too severely; and mourning New Yorkers, too gaily: "For ourselves, we think the present taste is to lighten a garb, grave, at best, by color rather than ornament."[39] Accompanying this new emphasis on taste was, once again, an arch sense of humor about fashionable self-display: "A widow's veil, then, is of double crape; and, no matter what the state of the atmosphere may be, woe to her if Mrs. Grundy should see her raise it before the prescribed twelve months may have passed. She may breathe comfortably after that, if she chooses, or go on blinding and stifling herself three or five years, if she chooses."[40]

As elegance, good taste, and personal style became the guiding concerns behind proper mourning attire, the funeral ritual itself was emerging as a powerful form of middle-class theater. Ironically, the growth of rural cemeteries on the outskirts of American towns and cities transformed the funeral procession into an event of great dramatic significance. "Whether it takes the form of pageantry; of mournful, simple silence; of noise and expressive behavior; of mock gaiety or real gloom, the funeral procession is a dramatic movement involving many actors. Although the performance may have its basis in an indispensable physical act, social participation in it cannot help but produce significant ceremonial overtones."[41] After 1850, the hearse became more imposing, evolving from a plain black car into a larger vehicle covered with plumes and fancy scrollwork, metal columns and a scrolled iron "goose neck" that supported an elaborate seat for the driver. By 1880, the funeral cortege had become a slow and solemn procession, led by the clergyman, who was followed in turn by the flower carriage, the honorary pallbearers, the active pallbearers, the hearse, the immediate family and relatives, and then the friends of the deceased. Sentimental mourning had been viewed primarily as a matter of private and intensely personal grief; high Victorian mourning, in contrast, was an elaborately ceremonial public ritual.[42]

The corpse itself soon returned to center stage in the drama of death. Between 1840 and 1880, hearses were designed increasingly to expose the caskets inside: originally a small closed box, the hearse evolved into a large car with full plate-glass sides and finally into a massive vehicle with a circular end of bent glass, called a Clarence front. More important, caskets were being designed to display their contents. In the early nineteenth century, coffins were plain wooden boxes with screwed-on lids. But in 1848, a patent was issued for the Fisk Metallic Coffin, which had a glass plate over the corpse's face. By 1862, metallic burial caskets featured a top of two large sections of plate glass, separated by a name plate. Finally, "in conjunction with the aesthetic and material upgrading of burial receptacles, and especially the casket with its 'jewel-box' emphasis, there followed a corresponding disposition to keep the body on display for a longer period." In 1846, the Frederick and Trump corpse cooler was patented: this was a cooling board on which the body lay, surrounded by a metal box that fit the torso and was filled with ice. Refrigeration techniques dominated corpse preservation from 1830 through the 1870s, although the use of ice still made display of the corpse something of a problem. But the Civil War stimulated experimentation with injection embalming by undertakers with army contracts for soldier burial, and by the 1880s, embalming fluid companies and embalming schools were providing undertakers with the materials and techniques required to keep a corpse on display for several days.[43]

The growing theatricality of middle-class funeral ritual after 1850, with its dramatic focus on the corpse, was made possible by the expanding professional role of the undertaker himself. By the late nineteenth century, the undertaker was evolving into the modern *funeral director,* who acted as a stage manager for the entire dramatic ritual of the funeral. As Victorian funeral ritual grew increasingly elaborate, only the undertaker could be expected to know all the ceremonial details requiring attention. The undertaker had to arrange the funeral ceremonies: to help select a casket, an appropriate funeral service, and the pallbearers; to provide relatives and friends with carriages; to determine the order of mourners in the funeral procession. One of his greatest responsibilities was

Funeral of General Charles G. Halpine, 1868. The coffin's glass top is divided by a silver plate inscribed with the corpse's name, age, and date of death.

to ensure that all mourners and funeral attendants enacted their parts in the ceremony properly. Even more important, however, the undertaker had to prepare the body for display: to wash and embalm the corpse, close its eyes and mouth, insert false teeth if necessary, sew its lips shut, close the jaw with a chin support, tint the face with a flesh-colored liquid, dress the body, and drape it with a sheet. In a ghoulish but significant sense, his greatest responsibility here was to ensure that the corpse enact its own final genteel performance with bourgeois propriety. In dying, the Victorian lady or gentleman was guilty of a total lapse in genteel performance: the corpse's first act was to lose control over eliminatory functions; it assumed a rigid and unattractive physical position and facial expression, and sooner or later it was bound to emit an unpleasant odor. So the undertaker stepped in, to clean the corpse, to alter its facial expression with cosmetics and, if necessary, with wire, to compose its limbs in as "natural" a position as possible, and to halt the process of decay that could give offense to genteel nostrils. The undertaker's task was to make certain that, even in death, the respectable Victorian remained genteel. He might use makeup, embalming fluid, hidden wires and threads and chin supports, and false teeth to assist that genteel performance, but these would be invisible to the mourners leaning over the Fisk Metallic Coffin or standing outside the Clarence front hearse. Even if a funeral attendant did catch sight of a hidden bit of mortuary technique, he was to ignore it and murmur, with genteel tact, "He looks asleep." No polite Victorian would ever acknowledge that a genteel acquaintance had become a vulgar corpse.[44]

In American funeral ritual after 1850, the genteel performance of the middle-class corpse was distinguished above all for its unabashed theatricality. Fully costumed, coated with makeup, surrounded by elaborate stage properties, and directed by a professional, the middle-class corpse undertook its final social appearance within a dramaturgical structure designed to establish its gentility for all eternity. In a larger sense, as I have argued, the genteel performance enacted by living middle-class men and women was becoming more openly and self-consciously theatrical. In the 1850s, important changes taking place in attitudes toward dress, etiquette, and mourning ritual suggest that the American middle classes were actually beginning to take pride in the theatricality of their social conduct. With pride middle-class men and women learned to mask their physical defects and assume a personal style in their dress, to

Parlor theater, 1863. The presence of the puppet stage points to a growing middle-class interest in theatricality.

accept the necessity of etiquette as a cloak for their inner characters, and to don mourning for effect, parade their grief publicly in funeral processions, and contemplate without flinching the studied effect of a corpse displayed in a glass-topped casket. Sentimental anxieties about the hypocrisy of social disguise and formal ritual were yielding before a growing middle-class fascination with the theatrical arts of everyday life.

This fascination was most evident in the explosive popularity of theatrical parlor games in the 1850s and 1860s. As they built parlor stages, donned costumes and stage makeup, and learned to perform amateur theatricals in their homes, the American middle classes openly embraced theatricality for its own sake—in effect, bringing the farce of *Fashion* into their own homes and laughing harder than ever at the theatricality of their social lives. In so doing, they entered a new phase of their cultural history.

Before 1850, the parlor game called the charade was a kind of riddle. As *The New Athenian Oracle,* published in London in 1806, pretentiously explained,

> To inform those who are not used to this species of wit, it may be proper to observe, that Charades are a kind of Rebus, imported from the French, and have this property, namely, that the subject, or word in question, called the *whole,* must be a noun substantive of two syllables; and each of these syllables, called the *first* and *second part,* must also be a noun substantive, and the whole compound word is to be described, or enlarged upon, by some elegant allusion.[45]

This quiet, erudite word game was well suited to a Protestant culture suspicious of ritual. But in the 1850s, a new form of entertainment called "Charades in Action" was sweeping the parlors of America. "This game," *Godey's Lady's Book* explained in 1854, "is, as its name expresses it, a charade, acted instead of spoken."[46] In "acting charades," each syllable of a word was performed as one act of a play, and then the entire word was enacted in the final scene. The first example of a charade in action published in *Godey's* was the word *courtship.* In the first act, a sailor is placed on trial for polygamy (*court*); in the second, sailors toil and passengers suffer seasickness on an ocean passage (*ship*); and in the third act, a young lover pleads his cause before the young lady he loves (*courtship*).[47] In the early stages of this new entertainment fad, *Godey's* instructed readers to maintain absolute silence during the performance. But in May 1855, *Godey's* published a charade with dialogue and explained, "This Charade differs from those we have previously given in being spoken instead of acted in dumb-show."[48] Once the verbal charade was transformed into the dramatic charade, middle-class Americans were soon performing a wide variety of theatricals in their parlors, including acting charades, acting proverbs, burlesques and farces, *tableaux vivants* or living pictures, charades in tableaux and shadow pantomimes. The private theatrical had emerged as the most popular form of middle-class parlor entertainment.

Guides to parlor theatricals began to pour off the American press, books such as *The Parlor Stage: A Collection of Drawing-room Proverbs, Charades and Tableaux Vivants, Hudson's Private Theatricals for Home Performances, Burlesque and Musical Acting Charades,* and *Parlor Theatricals; or, Winter Evenings' Entertainment.*[49] The early guides often endeavored to reassure their readers that parlor theatricals were a perfectly respectable form of entertainment. *The Sociable; or One Thousand and One Home Amusements,* published in New York in 1858, was careful to preface its offerings of theatrical home entertainment with the promise that "the greatest care has been taken to exclude everything that might possibly be objected to by the most rigidly fastidious." Its tableaux vivants, middle-class readers were assured, were "arranged by persons of taste, and form one of the most refined recreations that a mixed party can indulge in"; its charades contained only "good characters" and "healthy sentiments."[50] Other books that followed *The Sociable* adopted a similar tone of reassurance, comparing charades with school dialogues as "the most innocent and improving form of dramatic entertainment," and assuring their readers that "everything like style or unnecessary show will be avoided."[51] Obviously sentimental antipathy for theatricality was not to die overnight. But the abundance of guides to parlor theatricals published in the 1850s and 1860s clearly suggests a new middle-class interest in the use of the parlor as a stage.

When Shakespeare's melancholy Prince of Denmark, himself an amateur player, observed that "all the world's a stage," he was speaking metaphorically, but to say that the middle-class parlor in the 1850s was a stage is to speak the literal truth. If the instructions given in the popular guides were followed, middle-class Americans in the 1850s and 1860s did actually transform their parlors into small theaters. Parlor players constructed their stage by placing wooden boxes in a rectangle and laying beams across them; stout planks were laid across the beams, and the resulting platform was covered with carpet. Once the stage was built, "The next thing of importance is the curtain, behind whose friendly expanse the young comedians may arrange their scenes, and which may close silently upon their histrionic triumphs."[52] A light wooden frame was attached to the front of the stage, and a drop curtain of heavy green material—like that used in public theaters—was nailed to the top piece, with an intricate system of wires and pulleys enabling the prompter to raise and lower the curtain. Windows, closets, and doors provided theatrical entrances and exits, and a single door could be converted into two exits by means of a screen placed in front of it. For tableaux vivants, black muslin curtains were added at the back and the sides of the stage to frame the picture. Alternatively, the tableau could be performed in the back parlor before an audience seated in the front parlor: this arrangement ensured the invisibility of the stage hands superintending the lights and the special effects on either side of the tableau. For shadow pantomimes, a white sheet was stretched tightly across the doorway between the two parlors; the audience sat in total darkness in one parlor, while the performers worked in front of a single bright light in the other.[53]

With the stage constructed, parlor performers could turn their attention to the problem of special effects. For the tableau vivant several layers of gauze were stretched over the curtain frame to give a misty, dreamlike cast to certain scenes. Each living picture required a different arrangement of light and shadow, and stage lamps were placed with attentive care. Colored lights, made by burning various chemicals in a metal pan or by placing globes of colored water between the light and the tableau, were often used; for ghostly scenes, a dingy yellow tint was considered effective. Popular sound effects included thunder, made by shaking a piece of sheet iron, artillery, made by striking sheet iron in the middle with a drum stick, and a fire alarm bell, made by striking a gong slowly. Tableaux vivants were often accompanied by appropriate music, such as "Home Sweet Home" for "Papa's Birthday," and a military air for "Major André." In most tableaux the performers assumed their positions, the curtain was raised for thirty seconds, and then it was lowered. In the movable tableau, however, the performers held one pose for thirty seconds and then changed position at the sound of the stage manager's bell: "This being done in the presence of the audience, has a magnificent effect when well done." In some highly contrived tableaux vivants, the figures held their positions while a moving platform gently rotated them around the stage. In "Summer and Winter," for example, two women stood on a circular platform, supported by an upright revolving beam that extended through the bottom of the stage and was turned from below. The parlor audience to this contrived piece of stage machinery could thus witness the aged crony "Winter" slowly revolving out of sight, while the beautiful young woman "Summer" came into view.[54]

The painstaking attention to detail in the construction of the parlor stage and the contrivance of special effects suggests the enthusiasm with which middle-class Americans threw themselves into the new theatrical entertainments. The dramatic devices of raised stage and drop curtain, music and sound effects, colored lights and revolving platforms—all point to a growing middle-class fascination with theater-for-theater's sake. This fascination was even more evident in the stage costumes and stage makeup worn by amateur parlor players. The costumes suggested by instructional guides for charades and tableaux vivants were often fantastically elaborate. The character of Cordobello, the Italian brigand in the acting proverb "Honor among thieves," was to be dressed as follows:

A common black felt hat, with the left side fastened up by a showy buckle, holding a black ostrich plume—a short velvet or woollen jacket with brass buttons (easily sewed on for the occasion)—a gay scarf bound several times around the waist, with a large knot and long ends, and a brace of pistols thrust in it—a pair of knee breeches (made by cutting off the legs of an old pair of pantaloons), with a knot of red ribbons at the knees, and long stockings—a pair of pumps, with metal buckles, and a quantity of paste jewelry, chains, etc., make a very respectable brigand's costume, at the expense of next to nothing.

In conclusion Cordobello's costume designer writes, "This is merely one instance among many that might be mentioned, and will illustrate the ease with which the 'tinselled fascination of the stage' may be mimicked by the home fireside."[55] Charade enthusiasts apparently delighted in the art of transforming the most familiar objects from the home fireside into stage properties. For a charade of the coronation of Darius, the use of domestic items as props verged on the ridiculous:

Enter PERSIAN GENERALS in full armor of dish-cover breastplates, and turbans of rich shawls and scarfs. They lead on their Troops, carrying spears of brooms, and banners of fire-screens. The Generals bend the knee to Darius, who by his affable pantomime, wins their love. The Generals, drawing their swords of walking-sticks, deliver them to the king, who immediately returns them. A crown of jelly mould is placed on the head of Darius.[56]

Through such use of dish covers, brooms, and jelly moulds as costume accessories, middle-class Americans no doubt satisfied themselves that they were in fact mimicking the tinselled fascination of the stage right at their home firesides.

Important though stage costumes and props were, "A still more important part of dramatic preparation is what is technically termed the 'making up' of the characters, and one which requires some practice and observation."[57] Every good parlor stage manager had a box of good watercolors, some fine chalk, burnt cork, a few camel's-hair brushes, and a pot of dry rouge, and with these standard cosmetic aids could produce a variety of stock characters. The stage drunkard's face was given a flushed cast, with a few purplish spots on the cheeks and nose, while his emaciated wife and children had gaunt faces with dark shadows of blue paint, burnt cork, or india ink. Stage Indians were painted a copper color, and stage blacks were easily made up with burnt cork, as in the minstrel shows. Young actors and actresses were transformed into old characters with the application of a set of india-ink wrinkles, applied with a camel's-hair brush, and softened with a dusting of fine chalk. False moustaches, beards, and wigs in a variety of colors and patterns were considered a valuable addition to any parlor wardrobe. And any comic character could achieve the quality of caricature through the following technique: the actor applied a reddish brown tint to his face, assumed the emotional expression he wanted to project—a broad grin, a frown, a smirk, a simper, a scowl—and then traced the wrinkles made by this expression with a fine brush dipped in brown tint.[58]

Popular guides to private theatricals coached amateur players in a highly stylized and melodramatic acting method. Performers were advised to "study the different expressions and suitable actions of the passions," and to learn "a kind of code of expressions, or laws for the better regulation of frowns, smiles, and gestures." Love, for example, was to be expressed by pressing the heart, looking tenderly at the ceiling, gently swinging the body, and kissing a miniature or embracing a lock of hair. Rage "may be pictured to an almost maddening amount by the frequent stamping of the foot and the shaking of the fist." Stock despair involved sinking into a chair and spreading a hand through the hair with the fingers open "like a bunch of carrots"; hope involved raising a finger to the ear with a bright smile and a look of deep intensity. Finally, "DISDAIN is perhaps the easiest passion to be expressed. The dignified waving of the hand, and the scornful look, gradually descending from top to toe, are well known to all who have been mistaken for waiters at evening parties."[59] This stylized presentation of emotion was even more pronounced in tableaux, in which the facial expression was static. And in the shadow pantomime, the expressive powers of the performer were strained to the utmost, for the entire performance lay in the posture, the gestures, and the movements of the character-shadow behind the sheet. Even in the acting charade, however, emotion was to be enacted with painstaking self-consciousness, as in this Christmas dinner scene:

> The Visitors then take the Young Ladies, who appear dreadfully bashful, and drag them screaming and tittering under the Mistletoe, where they embrace them theatrically, by crossing their heads over their shoulders. Grandmother is delighted, and presses her sides with mirth, when one of Their Children takes her hand, and pulls her under the Mistletoe and kisses her. Grandfather pretends to be jealous, and the fun increases.[60]

In their parlor performances, middle-class men and women were clearly casting aside some of their sentimental aversions to theatrical conduct. In fact, they were learning to use costume, cosmetics, and the dramatic art of caricature as an integral part of their parlor social lives, and they were doing so with a high degree of self-consciousness. Many charades and parlor farces, for example, offered a play-within-a-play for the entertainment of polite audiences. Characters often appeared on stage wearing a disguise: in one play, for example, a beautiful young woman who seeks to avoid marriage to an ugly old man runs away and disguises herself as an Irish servant. In some charades a formal performance as well as an audience appear within the play: Scottish dancers, for example, perform before spectators who shower them with bouquets. Other

"Acting Charade—Stratagem," 1861. The character on the right has disguised himself as a geology tutor, Professor Ammonite, in order to gain access to his beloved.

charades and tableaux depict performers behind the scenes and out of character: a family of circus performers having lunch on the road or a motley collection of characters from Shakespeare relaxing in the dressing room of a theater. In these performances, the Victorian fascination with back-region activity is strongly evident. The most significantly self-conscious charades, however, were those that parodied the histrionic efforts of the performers themselves by ridiculing the melodramatic posturings of stagestruck characters. In the final scene from the charade "Dramatic," for example, a character named Ludovico Jones melodramatically performs a scene from a play called "Lost Father, or the Found Daughter," before a theater manager who coaches his performance. In the charade "Stagestruck," two cousins named Frederick and Cora are sent to the country to get over their mania for the stage, but in defiance of their irate relatives they continue to deliver ridiculous sequences of lines and scenes from Shakespeare. For the balcony scene from *Romeo and Juliet*, they actually construct their own charade-like stage-within-a-stage by placing a fender on a table for Cora to stand behind. Finally, Fred's father surrenders, saying, "Was there ever before such a pair of stage-struck idiots?"[61] The humor of his question lay in the ambiguity of "stage-struck idiots": was he referring to the characters of Frederick and Cora or to the polite young gentleman and lady who were assuming these roles on the parlor stage?

Another popular theme that points to the highly self-conscious nature of parlor theater was ritual. Many charades and tableaux vivants focused on simple domestic rituals such as christenings, weddings, or parlor scenes on St. Valentine's Day. Medieval rituals and pageants were also popular, and many were the parlor knight-ings of Sir Walter Raleigh by Elizabeth and the parlor celebrations of May Day in which peasants danced around the maypole and crowned the May queen. Even more pagan than this May Day ritual was a tableau called "The Idol," which featured a grotesque figure seated on a pedestal and flanked by two priests in long white robes and white veils; in the foreground men and women in long robes of various colors all knelt with their foreheads touching the ground. In a similarly rich and pagan tableau called "Cagliostro's Magic Mir-ror," a magician stood before a mirror in which the image of a lovely woman appeared to a frightened nobleman; at the magician's feet lay a lamp, a book, a naked sword, and a human skull. Finally, many tableaux represented scenes of Roman Catholic ritual. In "Penitent," a young girl dressed in white and holding a rosary knelt before a crucifix in her boudoir, while a monk stood before her with one hand pointing upward and the other inviting her to rise. This theme was repeated in a similar charade called "Novice," in which the kneeling girl was accompanied by a priest holding an open book, an abbess raising a pair of scissors to cut a long lock of the girl's hair, and several nuns, one of whom held out a long white veil.[62]

As discussed earlier, the sentimental antipathy toward social ritual had been rooted historically in Puritanism. Seventeenth-century English Puritans had actively opposed the pagan rituals of the peasantry, the court masques and pageants of the nobility, and the religious rituals of the Anglican church, which retained too many Roman trappings for Puritan satisfaction. In the parlor theatricals that achieved great popularity in the mid-nineteenth century, all these ancient rituals were reenacted as a form of entertainment: the pagan peasant ritual surrounding the maypole, the courtly ritual of knighthood, the Roman Catholic rituals of penance and monastic vocation. Now middle-class men and women sat in their parlors and politely applauded their own theatrical renditions of rich and once-forbidden rituals. Once the source of grave anxieties and righteous resistance, these rituals had become an important form of Victorian entertainment.

Why was the sentimental attack on theatricality as a form of hypocrisy rapidly being swept away by a flood of enthusiasm for private theatrical entertainment? Just as Frederick and Cora's performance of *Romeo and Juliet* in the charade "Stagestruck" was a play-within-a-play, the parlor theatrical itself was a play-within-a-play, an explicit theatrical performance taking place within the larger, implicit theatrical performance that was middle-class gentility. A number of structural parallels linked the parlor theatrical with the larger genteel performance. First of all, the charade, like the genteel performance, demanded a strict division of space between the front regions where the performance was given and the back regions where the mechanics of the performance were hidden from the audience. Many of the elaborate stage devices of the parlor theatrical—the drop curtain, the employment of folding screens for entrances and exits, the hidden lights and sound effects, the placement of the audience in one parlor and the performers in the other, the draping of gauze sheets across the doorway for tableaux vivants—served to reinforce the separation of front region

Parlor theatricals, 1867. Note the elaborate costumes and histrionic gestures of the players and the presence of the prompter backstage.

from back region and to render audience intrusion "backstage" virtually impossible. In the private theatrical, a stage manager ensured the separation of front regions from back regions, just as a hostess performed the same function for each parlor social encounter. Second, the private theatrical, like the genteel performance, demanded from the audience a tactful recognition of what the performance was about. In dramatic charades, this demand for recognition was made explicit, as the audience was invited to participate in the performance by guessing what word or proverb was being enacted. Within the rules of the game, the audience that succeeded in guessing the charade thus won the privilege of performing in turn, just as in the genteel performance any lady or gentleman who tactfully affirmed the gentility of another was thereby demonstrating her or his own gentility. Even within some parlor farces, performers would turn to the audience and demand that its members guess the meaning of the performance. Third, in the charade or parlor farce as in the genteel performance, the audience was carefully restricted, as suggested in the term *private* theatrical. No vulgar intruders who might undermine the performance through their lack of tact would be permitted to witness a parlor theatrical.

Not only was the structure of the private theatrical similar to that of the genteel performance; the expressive content of the charade, farce, or tableau was similar to that of polite parlor conduct. The stylized and controlled emotional self-expression demanded of parlor players strongly resembled the demonstration of right feeling demanded by sentimentalism. To strike the appropriate emotional expression and pose and, in the tableau vivant, to maintain them with flawless self-discipline for half a minute: this was a frozen caricature of the genteel performance. The parlor performer was thus virtually sculpted into genteel propriety. In fact, many tableaux did feature human sculptures or portraits. In "The Statue Bride," for example, a young woman dressed in white and holding a bouquet stood on a pedestal painted to resemble marble and set in a niche draped with black or dark red curtains. Her face, arms, hands, and all exposed parts of her figure were whitened with chalk, and she stood perfectly still, in unquestionably flawless gentility.[63] Given the high demands of genteel propriety, it is not surprising that private theatricals were praised as an excellent form of training in genteel expressiveness, especially for young people: "As an educational agent, the amateur drama can hardly be too highly

esteemed; for it teaches the young performer elocution, gesticula-
tion, ease of manner, and a certain knowledge of the emotions and
passions of humanity, which can hardly be acquired elsewhere."[64]
Parlor players often emphasized the connection between the
parlor theatrical and the larger genteel performance of which it was
a part by freely crossing the invisible boundary between stage and
audience and by dropping briefly out of their stage characters to
reveal themselves in their private characters. In other words, they
delighted in subverting the play by revealing its theatricality. In
charades and certain farces the players openly invited their audience to comment on the meaning of the performance. In those
scenes mentioned earlier, in which circus performers ate lunch by
the side of the road or a jumble of Shakespearean actors relaxed
together in the greenroom, the parlor amateurs implicitly pointed
to the fact that they too lived more of their lives out of character
than in character. Within what was one of the most self-consciously
theatrical of all parlor theatricals, "Irresistibly Impudent," the
Prompter actually emerged from backstage to argue with a player
who had forgotten his lines, and then appealed to the audience for
vindication. Then, when the heroine's father refused to give his
blessing to her union with her lover, a character named Dick said,
"Oh! but you must; we want to finish the play, and it will never do to
end it without the parent's blessing." The father finally relented,
and Dick said to the audience, "You knew it would end that way,—
didn't you? A farce always does. The parent relents—the lovers are
made happy—and as a matter of course, down comes the curtain."[65]
Through such techniques as these, the parlor theatrical continually emphasized the fact that the players were all performers, and
repeatedly drew the audience onstage as well, thus suggesting that
all the world was a stage and all men and women merely players.
Many popular private theatricals succeeded in collapsing the distinction between the overt theatricality of the play and the implicit
theatricality of all parlor social conduct. The message of parlor
theatricals was simply this: middle-class social life was itself a charade. This message was reaffirmed in dozens of plot lines whose
main theme was the theatricality of the struggle for middle-class
gentility. Many of these were patterned on Anna Cora Mowatt's
play, as numerous fashionable coquettes, some named Seraphina,
welcomed courtship from lisping dandies and bogus counts. What
distinguished these treatments of fashion from the sentimental
attack was their broad sense of humor. To emphasize how ludicrous

was the fashionable struggle for gentility, some satirical spoofs planted an unseen audience in the picture to laugh onstage at the genteel performers. In a tableau called "The Dancing Lesson," a very serious dancing master and the very serious young lady who is his student stand in perfect dance position, while a little girl and an Irish servant, convulsed with laughter, mimic their efforts. In a tableau on the proverb "They are chips from the old block," a lady in full evening dress admires herself in a mirror while her daughter tries on her mother's headdress and mimics her exact attitude; a father in full evening dress with white kid gloves and curled hair enters the room accompanied by his son, identically dressed, and each adjusts his pet curl; while the valet and the lady's maid stand hidden behind the mirror and point derisively at these fashionable pretenders.[66] In both of these tableaux, the onstage spectators at the genteel performance were themselves nonparticipants, since servants and children were not bound by the same restraints as middle-class adults.

The rage for parlor theatricals that swept through middle-class culture after 1850 testified to a growing acceptance by the American middle classes of the underlying theatricality of all their claims to genteel social status. In tableaux such as "The Dancing Lesson" and "Chips from the old block," parlor performers and their audiences laughingly admitted that middle-class social climbers were all performers trying to pass for what they were not. Gentility, they suggested, was an assumed role, a part to be played by wearing the right clothing, cultivating the proper manners, and engaging in the correct forms of social ritual. Even as middle-class Americans were beginning to embrace a new theatricality in their dress, etiquette, and mourning ritual, they were examining, in their parlor theatricals, the source of that larger theatricality in the demands of the genteel performance. By suggesting that all parlor social life was a form of charade, they were in a sense anticipating the idea formulated by Erving Goffman, that personal conduct in societies based on the premise of upward mobility is characterized by a highly theatrical attention to the presentation of self. The struggle for genteel status, they were coming to admit, was a confidence game.

This new acceptance of the theatricality of middle-class social life was a product in part of the surge of economic self-confidence experienced by the bourgeois classes in America. At mid-nineteenth century, America was entering what E. J. Hobsbawm has called "the era of the triumphant bourgeois." In the "age of capital," from 1848 to 1875, an unprecedented economic prosperity created a "bourgeois world" dominated by men of substance, financial power, and influence and by women whose major social role was to demonstrate their husbands' substance by spending money lavishly on summer holidays, ornate houses and furnishings, and elaborate dress. On a grand scale, Hobsbawm argues, the bourgeois classes celebrated their new economic self-confidence in "giant new rituals of self-congratulation" such as the Crystal Palace Exhibition in London in 1851, and the Philadelphia Centennial Exposition in 1876.[67] On a smaller but more significant scale, I would argue, they developed personal rituals of self-congratulation: of extravagant self-display through dress, of elaborate social formalism in their etiquette, of public pageantry in their funerals. With pomp and with pride they celebrated their cultural dominance in a form not unlike the masque that displayed the power of the Elizabethan and Stuart nobility—the parlor theatrical. Within this new atmosphere of worldly self-confidence, American middle-class culture cast aside its sentimental uncertainty about all forms of theatricality and entered an era of what Thorstein Veblen would soon term "conspicuous display."[68]

The self-confidence that began to characterize middle-class culture after 1850 was not, however, solely the product of material prosperity. Bourgeois life was still riddled with social and economic insecurities: about personal failure, financial panics and depressions, political corruption, the urban masses and the influx of immigrants, and growing labor discontent, to name a few. The dangerous world beyond the walls of the middle-class home seemed no less a confidence game after 1850 than before; Mark Twain aptly captured this sense of the era in calling it the "Gilded Age."[69] Nevertheless, within the middle-class home and, more specifically, within the social sphere defined by the parlor, an intricate system of social forms had been hammered out within which middle-class men and women might place tentative confidence in one another without relying on each other's perfect sincerity. Polite society, they were beginning to recognize, could never rest on the sincere adherence to Christian law of all its participants. But it could insist that all members assume an outward appearance of virtue. As Sarah J. Hale wrote in 1868, society could not enforce a Christian trust among all men, but it could insist upon that "confidence in the good intentions of our neighbors" without which social intercourse would prove impossible. With these words Sarah Hale, sentimental writer and onetime editor of *Godey's Lady's Book,* set forth the fundamental new assumption on which bourgeois social life would rest after mid-century. By the 1850s and 1860s, the American middle classes were learning to distinguish between an evangelical Christian trust based on heartfelt sincerity, and bourgeois social confidence based on proper social forms; and they were deciding to rely upon the latter. They were learning to place confidence not in the sincere countenance but in the social mask; to trust not in simple dress but in elaborate disguise. Finally, they could rest secure in the knowledge that heart cannot meet heart in a world of strangers, and in the recognition that the uncloaked heart is the most dangerous acquaintance of all. And their new acceptance of social masks and disguises was playfully acted out in the parlor theatricals that became so popular after 1855. In the elaborately costumed and heavily made-up amateur player, Victorian Americans directly confronted the figure of the stranger in the parlor and deprived him of his powers of contamination through simple laughter. In the deepest sense, their laughter signified their worldly new realization that all characters were forms of disguise, and their new belief that only disguise ensured safety in the parlor. "Hypocrisy," D. Mackellar observed in 1855, "is the homage that vice pays to virtue."[70] Increasingly, middle-class Americans accepted that homage in lieu of true virtue.

The new homage to virtue meant an adherence to the hundreds of codified rules governing every aspect of middle-class conduct after 1830. Within those rules, middle-class men and women were finding ways of negotiating the dangerous world of strangers with minimal risk. No longer did they seek to ensure that all personal conduct be guided by the sentimental ideal of the transparent soul. Instead they began to rest easy in the knowledge that the right people would always behave in the right way, that genteel men and women would know and obey the mutually agreed upon rules of polite society, even though their conduct masked the blackest of hearts. Parlor society, like the world outside the home, was a confidence game, but it was a game with well-defined rules designed to ensure that no player would be hurt. And smart participants who played by the rules might win the game and claim their prize: the recognition of their genteel standing in the bourgeois world. In the most fundamental sense, the criteria by which middle-class gentility was assessed had shifted from a sentimental demand for transparent sincerity to a worldly Victorian demand for a skillful social performance. Whereas the sentimentalist had judged an individual's claim to gentility in terms of the sincerity of his or her expression of right or genteel feeling, the worldly new Victorian judged such a claim by assessing the skillfulness of his or her avowedly theatrical performance of gentility. The sentimental ideal of transparent feeling in social intercourse was yielding to an increasingly frank reverence for social expertise.

Ironically, the many social laws and rituals that went into the skilled performance of middle-class gentility after mid-century had originated in sentimental anxieties about theatricality in face-to-face social conduct. To escape the hypocrisy of fashionable forms and rituals, sentimentalists expressed a belief in sentimental typology, which stated that all forms of dress and conduct should be the outward marks of inner character. Sentimental typology had provided a way to link true character with apparent character, the inner self with the social mask or disguise. But sentimental typology had generated an almost obsessive demand for dress styles that were simple or "transparent," for polite forms that were social expressions of "right feeling," and for mourning ritual that was perfectly sincere. In their efforts to meet the demand for perfect social sincerity, the sentimental arbiters of middle-class conduct had to expand constantly the polite forms and rituals that shaped their social intercourse. The quest for sincerity of form thus inevitably turned and destroyed itself, for when sincerity became a matter of style or of fashion, sentimental typology was rendered meaningless. As Lionel Trilling has observed,

> If sincerity has lost its former status, if the word itself has for us a hollow sound and seems almost to negate its meaning, that is because it does not propose being true to one's own self as an end but only as a means. If one is true to one's own self for the purpose of avoiding falsehood to others, is one being truly true to one's own self? The moral end in view implies a public end in view, with all that this suggests of the esteem and fair repute that follow upon the correct fulfillment of a public role.[71]

The more the middle classes strived for sincerity of form, in short, the more all social forms smacked of insincerity.

Because of this built-in tendency for self-destruction, sentimentalism in its purest form shaped middle-class culture for a relatively brief period, from about 1830 to about 1850. The fragility of the sentimental ideal must not, however, be overestimated. Sentimentalism has proved to be a very enduring strain within American culture; the middle-class acceptance, at mid-nineteenth century, of the theatricality of social conduct was neither complete nor permanent. Repeatedly throughout American history, the sentimental impulse has returned to convince middle-class men and women of the hypocrisy of their social lives and to stress the importance of establishing sincere social forms as a way of restoring confidence to the entire American social order. Middle-class Americans have continued to express grave anxieties about the hypocrisy of fashion and of ritualistic social forms; they have continued to be both fascinated and repelled by the images of the confidence man and the painted woman; they have continued to regard transparency as a sound moral ideal for all personal conduct. In the long run, sentimentalism has shaped a crucial cultural tension in middle-class American views of what constitutes proper social conduct, a tension between the desire for sincerity and the demand for formality. The reason for this underlying concern about the sincerity of culture may be stated simply: the problem is endemic to a society of men and women on the make, of geographical and social movers, of men and women who are constantly assuming new identities and struggling to be convincing in new social roles. Within this context of social mobility, sentimentalism—the cultural response to the threat of a nation of confidence men and painted women—has become a permanent component of middle-class culture.

Conclusion

On his famed travels through Jacksonian America, Alexis de Tocqueville was struck most forcefully by one distinguishing characteristic of American society: "the general equality of condition among
the people." In *Democracy in America,* Tocqueville discussed how that
equality of condition shaped not just American politics and law, but
national opinions, sentiments, and customs as well. His analysis of
democratic culture focused on the peculiar "restlessness of temper"
that plagued the American anxious to improve his condition. "It is
strange to see," he wrote, "with what feverish ardor the Americans
pursue their own welfare, and to watch the vague dread that
constantly torments them lest they should not have chosen the
shortest path which may lead to it." In sweeping away the privileges
of the few, American democracy had opened the way to a universal
scramble for distinction in which most men were doomed to disap-
pointment, for "when men are nearly alike and all follow the same
track, it is very difficult for any one individual to walk quickly and
cleave a way through the dense throng that surrounds and presses
on him." Consequently, the ambitions of American democrats were
insatiable: "They can never attain as much as they desire. It perpet-
ually retires from before them, yet without hiding itself from their
sight, and in retiring draws them on. At every moment they think
they are about to grasp it; it escapes at every moment from their
hold."[1] If Tocqueville's analysis was accurate, as Edwin C. Rozwenc
has observed, "then we can assume that the American in the
Jacksonian generation had a peculiar problem of self-identification
and self-esteem."[2]

Tocqueville's assertion of the general equality of condition among the American people has recently come under attack from the new social historians, whose work has uncovered wide inequities in the distribution of wealth during the Jacksonian era. But his insights still prove useful to historians of middle-class culture in the antebellum period. Many middle-class Americans firmly believed in the openness of their society and manifested their faith in that restlessness of temper that Tocqueville found central to the American character. In the broadest sense, what Tocqueville was addressing with his provocative insights into democratic culture was "the problem of status in the Jacksonian era." As Rozwenc has suggested, rapid economic and social changes between 1820 and 1850 "deranged the previously established bases of personal identification and of social status."[3] But Tocqueville's picture of the American democrat makes possible a more subtle analysis. Marvin Meyers has accurately described Tocqueville's democrat as follows: "With all the parts of his universe, himself included, in erratic motion, with no fixed terminus and no secure resting place, the democrat develops an acute awareness of loss and failure."[4] The American democrat— that is to say, the middle-class American—had no status in the strict sense of the term; he occupied no fixed position within a well-defined social structure, and his vague sense of restlessness and dread sprang from his liminality, his betwixt-and-between social condition. Because he lived suspended between the facts of his present social condition and the promise of his future, because he held a vertical vision of life in an allegedly fluid and boundless social system, he was plagued with anxiety concerning his social identity. Middle-class concerns about placelessness were expressed through the figure of the confidence man, the archetypal man-on-the-make who threatened to contaminate all he encountered with the depravity of his own nature. The confidence man threatened to infect the rising generation with his own hypocrisy, a trait he shared with the liminal trickster figures of many primitive cultures. The powerful symbol of the confidence man expressed antebellum concerns about the replacement of a traditional hierarchical social structure with a modern system in which no man occupied a fixed social position. In the open society, it was feared, because all men were on the make, all men were in danger of becoming confidence men, whose claims to a new and higher social status were a dangerous form of hypocrisy.

Antebellum concerns about the confidence man were particularly acute due to the rapid expansion of the urban world of strangers. As the urban stranger, the confidence man served to express the middle-class fear that success among strangers demanded not character formation, but a manipulation of those surface impressions of dress and conduct that were so crucial to urban life. Hypocrisy, it was feared, paid off in an urban environment. In a broader sense, however, the figure of the confidence man as urban stranger attests to an antebellum crisis in the rules and conventions of social conduct. Traditional norms governing face-to-face conduct had operated in a world where men and women came to know one another gradually over a long period of time, within a well-defined social context of family and community. In that world, confidence might be offered or denied to another on the basis of long-term mutual knowledge. But the social and economic changes of the eighteenth and early nineteenth centuries had disrupted these older norms and left a vacuum of prescriptive guidance on how to interact safely with others. This crisis was captured symbolically in the condition of the youth just entering the antebellum world of strangers. Detached from his family, friends, and local community, alone and placeless, he stood on the threshold of a dangerous social world roamed by hypocritical strangers who would dupe and destroy him if he so much as looked at or spoke with them. In a world of confidence men the individual dared not connect with anyone. Tocqueville expressed very powerfully this isolation of the American democrat: "Thus, not only does democracy make every man forget his ancestors, but it hides his descendants and separates his contemporaries from him; it throws him back forever upon himself alone and threatens in the end to confine him entirely within the solitude of his own heart."[5]

To resolve this antebellum crisis of social confidence, a new system of cultural forms was needed within which Americans seeking to rise in the world of strangers might meet without fear of moral or psychological injury. In response to this need, hundreds of manuals on conduct-of-life began to pour off American presses after 1830. Central to that new system of cultural forms set forth in these manuals was the demand for perfect sincerity. The hypocrisy of life in the marketplace and on the city street, according to that sentimental ideal, had to be counteracted by the sincerity of socail intercourse in the parlor. This sentimental demand for a transparent display of feeling proved to be a powerful shaping force in three areas of middle-class culture: dress, etiquette, and the social ritual of mourning the dead. The sentimental ideal of dress insisted that a woman's clothing should serve not as a disguise but as a transparent reflection of her soul. The sentimental ideal of etiquette demanded that politeness be the sincere outward demonstration of inner virtue. And the sentimental ideal of mourning dictated that mourners dress and behave in a ritual designed to demonstrate the perfect sincerity of their grief.

In its initial impulse the sentimental demand for sincerity was a defensive strategy against the perceived dangers of placelessness in the open society and of anonymity in the urban world of strangers—two social conditions that were believed to breed confidence men. But as the new rules of conduct were articulated and formalized, sentimentalism emerged as an offensive strategy for defining what it was to be middle-class in America. The code of polite conduct defined middle-class gentility by dictating how the "right" people would meet face-to-face in polite society. Most important, sentimentalism defined middle-class gentility negatively, through social rituals of exclusion. Despite its hostility to fashion, sentimentalism was, in sociological terms, a form of fashion: its rules of conduct served first as a barrier to be surmounted by those who wished to enter the ranks of the genteel, and second as a standard that could be erected to assess the efforts of those men and women still seeking admittance. The sentimental barrier against social upstarts was erected at the entrance to the parlor, where the calling cards of the socially unworthy would be rejected with the significant message, "not at home." In a literal sense, liminal men and women stood poised on the threshold of gentility and were admitted or excluded on the basis of their adherence to the sentimental code of conduct. In this way the parlor was itself a metaphor for genteel social status; just as its spatial borders were patrolled by servants who received their instructions from vigilant hostesses, the boundaries of gentility were being carefully patrolled so the unworthy could not pass. The central demand of the sentimental code for sincerity was intended to weed out those social aspirants who were merely "passing," whose new social identity was a superficial gloss over a fundamentally vulgar nature.

Even as the sentimental middle classes erected barriers to define their own social status through the exclusion of others, however, they sidestepped the difficult issue of class distinctions. The American republic, it was widely agreed, was a classless society: "It is a glorious thing that we have no serfs, with the large and unfortunate

exception of our slaves—no artificial distinctions—no acknowledged superiority of blood—no station which merit may not
fill—no rounds in the social ladder to which the humblest may not
aspire."[6] So powerful was this myth that even Karl Marx affirmed it:
social classes in America, he wrote at mid-century, were "in a
constant state of flux."[7] Despite widespread signs of growing stratifi-
cation in Jacksonian society, despite the reality of severe limitations
on upward social mobility, there were few expressions of class-
consciousness in antebellum America; in stark contrast to Old
World society, Americans believed, theirs was a uniquely open social
system. "Why, sir," protested an American to an Englishman in
Francis Grund's satirical *Aristocracy in America,* "this is a republican
country; we have no *public* distinction of classes."[8] Grund's irony was
at work in the emphasis on the word *public.* Privately, American
society was rife with distinctions, often based on behavioral criteria
so refined as to be invisible to European observers, accustomed as
they were to more overt class distinctions. In the private class system
of American middle-class society, individual claims to gentility were
assessed according to sentimental criteria. To be genteel, simply
stated, was to be sincere, and sincerity was not an economic category, it was a matter of morality. Sentimentalism thus shored up the
myth of a classless America by professedly excluding from genteel
status only the insincere—confidence men and painted women, who
were barred for their hypocrisy, as demonstrated in their failure to
meet the moral demands of the sentimental code. Sentimentalism
offered an unconscious strategy for middle-class Americans to
distinguish themselves as a class while still denying the class structure of their society, and to define themselves against the lower
classes even as they insisted they were merely distinguishing themselves from vulgar hypocrites. In fact, those barred from polite
society may have been too poor, too closely linked with manual
labor, or too nouveau for admission to a given set. But within the
terms of sentimental culture, they were excluded for their hypocrisy.

In its purest form, the sentimental culture of the early Victorian
period was yielding by mid-century to the new theatricality of high
Victorian middle-class culture. To some extent sentimentalism was
destroyed by its own internal contradictions: the sincere ideal
subverted itself by establishing fixed formulas governing proper
middle-class dress, etiquette, and social ritual, formulas which in-
tensified middle-class concerns about the problem of hypocrisy

because they permitted social pretenders to enter the parlor in the guise of the sincere ideal. Sentimental culture in the 1830s and 1840s assumed the pattern of a vicious circle: middle-class demands for sincerity were formalized in sincere social forms and rituals; these formal prescriptions generated heightened concerns about the hypocrisy of middle-class social conduct; these anxieties were in turn embodied in ever more sincere social forms; and the circle began again. By the 1850s, however, middle-class Americans were beginning to break out of the vicious circle established by the sentimental ideal of sincerity and to embrace more avowedly theatrical cultural forms. Proper dress gradually came to be accepted as a legitimate form of disguise; proper etiquette was increasingly viewed as a means of masking and thus controlling unacceptable social impulses; and mourning ritual was coming to be a form of public theater, designed to display the perfect gentility of its participants. The growing theatricality of middle-class culture in the 1850s and 1860s was best exemplified in the new vogue of parlor theatricals that first emerged as a popular form of entertainment in the mid-1850s. In playing charades and staging pantomimes and burlesques in their parlors, middle-class Americans proved willing to engage in forms of conduct that would have been condemned a decade earlier as dangerously hypocritical. The parlor theatricals of the late 1850s and 1860s proved to be a highly self-conscious emblem of middle-class culture, with its new acceptance of the social arts of disguise, masking, and theatrical ritual, and its new willingness to admit their function in a culture centered on the promise of upward social mobility.

In effect, what had happened within middle-class culture by mid-century was this: the sentimental demand for sincerity that had given rise to the complex code of genteel conduct had fallen away, leaving behind the social forms themselves. Those social forms could now be accepted for what they were, a theatrical performance of gentility. They had succeeded in laying to rest those anxieties that had initially given rise to the spectre of the confidence man, the anxieties evoked by the demands of meeting strangers in an open social system. Middle-class Americans might still have been unwilling, after 1850, to confide in one another, but they were now willing to confide in the social forms themselves, for it was in adhering to those forms that they defined their genteel social status, both individually and collectively, as a class. And it was in their genteel standing as a class that they were ultimately willing to place their confidence. The rigid code of Victorian social conduct that defined the American genteel after mid-century served to resolve the middle-class problem of self-identification and social status that had so troubled the Jacksonian generation. The new theatricality of middle-class culture after 1850 was thus part of that critical historical transformation "from boundlessness to consolidation": the American middle classes were leaving behind the boundless social system of the Jacksonian era and consolidating as a class with social borders clearly defined by detailed criteria of social expertise.[9] In their overtly theatrical adherence to a formal code of conduct, middle-class Americans abandoned the apologetic manner of the sincere ideal and proudly claimed their right to social distinction.

Sentimentalism, the system of values that established guidelines for middle-class conduct in antebellum America, proved critical to the historical development of the middle-class culture that had clearly established its dominance in American society by mid-century. To be middle-class in antebellum America, according to sentimentalists, was to be sincere and to demonstrate one's sincerity through the proper forms of dress, courtesy, and social ritual. Perhaps it is not entirely inaccurate to label sentimentalism a form of hypocrisy, if by hypocrisy we mean to suggest the adoption of any conduct that is not instinctual or natural. Victorian gentility demanded an adherence to social conventions that many twentieth-century Americans must find intolerably artificial and restrictive. But such a critique itself rests finally on the sentimental assumption that all arbitrary social forms are hypocritical, a view that would render meaningless all cultural history. In studying middle-class culture in mid-nineteenth century America, it is far more useful to recognize the importance of the middle-class concern—amounting at times to an obsession—about the problem of hypocrisy in a modernizing world; and to treat seriously the sentimental demand for sincerity in face-to-face social interaction. For it was through their definition of the problem of hypocrisy, and their efforts to resolve that problem in the sentimental cult of sincerity, that Americans seeking to rise in the urban world of strangers became resolutely middle-class.

Epilogue

The Confidence Man in Corporate America

The transition from the sentimental culture of early Victorianism to the theatrical culture of high Victorianism demonstrates a sharp decline in middle-class concerns about the problem of hypocrisy in American society. This major cultural shift thus points to a reorientation of middle-class attitudes toward social mobility after mid-century. For the sincere ideal of sentimental culture had been nurtured, in part, by middle-class anxieties about the dangers of placelessness in an open society. By the second half of the nineteenth century, middle-class Americans were coming to accept the idea of a social system filled with liminal men in pursuit of the main chance. With that new willingness to accept a society of men on the make came a new view of that archetypal man-on-the-make, the confidence man. By the late nineteenth century, the confidence man no longer stalked the pages of advice literature as a symbol of the dangers of placelessness in a society of self-made men. In fact, the confidence man was actually becoming a kind of model for ambitious young Americans to emulate. After 1870, a new success literature was emerging that effectively instructed its readers to cultivate the arts of the confidence man in order to succeed in the corporate business world. This new strain in success ideology peaked in 1936 with the publication of Dale Carnegie's *How to Win Friends and Influence People*. But the direction of American success mythology was already evident by 1868, when the most popular spokesman for success of his generation, Horatio Alger, Jr., published his first successful novel, *Ragged Dick*.

The story of a young bootblack's rise to middle-class standing,

Ragged Dick is an excellent example of the "rags-to-respectability" success formula of Horatio Alger.[1] The reader first finds Dick dressed in filthy rags and sleeping soundly in a wooden box on the street in New York City. He is a lively, good-humored orphan of fourteen who spends his days shining shoes and his evenings wasting his nickels and dimes at the Old Bowery Theatre and an occasional gambling house. But Ragged Dick's life is transformed when he meets respectable Mr. Whitney and his nephew Frank. Fired with a new desire for respectability, Dick abandons his old way of life: he dons the new suit given him by Mr. Whitney, hires a room, takes in an educated fellow bootblack as his tutor, opens a savings account, begins to attend church, and enters society at the home of his Sunday school teacher. In the final chapter Dick secures his respectability by saving the life of a little boy who has fallen off the Brooklyn ferry, and thus earning a clerkship in the counting room of the boy's grateful father. In symbolic affirmation of his new middle-class identity, he changes his name from Ragged Dick to "Richard Hunter, Esquire" and in the last line of the novel is hailed by his roommate as "a young gentleman on the way to fame and fortune."[2]

It was most fortunate for the young bootblack that a merchant's son chose the morning of Dick's visit to Greenwood, Brooklyn's rural cemetery, to fall into the East River. But Dick's rise to respectability was not entirely due to lucky breaks. Early in the novel, he displays a number of personal qualities that distinguish him from the bootblacks around him. First, Dick is aggressive. He is openly critical of his friend Johnny Nolan who "ain't got no ambition. I'll bet he won't get five shines today." Dick, by contrast, has an "eye to business"; he is forever hustling up customers by looking "sharply in the faces of all who passed, addressing each with, 'Shine yer boots, sir?' " More important than Dick's salesmanlike aggressiveness, however, is his energetic drive in seizing the main chance. When he overhears Mr. Whitney telling his nephew Frank that he is too busy to show him the city, Dick, "being an enterprising young man, . . . thought he saw a chance for a speculation, and determined to avail himself of it." He steps forward and offers himself as Frank's guide, a service which earns him a new suit, a five-dollar bill, and some invaluable advice on how to rise in the world. Similarly, when the little boy falls off the ferry, Dick dives to the rescue without a second thought and is praised by a boatman for his "pluck." When Alger spoke of his boy heroes' pluck, he referred not simply to their courage but to the aggressiveness of their pursuit of success.[3]

Dick is also distinguished from the bootblacks around him by his charm, his powers of personal attraction. He is early recommended to the reader as a good-looking boy, with "a frank, straight-forward manner that made him a favorite." He is also something of a stand-up comic, "always ready to joke," especially with his customers, who respond well to his self-deprecatory banter. "I have to pay such a big rent for my manshun up on Fifth Avenoo," he says to one, "that I can't afford to take less than ten cents a shine." Sometimes Dick uses humor as a sly form of flattery, as when he chatters with the "slatternly servant" of the boardinghouse where he plans to rent a room. "Well, Queen Victoria," he says when the girl comes to the door, "is your missus at home?" When the stupid girl replies that her name is Bridget, Dick continues, "Oh indeed! . . . you looked so much like the queen's picter what she gave me last Christmas in exchange for mine, that I couldn't help calling you by her name." Much of Dick's charm lies in his ability to please those around him by making them laugh. And the usefulness of his charm is very evident, whether he is entertaining his customers while shining their shoes or reassuring Mr. Whitney about his suitableness as a tour guide for Frank.[4]

The third quality that distinguishes Dick from his fellow boot-blacks is the most significant: it is his skill as a confidence man. Almost immediately after praising Dick for his frank, straightfor-ward manner, Alger confessed with ill-concealed delight that his hero sometimes

> played tricks on unsophisticated boys from the country or gave a wrong direction to honest old gentlemen unused to the city. A clergyman in search of the Cooper Institute he once directed to the Tombs Prison, and, following him unobserved, was highly delighted when the unsuspicious stranger walked up the front steps of the great stone building on Centre Street, and tried to obtain admission.

Three confidence games are played by the street-wise bootblack in the course of the novel. In the first, Dick convinces a hideous old woman selling apples on the street that he is a government official sent to collect her taxes, and offers to take his payment in fruit. For his next trick Dick actually beats another confidence man at his own game. A stranger shows Dick and Frank a fat wallet that he has just picked off the sidewalk and offers to let Dick return it to its rightful owner if the boy will give him twenty dollars as his share of the reward. Dick disingenuously assents and hands him a bill, and the stranger hurries away. Dick then shows Frank that the wallet is stuffed with blank paper and explains that he has slipped the stranger "a dry-goods circular got up to imitate a bank-bill." Before long, the furious pocketbook dropper returns to demand his wallet. Dick refuses, and the two tricksters begin to argue:

"You gave me a bogus bill," said the man.
"It's what I use myself," said Dick.
"You've swindled me."
"I thought it was the other way."

At last the angry man leaves the field in defeat, and Dick smugly tells Frank, "I aint knocked round the city streets all my life for nothin'." In his third confidence game Dick tracks down a swindler who has tricked a rural greenhorn out of fifty dollars in cash by offering him a check for sixty dollars on a bogus bank. Again, he out-cons a confidence man, by falsely informing him that a police-man will seize him unless he returns the cash to Dick. In the second part of his own game, Dick relocates the swindler's victim and calls out, "Have you found your money?" The unhappy bumpkin begins to cry and Dick returns his money. Then, when the grateful youth invites him to the country, Dick concludes his game by replying that he would like to bring his wife. "Jonathan stared at him in amaze-ment, uncertain whether to credit the fact of his marriage. Dick walked on with Frank, leaving him in an apparent state of stupefac-tion, and it is possible that he has not yet settled the affair to his satisfaction." The country youth has been taken in by two confi-dence men, one of whom is Alger's boy hero, whose skill as a trickster enables him successfully to negotiate the moral wilderness of New York.[5]

The success formula elaborated in the works of Horatio Alger represented a significant departure from the antebellum success myth. In the first half of the nineteenth century, middle-class Americans believed that the key to success was character formation: any man who cultivated the virtues of industry, sobriety, and frugality might triumph over circumstances to rise as high as he desired. Underpinning this formula for success was a supernatural-istic cosmology, the belief that a benevolent God operating in a universe of reason and law would reward virtue with worldly success. This nineteenth-century association of personal virtue and material prosperity was rooted in the American Puritan tradition. But seventeenth-century Calvinists, as Max Weber showed in *The Protestant Ethic and the Spirit of Capitalism,* worked hard in their callings for the greater glory of God. By the nineteenth century the idea of calling had been subtly secularized; men now directed their attention less to hard work for the greater glory of God, and more to character formation as a bulwark against temptation in a dangerous world. Nonetheless, Americans in the first half of the century continued to hold fast to the traditional Protestant synthesis of the religious and the secular callings. Within the new, theologically liberalized version of the Protestant ethic, the man who diligently practiced the ascetic self-discipline that had been definitively set forth by Benjamin Franklin would be rewarded in this lifetime with worldly prosperity. He who cultivated industry, sobriety, and frugality had merely to stand and wait for the success that would inevitably be bestowed upon him by a benevolent and fair-minded God.[6]

Horatio Alger's *Ragged Dick* did not abandon the character ethic completely: even before Dick launches his pursuit of respectability, he displays some honesty, great industry, and complete self-reliance. But Dick's rise depends on three qualities new to American success ideology: aggressiveness, charm, and the arts of the confidence man. Throughout his approximately 120 novels Horatio Alger betrayed his conviction that character alone could no longer ensure success in the new world of postbellum America. Some historians of American success mythology have seen Horatio Alger as a "nostalgic spokesman for a dying order"—an order of small businesses and partnerships, not large corporations; of mercantile firms, not industrial enterprises; of moderate economic security, not vast fortunes.[7] In this view, Alger

> is able to present the traditional pattern of middle-class economic ideals in late nineteenth-century dress and fill the bustling streets and thoroughfares of a nineteenth-century industrial metropolis with a nostalgic reincarnation of the ideal *eighteenth-century* merchant and his noble young apprentice.[8]

Nonetheless, the success formula established by Horatio Alger departed significantly from the character ethic embraced by middle-class Americans before the Civil War. At the center of that new formula was a demand not for ascetic self-discipline, but for the arts of social manipulation. Ultimately, Dick's aggressiveness and his charm were subsumed under his larger skill as a confidence man.

Before the middle of the nineteenth century, few books had been devoted entirely to economic self-help; character formation was more a moral than an economic concern, and explicit discussions of how to succeed appeared primarily in stray chapters of the advice manuals. But after the Civil War, success manuals "swelled from a trickle to a flood"; four out of five success guides published before 1900 appeared after 1865.[9] These new success guides repeatedly stressed the personal qualities so essential to Ragged Dick's success. First, ambitious young men were encouraged to be aggressive: "Fortune," one manual advised, "favors the bold."[10] Indeed, it was asserted, fortune favored the impudent: "A man without impudence where impudence is needed, is a poor unfortunate child, one that had better have been born in some honester world."[11] In a dishonest world, success demanded boldness, energy, "push," decision, earnestness, "true grit," and above all, the Algerian quality of pluck.[12] Just as Ragged Dick had aggressively stepped forward to capitalize on Mr. Whitney's need for a tour guide, readers of late nineteenth-century success manuals were urged to go forth and seize the main chance. "Pluck," they were told, "is everything. You may just as well be contented and satisfied to remain where you are as to expect to meet with any degree of success in any business you may engage in, unless you are possessed with an abundance of this essential element."[13] And just as Ragged Dick had aggressively hustled customers on the streets of New York, ambitious young men were encouraged to call attention to themselves and their abilities through what one writer called "self-trumpeting":

> Not only in trade, but in all the professions, self-trumpeting is now acknowledged to be the great talisman of success, and the man who can blow his horn the longest and loudest is regarded as the most likely to reach the pinnacle of riches and respectability, if not of honor.[14]

The second quality displayed by Ragged Dick that was stressed throughout the success manuals of the period was his charm. Because "a cheery face and a civil tongue go a long way towards helping one on the road to fortune," the ambitious youth was urged to "cultivate the friendly spirit."[15] Cheerfulness and a good sense of humor were critical to success because, in the words of Matthew

Hale Smith, "wit and humor are magnetic."[16] In smiling and bantering with his customers and his patrons, Ragged Dick had been exerting a magnetic force that was, in Smith's view, essential to his rise. By the late nineteenth century, personal magnetism was regarded as one of the most important qualities to be cultivated by ambitious youth.[17] Personal magnetism was that which enabled a man to compel others "to follow and obey him whether they will or not."[18] But magnetism was a subtle form of domination that could "move upon others, bending them as the wind sways a field of grain."[19] The man of magnetism thus possessed in abundance what the new success literature called "executive ability," the art of acting as a "master and manager of human conduct."[20] Ragged Dick, though only a bootblack, through his charm had exerted powers of executive ability that had assisted his rise to respectability. Within the new success formula emerging in the late nineteenth century, only the man of magnetism could rise in society because only he could manage the men around him. The "art of handling marble," wrote Newell D. Hillis in 1896, "is nothing compared to the art of handling men."[21]

Personal magnetism was, of course, one of the salient characteristics of the confidence man, and the new emphasis placed on executive management pointed to a growing willingness to regard success as a form of confidence game. In late nineteenth-century success ideology, the manipulation of others through artifice was coming to be accepted as a necessary executive skill: "There are arts by which we read the hearts of men, and artifices by which we mould them to our purposes. The human heart is an engine to be operated and controlled like other engines."[22] The "first and fundamental principle" of all "dealings with men" is "that it is not enough for us to *do*, we must also *seem* . . . it is no unimportant matter to keep up appearances."[23] Whereas antebellum advice literature had cautioned young men never to cultivate outward appearances at the expense of inner realities, postbellum success manuals advised their readers about how to manipulate appearances to their own advantage. The demand of the older character ethic for diligent industry, for example, was yielding in the late nineteenth century to a new emphasis on "putting on the appearance of business"—that is, of appearing to be busy even when one was idle. One manual approvingly told the story of a new young physician who quickly established a vast practice by putting on the appearance of a vast practice: he spent every day driving his horses into the country and pushing them until they were white with foam, until the townspeople came to believe he must be very busy and began to seek his medical care.[24] Similarly, late nineteenth-century manuals instructed their readers to keep up a good front when business was bad: "Convince the public that business is looking up; be jovial in spirits, for bad news spreads quickly. If there is an opportunity to boom business, so do; don't pull a long face, but hold up your head and look pleasant."[25] Just as Ragged Dick had jovially informed customers that he lived in a Fifth Avenue mansion, the smart businessman was to maintain an appearance of prosperity even when on the brink of ruin. As one magazine article of the period admitted, "a tinge of charlatanism seems, indeed, almost necessary to a career, whether in business, literature, art, or science."[26]

Antebellum advice manuals had condemned magnetism as the illicit art of the confidence man, deplored the use of artifice to manage the conduct of others, criticized all attention to falsely keeping up appearances, and forbidden professional charlatanism in any form. By the late nineteenth century such concerns had virtually disappeared not only from success manuals but also from books of moral advice for young men. In fact, the wily confidence man himself had all but vanished from the pages of this literature. Although young men were still warned against the evils of the gambling den and the theater, of liquor and loose women and lewd literature, they received few warnings about the evil seducer who would try to lure them to such vices. Even when the youth was warned against evil companions, they were not usually represented as confidence men, but simply as bad influences over his development.[27] The major reason for the confidence man's disappearance from advice literature was the growing acceptance of the idea that the young American on the make had to become a kind of confidence man himself in order to succeed.

Nineteenth-century self-improvement literature did retain a moralistic tone until nearly the turn of the twentieth century. Most success manuals written between 1870 and 1900, like those of the antebellum period, stated at least cursorily that the cultivation of industry, sobriety, and frugality were important to the pursuit of success. But by the 1870s, the character ethic that had dominated ideas about success was weakening. By the last decades of the century, according to John Cawelti, the "final breakdown of the old ideal of self-improvement before the demands of a new social and economic order" was symbolized in the New Thought movement, which attempted to codify the laws of magnetism within a pseudo-scientific framework involving phrenology, animal magnetism, spiritualism, and mesmerism.[28] Once, the American youth had been urged simply to form a virtuous character and then wait for success to come to him; now he was taught to cultivate the proper "scientific" techniques in order to wrest success from life.

What were the reasons behind this late nineteenth-century decline of the character ethic? First, middle-class Americans were growing more aware of the class structure of their industrial society: "The inequities that characterized the period—the enormous accumulation of wealth by a few, on the one hand, and the poverty of the masses of men, on the other—strained the faith of even the most credulous."[29] A suspicion arose that the ordinary man had fewer chances of success than at an earlier time: "Croakers say that the time for young men to compete for the prize has passed,—that the coveted places of thrift and honor are over-crowded, and that now young men must content themselves with a back seat and small acquisitions."[30] Growing doubts about the openness of the American social system were often expressed in discussions of the importance of aggressiveness to the pursuit of success. "While there is so much striving and struggling, so much pulling and pushing, so much joggling and jostling, a man would be driven to starvation, if he did not leave his modesty at home when he started out for the contests of the day."[31] The character ethic may have continued to shape the attitudes of some prominent businessmen toward their own success, but Social Darwinism was nonetheless evident in passages such as this: "We move in accordance with immutable law, not luck, and play our characters on the stage of life, not as the puppets of chance, but as the product and result of everlasting pressing on for supremacy."[32] The antebellum character ethic had rested on the belief that in an open society anyone who was morally deserving might rise to social and economic prominence. By the late nineteenth century that faith was being eroded by the conviction that the upper ranks of American society were beginning to close.

A second reason for the erosion of the character ethic was "the crisis of faith in the Gilded Age."[33] The traditional association of personal virtue and material prosperity had been held together by a supernaturalistic cosmology, the Protestant faith in an ordered universe presided over by a benevolent deity who actively guided the affairs of men to ensure the material rewards of ascetic self-discipline. By the late nineteenth century, that cosmology was under challenge from Darwinism and scientific naturalism, higher biblical criticism and the study of comparative religions, and the rise of philosophical positivism.[34] This growing unwillingness to place confidence in a supernaturalistic cosmology was most evident in the rise of the pseudoscientific "laws of success," especially the law of magnetism.[35] In the law of magnetism, the older faith that virtue would be rewarded with success in a moral universe yielded to a new insistence that only a skillful manipulation of magnetic forces would ensure success in a scientific universe.

The third and most important reason for the late nineteenth-century decline of the character ethic was the gradual replacement of an earlier entrepreneurial pattern of success with a predominantly white-collar pattern. The character ethic, with its emphasis on ascetic self-discipline, had been well suited to an early industrial capitalist stage of economic development dominated by self-employed entrepreneurs along the model of Benjamin Franklin. The new success formula emerging late in the nineteenth century was tailored to the demands of large-scale corporate capitalism:

> The imperatives of attracting attention in a large organization and winning notice and patronage among myriad competitors put a further premium on self-confidence and dynamic personality. By the end of the nineteenth century, self-help books were dominated by the ethos of salesmanship and boosterism.[36]

Within the new corporate context, personality skills, such as that subtle quality called charm, were more useful to the ambitious youth than the qualities of industry, sobriety, and frugality; executive ability or management—the art of manipulating others to do what you want them to do—was far more valuable than the ascetic self-discipline of an earlier era. In sentimental America, the term *influence* had meant the moral force exerted by one character upon another, a force that could either uplift or contaminate. By the late nineteenth century, influence had been adapted to the new success formula as a hard-nosed business technique designed to advance its practitioner at the expense of others within his organization.[37] The central skill demanded within the new success formula was the art of social manipulation that had been cultivated to perfection by the antebellum trickster. The executive manager emerging in this new phase of industrial capitalism was, in Donald Meyer's term, a "psycho-social organizational symphonist"—a corporate version of the antebellum confidence man.[38]

In *The Culture of Narcissism: American Life in an Age of Diminishing Expectations,* Christopher Lasch has discussed in sweeping terms this transformation of American success mythology. Lasch traces the origins of the new formula to the "bureaucratization of the corporate career" which forced "ambitious young men . . . to compete with their peers for the attention and approval of their superiors." With the rise of corporate business structure, the self-made man has undergone a complete transformation:

> In earlier times, the self-made man took pride in his judgment of character and probity; today he anxiously scans the faces of his fellows not so as to evaluate their credit but in order to gauge their susceptibility to his own blandishments. He practices the classic arts of seduction and with the same indifference to moral niceties, hoping to win your heart while picking your pocket. The happy hooker stands in place of Horatio Alger as the prototype of personal success.

As the management of interpersonal relations came to be considered the key to personal advancement in the late nineteenth century, Lasch argues, "The captain of industry gave way to the confidence man, the master of impressions." In the twentieth century, the classic statement of this new model for success has been Dale Carnegie's *How to Win Friends and Influence People.* As preached by Carnegie and other more recent proponents of the new formula, the art of success is the projection of "winning images." The hallmark of mid- to late-twentieth-century success manuals has been "their lack of interest in the substance of success" and the "candor" of their insistence "that appearances—'winning images'— count for more than performance, ascription for more than achievement." Lasch's use of the term *candor* here is ironic. For the insistence of twentieth-century success manuals on winning images, in a sense, betrays anything but a high valuation of sincerity per se. The pursuit of a winning image, whether reflected in the charm of Ragged Dick or in the mid-twentieth-century formula that Lasch savagely calls "the deadly game of intimidating friends and seducing people," is a confidence game that demands of its players precisely those personal qualities that were condemned by middle-class sentimentalists in the antebellum period.[39]

The replacement of the captain of industry with the confidence man in American success mythology clearly demonstrates a critical shift in middle-class attitudes toward the sincere ideal. As Donald

Meyer has argued in *The Positive Thinkers,* Dale Carnegie's formula for winning friends and influencing people effectively absorbed the sincere ideal into a system of twentieth-century corporate gamesmanship. Carnegie's system, in Meyer's view, endeavored "to bring the occasion of insincerity into the heart—and make it sincere." Carnegie's secret for winning friends and influencing people was to make others feel important by smiling at them, and Carnegie insisted on the sincerity of those smiles. But he did not offer any instruction on how sincerely to like people; in fact, despite its title, his book has virtually nothing to say about friendship. What, then, was sincere about the smile of the ambitious follower of the Carnegie system? "It was rather that the man who used smiles must believe in the smiles directed at him. His sincere smile was his allegiance to the system of smiles." Carnegie's purpose was to train men in a very special type of corporate salesmanship, "the salesmanship of the system selling itself to itself." But the problem of sincerity was not so easily resolved, for "trying to solve the problem of sincerity by self-manipulation involved one in an infinite regression, an endless effort to disarm oneself as well as others." Meyer sees Carnegie's formula as a kind of self-hypnosis, "a self-automated caricature of [the] personal-magnetism ideal." This "spiritual automation, new style" ultimately presented the spectacle of the salesman trying to sell himself to himself, like a confidence man who acts as his own "mark."[40]

On one level, the sentimental ideal of sincerity has continued to be an important strain in American middle-class life and has provided a recurring formula for self-criticism within a culture still plagued with the problems of social mobility. But on another level, the corporate gamesmanship of Dale Carnegie and his many imitators points to a complete transformation of the sincere ideal in twentieth-century middle-class culture. Perhaps the best expression of the corporate impact on the sincere ideal lies in Dale Carnegie's "Seven Rules for Making Your Home Life Happier." In this final section of *How to Win Friends and Influence People,* Carnegie unabashedly states how his principles of corporate social interaction may be applied to domestic life. "No woman," he writes, quoting Dorothy Dix, "can ever understand why a man doesn't put forth the same effort to make his home a going concern as he does to make his business or profession a success." Having thus stated that success in marriage demands the same social skills as success in business, Carnegie and Dix continue:

Every man knows that he can jolly his wife into doing anything, and doing without anything. He knows that if he hands her a few cheap compliments about what a wonderful manager she is, and how she helps him, she will squeeze every nickle [sic]. Every man knows that if he tells his wife how beautiful and lovely she looks in her last year's dress, she wouldn't trade it for the latest Paris importation. Every man knows that he can kiss his wife's eyes shut until she will be blind as a bat, and that he has only to give her a warm smack on the lips to make her dumb as an oyster.

And every wife knows that her husband knows these things about her, because she has furnished him with a complete diagram about how to work her.[41]

"So," Carnegie concludes, "if you want to keep your home life happy, Rule 6 is, *Be courteous*."[42] Popular views of domestic courtesy had come a long way from the sentimental ideal of a century earlier. To antebellum sentimentalists, any man who used cheap compliments and sexual attention to manipulate a woman to do what he wanted could only have been understood as an evil seducer. Any man or woman whose social relationships were calculated on the basis of a complete diagram on how to work others would have been condemned as a confidence man or a painted woman. In the success mythology of twentieth-century corporate America, the confidence man has been effectively welcomed into the mainstream of American middle-class culture.

Notes

Preface

1. W. L. Burn, *The Age of Equipoise: A Study of the Mid-Victorian Generation*, p. 43.
2. See Lytton Strachey, *Eminent Victorians;* Walter E. Houghton, *The Victorian Frame of Mind, 1830–1870*, chap. 14; Steven Marcus, *The Other Victorians: A Study of Sexuality and Pornography in Mid-Nineteenth-Century England;* E. J. Hobsbawm, *The Age of Capital, 1848–1875*, pp. 232–37; Charles Dickens, *The Life and Adventures of Martin Chuzzlewit* (Boston: Fields, Osgood and Co., 1861); Burn, *Age of Equipoise*, chap. 1.
3. See E. Douglas Branch, *The Sentimental Years, 1836–1860: A Social History*, preface; Herbert Ross Brown, *The Sentimental Novel in America, 1789–1860;* Ann Douglas, *The Feminization of American Culture*, p. 12.
4. Houghton, *Victorian Frame of Mind*, p. 424.
5. Burn, *Age of Equipoise*, p. 43.
6. See A. Douglas, *Feminization of American Culture*, pp. 290–93.

Chapter 1

1. Albert Barnes, introduction to *Young Man's Closet Library*, by Robert Phillip (1857), quoted in Joseph F. Kett, *Rites of Passage: Adolescence in America, 1790 to the Present*, p. 95. For statistics on publications, see Kett, *Rites of Passage*, p. 95; Carl Bode, *Antebellum Culture*, p. 125.
2. Eugene Arden, "The Evil City in American Fiction," p. 261.
3. *The Autobiography of Benjamin Franklin* (New York: Random House, 1944), pp. 29–30.
4. John Todd, *The Young Man: Hints Addressed to the Young Men of the United States*, p. 122.

211

5. *Autobiography of Benjamin Franklin,* pp. 40, 48, 37–48.

6. Henry Ward Beecher, *Seven Lectures to Young Men, on Various Important Subjects: Delivered Before the Young Men of Indianapolis, Indiana, during the Winter of 1843–4,* preface.

7. David Magie, *The Spring-time of Life; or, Advice to Youth,* p. 9.

8. Rufus W. Clark, *Lectures on the Formation of Character, Temptations and Mission of Young Men,* p. 28.

9. William A. Alcott, *Familiar Letters to Young Men on Various Subjects. Designed as a Companion to the Young Man's Guide,* pp. 180–81.

10. Jared Bell Waterbury, *Considerations for Young Men,* p. 27.

11. For a discussion of the sentimental concept of influence, see Ann Douglas, *The Feminization of American Culture,* chap. 2.

12. Magie, *Spring-time,* p. 68.

13. Ibid., p. 21.

14. Beecher, *Seven Lectures,* p. 91.

15. Clark, *Lectures,* p. 198.

16. Magie, *Spring-time,* p. 42.

17. For discussions of mesmerism in nineteenth-century America, see John D. Davies, *Phrenology, Fad and Science: A Nineteenth-century American Crusade,* chap. 11; Madeline B. Stern, *Heads and Headlines: The Phrenological Fowlers,* chap. 5, passim; Gail Thain Parker, *Mind Cure in New England from the Civil War to World War I,* pp. 3–4, passim. The miasmic theory of cholera is discussed in Charles E. Rosenberg, *The Cholera Years: The United States in 1832, 1849, and 1866.*

18. Clark, *Lectures,* p. 185; Beecher, *Seven Lectures,* p. 89.

19. Beecher, *Seven Lectures,* p. 78.

20. Clark, *Lectures,* pp. 170–71.

21. Waterbury, *Considerations,* p. 67.

22. Beecher, *Seven Lectures,* p. 90.

23. Waterbury, *Considerations,* p. 104.

24. Clark, *Lectures,* pp. 185, 36–37.

25. Beecher, *Seven Lectures,* pp. 100–01.

26. See Johannes Dietrich Bergmann, "The Original Confidence Man," pp. 560–77; Michael S. Reynolds, "The Prototype of Melville's Confidence Man," *PMLA* 86 (October 1971): 1009–13; Neil Harris, *Humbug! The Art of P. T. Barnum,* pp. 224–25.

27. Review in Boston *Evening Transcript,* 10 April 1857, quoted in Bergmann, "The Original Confidence Man," p. 574.

28. Bergmann, "The Original Confidence Man," p. 574.

29. Roger Lane, *Policing the City: Boston 1822–1885,* pp. 143–44.

30. Lane, *Policing the City,* p. 54.

31. Quoted in Lane, *Policing the City,* p. 69.

32. Quoted in Herbert Asbury, *Sucker's Progress: An Informal History of Gambling in America from the Colonies to Canfield,* p. 158.

33. Ibid., p. 160.

34. Quoted, ibid.

35. [Ferdinand Longchamp], *Asmodeus in New-York* (New York: Longchamp and Co., 1868; reprint ed., New York: Arno Press, 1975), p. 141.

36. *Wood's Illustrated Handbook of New York City*, quoted in R. Richard Wohl, "The 'Country Boy' Myth and Its Place in American Urban Culture: The Nineteenth-century Contribution," p. 104.

37. Bernard Bailyn, *The Ideological Origins of the American Revolution*, p. 56.

38. *New York Evening Post*, 16 November 1747; quoted in Bailyn, *Ideological Origins*, p. 233.

39. In addition to Bailyn, see Gordon S. Wood, *The Creation of the American Republic, 1776–1787*, pt. 1; and Robert E. Shalhope, "Toward a Republican Synthesis: The Emergence of an Understanding of Republicanism in American Historiography," pp. 49–80.

40. Artemus Bowers Muzzey, *The Young Man's Friend*, p. 116.

41. Edwin Hubbell Chapin, *Duties of Young Men, Exhibited in Six Lectures; with an Anniversary Address, Delivered before the Richmond Lyceum*, p. 204.

42. George Forgie, *Patricide in the House Divided: A Psychological Interpretation of Lincoln and His Age*, p. 13.

43. Ibid., chap. 1.

44. Fred Somkin, *Unquiet Eagle: Memory and Desire in the Idea of American Freedom, 1815–1860*, chap. 1.

45. David B. Davis, "Some Themes of Countersubversion: An Analysis of Anti-Masonic, Anti-Catholic, and Anti-Mormon Literature," in Davis, ed., *The Fear of Conspiracy: Images of Un-American Subversion from the Revolution to the Present*, pp. 9–22.

46. Marvin Meyers, *The Jacksonian Persuasion: Politics and Belief*, p. 23.

47. Quoted in Somkin, *Unquiet Eagle*, p. 32.

48. Forgie, *Patricide*, p. 15.

49. G. Wood, *Creation of the American Republic*, p. 100.

50. Michael Kammen, *A Season of Youth: The American Revolution and the Historical Imagination*.

51. Waterbury, *Considerations*, p. 103.

52. Joel Hawes, *Lectures Addressed to the Young Men of Hartford and New-Haven*, p. 41.

53. Waterbury, *Considerations*, p. 104.

54. Todd, *Young Men*, p. 136.

55. James A. Henretta, *The Evolution of American Society, 1700–1815: An Interdisciplinary Analysis*, chap. 2; Philip J. Greven, *Four Generations: Population, Land, and Family in Colonial Andover, Massachusetts;* Kenneth A. Lockridge, "Land, Population, and the Evolution of New England Society, 1630–1790," in Gary B. Nash, ed., *Class and*

Society in Early America, pp. 149–66; Stuart Bruchey, *The Roots of American Economic Growth 1607–1861: An Essay in Social Causation;* Joseph F. Kett, "Growing Up in Rural New England, 1800–1850," in Tamara K. Hareven, ed., *Anonymous Americans: Explorations in Nineteenth Century Social History,* pp. 1–16; Allan Horlick, *Country Boys and Merchant Princes: The Social Control of Young Men in New York,* p. 11; Paul E. Johnson, *A Shopkeeper's Millennium: Society and Revivals in Rochester, New York, 1815–1837.*

　　56. Henretta, *Evolution,* chaps. 1, 2, 4; Greven, *Four Generations;* Bernard Bailyn, *Education in the Forming of American Society: Needs and Opportunities for Study;* David Montgomery, "The Working Classes of the Preindustrial American City, 1790–1830," pp. 3–22; Johnson, *A Shopkeeper's Millennium;* Michael B. Katz, *The People of Hamilton, Canada West: Family and Class in a Mid-Nineteenth-Century City,* p. 212.

　　57. Nancy F. Cott, *The Bonds of Womanhood: "Woman's Sphere" in New England, 1780–1835,* pp. 187–88.

　　58. Beecher, *Seven Lectures,* p. 94.

　　59. Muzzey, *Young Man's Friend,* p. 107.

　　60. Beecher, *Seven Lectures,* p. 96.

　　61. Todd, *Young Man,* pp. 31–32.

　　62. Muzzey, *Young Man's Friend,* p. 117.

　　63. Robert Kelley, "Ideology and Political Culture from Jefferson to Nixon," p. 541. Also see Ronald P. Formisano, "Deferential-Participant Politics: The Early Republic's Political Culture, 1789–1840," pp. 473–87; Michael Wallace, "Changing Concepts of Party in the United States: New York, 1815–1828," pp. 453–91.

　　64. Bertram Wyatt-Brown, "Prelude to Abolitionism: Sabbatarian Politics and the Rise of the Second Party System," p. 340.

　　65. Muzzey, *Young Man's Friend,* p. 131.

　　66. Chapin, *Duties,* p. 92; Alexis de Tocqueville, *Democracy in America,* 1: 264–80.

　　67. See Edwin C. Rozwenc, ed., *Ideology and Power in the Age of Jackson,* introduction.

　　68. Lynn L. Marshall, "The Strange Stillbirth of the Whig Party," p. 449.

　　69. Leonard Richards, *Gentlemen of Property and Standing: Anti-Abolition Mobs in Jacksonian America.*

　　70. Clark, *Lectures,* pp. 178–79.

　　71. Alcott, *Young Man's Guide,* p. 158.

　　72. Ibid., p. 160.

　　73. Beecher, *Seven Lectures,* p. 53.

　　74. Ibid.

　　75. Clark, *Lectures,* p. 225.

　　76. Magie, *Spring-time,* p. 155.

　　77. Clark, *Lectures,* p. 267.

　　78. Beecher, *Seven Lectures,* p. 121.

79. Ibid., p. 33.
80. Douglass C. North, *The Economic Growth of the United States;* Bruchey, *Roots of Economic Growth.*
81. James A. Henretta, "Families and Farms: Mentalité in Pre-industrial America," pp. 3–32.
82. Meyers, *Jacksonian Persuasion,* p. 26.
83. Beecher, *Seven Lectures,* pp. 52, 32, 33, 105.
84. Henretta, *Evolution,* p. 165.
85. Ibid., p. 211.
86. Muzzey, *Young Man's Friend,* p. 119.
87. See Perry Miller, *The New England Mind: From Colony to Province,* pp. 33–39. For an excellent discussion of the enduring power of the jeremiad from the seventeenth to the nineteenth century, see Sacvan Bercovitch, *The American Jeremiad.*
88. See G. Wood, *Creation of the American Republic;* A. Douglas, *Feminization of American Culture;* Daniel Calhoun, *Professional Lives in America: Structure and Aspiration, 1750–1858,* chaps. 1, 4; Richard D. Brown, "Modernization and the Modern Personality in Early America, 1600–1865: A Sketch of a Synthesis," pp. 201–28.
89. Clark, *Lectures,* p. 105.
90. Ibid., p. 98.
91. Hawes, *Lectures,* pp. 15–16.
92. Beecher, *Seven Lectures,* pp. 169–70, 193.
93. Henretta, *Evolution,* p. 212.
94. See John W. Ward, *Andrew Jackson: Symbol for an Age;* William G. McLoughlin, Jr., *Modern Revivalism: Charles Grandison Finney to Billy Graham* (New York: Ronald Press Co., 1959), chap. 1; Herman Melville, *Moby Dick* (Indianapolis: Bobbs-Merrill, 1964); Nathaniel Hawthorne, *The Blithedale Romance* (New York: W. W. Norton and Co., 1978); Alcott, *Young Man's Guide,* p. 55; Ralph Waldo Emerson, *Representative Men: Seven Lectures* (Boston: Phillips, Sampson and Co., 1850), pp. 219–53; William Ellery Leonard, *Byron and Byronism in America* (Boston: Nichols Press, 1905), chap. 2; Clark, *Lectures,* pp. 92–95.
95. Mary Douglas, *Purity and Danger: An Analysis of Concepts of Pollution and Taboo,* p. 102.
96. Clark, *Lectures,* pp. 134–36; Beecher, *Seven Lectures,* p. 169.
97. Magie, *Spring-time,* p. 188.
98. Hawes, *Lectures,* p. 65.
99. Chapin, *Duties,* p. 137.
100. Ibid., p. 212.
101. Hawes, *Lectures,* p. 81.
102. Clark, *Lectures,* p. 72.
103. Chapin, *Duties,* pp. 34–35.
104. Arnold van Gennep, quoted in Victor Turner, *The Ritual Process: Structure and Anti-Structure,* p. 94.
105. Kett, *Rites of Passage,* p. 31.

106. Turner, *Ritual Process*, p. 95.

107. See Irvin G. Wyllie, *The Self-Made Man in America: The Myth of Rags to Riches;* John G. Cawelti, *Apostles of the Self-Made Man: Changing Concepts of Success in America;* Richard M. Huber, *The American Idea of Success.*

108. Cawelti, *Apostles*, p. 42.

109. Alcott, *Young Man's Guide*, p. 29.

110. Magie, *Spring-time*, p. 251.

111. Edward Pessen, ed., *Three Centuries of Social Mobility in America*, pt. 2. In this collection, see Stuart Blumin, "Residential and Occupational Mobility in Antebellum Philadelphia," pp. 59–92; Pessen, "The Myth of Antebellum Social Mobility and Equality of Opportunity," pp. 110–21. Also see Stephan Thernstrom, *Poverty and Progress: Social Mobility in a Nineteenth Century City;* Pessen, *Riches, Class, and Power before the Civil War;* Pessen, *Jacksonian America: Society, Personality, and Politics*, chap. 5; Clyde Griffen, "Making It in America: Social Mobility in Mid-nineteenth-century Poughkeepsie," pp. 479–99.

112. Blumin, "Antebellum Philadelphia," p. 91.

113. Thernstrom, *Poverty and Progress*, chap. 6; Calvin Colton, quoted in Rozwenc, ed., *Ideology and Power*, p. 356.

114. See Burton J. Bledstein, *The Culture of Professionalism: The Middle Class and the Development of Higher Education in America*, pp. 8–25.

115. Turner, *Ritual Process*, p. 107.

116. See Constance Rourke, *American Humor: A Study of the National Character*, chap. 2; Susan Kuhlmann, *Knave, Fool, and Genius: The Confidence Man as He Appears in Nineteenth Century American Fiction*, chap. 1.

117. Kenneth S. Lynn, *Mark Twain and Southwestern Humor* (Boston: Little, Brown and Co., 1959), p. 78; Johnson Jones Hooper, *Adventures of Captain Simon Suggs*, quoted in Cawelti, *Apostles*, p. 71.

118. Rourke, *American Humor*, chap. 1; Warwick Wadlington, *The Confidence Game in American Literature*, chap. 1.

119. *The Life of P. T. Barnum* (New York: Redfield, 1855), dedication. Also see Harris, *Humbug!*, chap. 8.

120. Quoted in Rourke, *American Humor*, p. 73.

121. Quoted in Harris, *Humbug!*, p. 212.

122. George W. Pierson, "The M-Factor in American History," p. 286.

123. See Kuhlmann, *Knave, Fool, and Genius*, preface.

124. William R. Taylor, *Cavalier and Yankee: The Old South and American National Character.*

125. Wadlington, *Confidence Game*, pp. 10–11. For an excellent discussion of the confidence man as a covert American cultural hero, see Gary Lindberg, *The Confidence Man in American Literature.*

126. Cawelti, *Apostles*, pp. 73–75; Somkin, *Unquiet Eagle*, chap. 1.

Chapter 2

1. Clark, *Lectures,* p. 1♔.
2. Hawes, *Lectures,* p. 76.
3. After 1660, every edition of the Connecticut laws issued this order; see David H. Flaherty, *Privacy in Colonial New England,* p. 173.
4. Ibid., pp. 173–74.
5. See Lyn H. Lofland, *A World of Strangers: Order and Action in Urban Public Space,* chap. 1.
6. See Zane L. Miller, *The Urbanization of Modern America: A Brief History,* chap. 2; Kenneth T. Jackson and Stanley K. Schultz, eds., *Cities in American History,* introductions to pts. 1 and 3.
7. Lofland distinguishes three major reasons why population growth generates anonymity: (1) individual biophysical limitations on the ability to recognize others, a limitation which she guesses to arise at 3,000 to 4,000 people; (2) structural limitations to knowing others due to increasing occupational differentiation, and (3) time limitations to knowing all those who have recently arrived or are just passing through. In a city of 10,000 or more, she estimates, there are clearly too many people for one to know personally, enough occupational differentiation to pose structural obstacles to knowing others, and a competitive advantage over other cities in drawing immigrants that presents temporal limitations on knowing others. See Lofland, *World of Strangers,* pp. 8–12.
8. In 1820, only 12 cities had over 10,000 inhabitants, and only 2 of these had populations of over 100,000; in 1860, 101 cities exceeded 10,000 people, with 8 numbering over 100,000 and the city of New York passing the 1,000,000 mark. See Z. Miller, *Urbanization,* p. 26. For statistics on the multiplication of cities with populations of 5,000, 10,000 or 20,000 between 1820 and 1860, see Stuart M. Blumin, *The Urban Threshold: Growth and Change in a Nineteenth-century American Community,* pp. 1–10.
9. Peter R. Knights, *The Plain People of Boston, 1830–1860: A Study in City Growth,* chap. 4. Knights's work reveals that the population turnover within a given city is much greater than censuses indicate, because each population stream had a counterstream, and large total movements produced small net population changes. At least twice as many households passed through the city of Boston in each of the three decades before the Civil War as lived in the city at the start of any of these decades. The annual turnover rate among Boston residents in the 1830s was roughly 30 percent, and in the 1840s, about 40 percent, in contrast to a mid-twentieth-century American turnover rate of around 20 percent.
10. Ibid.
11. Sam Bass Warner, Jr., *The Private City: Philadelphia in Three Periods of Its Growth,* chap. 3.

12. Lydia Maria Child, quoted in Paul Boyer, *Urban Masses and Moral Order in America, 1820–1920,* p. 73.

13. Eric W. Carlson, ed., *Introduction to Poe: A Thematic Reader* (Glenview, Ill.: Scott, Foresman and Co., 1967), pp. 257, 261, 264.

14. Quoted in Boyer, *Urban Masses,* p. 5.

15. James Dabney McCabe [Edward Winslow Martin], *The Secrets of the Great City: A Work Descriptive of the Virtues and Vices, the Mysteries, Miseries and Crimes of New York City* (Philadelphia: Jones, Brothers and Co., 1868), pp. 37–38.

16. Francis Lieber, *Letters to a Gentleman in Germany Written After a Trip from Philadelphia to Niagara* (Philadelphia, 1834), p. 60.

17. McCabe, *Secrets of the Great City,* pp. 89–92.

18. David Meredith Reese, *Humbugs of New-York: being a Remonstrance against Popular Delusion; whether in Science, Philosophy, or Religion* (New York: John S. Taylor, 1838), p. 17; E. H. Chapin, *Moral Aspects of City Life* (New York: Henry Lyon, 1854), p. 18.

19. For a good bibliography of such literature, see Bayrd Still, *Urban America: A History with Documents,* pp. 504–05.

20. Wohl, "The 'Country Boy' Myth," p. 87.

21. Lofland, *World of Strangers,* chaps. 2, 3. Also see Gideon Sjoberg, *The Preindustrial City, Past and Present* (New York: Free Press, 1960).

22. Sam Bass Warner, Jr., *Streetcar Suburbs: The Process of Growth in Boston, 1870–1900,* chap. 1; Warner, *Private City,* chap. 3; Z. Miller, *Urbanization,* pp. 40–45.

23. Robert Park, "The City: Suggestions for the Investigation of Human Behavior in the Urban Environment," in Richard Sennett, ed., *Classic Essays on the Culture of Cities,* p. 126.

24. Alcott, *Young Man's Guide,* p. 73.

25. Erving Goffman, *The Presentation of Self in Everyday Life,* pp. 36, 245.

26. Clark, *Lectures,* p. 28.

27. *The Young Man's Own Book: A Manual of Politeness, Intellectual Improvement, and Moral Deportment, calculated to Form the Character on a Solid Basis, and to Insure Respectability and Success in Life,* p. 196; Alcott, *Young Man's Guide,* p. 88.

28. Samuel G. Goodrich [Peter Parley], *What to Do, and How to Do It; or, Morals and Manners Taught by Examples,* p. 28.

29. *Young Man's Own Book,* p. 161.

30. Horace Mann, *A Few Thoughts for a Young Man: A Lecture, Delivered Before the Boston Mercantile Library Association, on its 29th Anniversary,* p. 21.

31. Alcott, *Young Man's Guide,* pp. 131–32.

32. Timothy S. Arthur, *Advice to Young Men on their Duties and Conduct in Life,* p. 108.

33. Clark, *Lectures,* p. 133.

34. John Todd, *Young Man*, p. 106.

35. Beecher, *Seven Lectures*, p. 92; Alcott, *Young Man's Guide*, p. 358.

36. Goffman, *Presentation of Self*, esp. chap. 6.

37. Magie, *Spring-time*, p. 173.

38. Clark, *Lectures*, p. 29.

39. See Edmund S. Morgan, *Visible Saints: The History of a Puritan Idea;* Perry Miller, *The New England Mind: The Seventeenth Century;* William Haller, *The Rise of Puritanism.*

40. Daniel B. Shea, Jr., *Spiritual Autobiography in Early America*, p. 87. Also see P. Miller, *The New England Mind: The Seventeenth Century,* and *The New England Mind: From Colony to Province,* chap. 5; Morgan, *Visible Saints,* and *The Puritan Family: Religion and Domestic Relations in Seventeenth-century New England;* Haller, *Rise of Puritanism;* Philip J. Greven, *The Protestant Temperament: Patterns of Child-rearing, Religious Experience, and the Self in Early America,* chap. 3.

41. Shea, *Spiritual Autobiography,* p. 187.

42. John Bunyan, *Grace Abounding to the Chief of Sinners,* ed. Roger Sharrock (London: Oxford University Press, 1966), p. 15.

43. Quoted in Shea, *Spiritual Autobiography,* p. 177.

44. Quoted in Greven, *Protestant Temperament,* p. 74.

45. Quoted, ibid., p. 89.

46. Quoted in Morgan, *Puritan Family,* pp. 1–2.

47. *Paradise Lost,* bk. 1, lines 34–36; bk. 3, lines 681–85.

48. Quoted in Greven, *Protestant Temperament,* p. 89.

49. Shea, *Spiritual Autobiography,* p. 192.

50. Muzzey, *Young Man's Friend,* p. 36.

51. Paul E. Johnson, "A Shopkeeper's Millennium: Society and Revivals in Rochester, New York, 1815–1837" (Ph.D. diss., University of California at Los Angeles, 1975), p. 213.

52. Waterbury, *Considerations,* p. 136.

53. Muzzey, *Young Man's Friend,* p. 37.

54. Clark, *Lectures,* p. 226.

55. *Young Man's Own Book,* p. 257.

56. Beecher, *Seven Lectures,* p. 64.

57. Hawes, *Lectures,* p. 112.

58. Todd, *Young Man,* p. 76.

59. Hawes, *Lectures,* p. 109.

60. Muzzey, *Young Man's Friend,* pp. 40–41.

61. Magie, *Spring-time,* p. 308.

62. Muzzey, *Young Man's Friend,* p. 142.

63. Todd, *Young Man,* pp. 63–64.

64. Ibid., p. 71.

65. John Stevens Cabot Abbott, *The School-boy; or, A Guide for Youth to Truth and Duty,* p. 38.

66. Ibid., p. 55.

67. Clark, *Lectures*, p. 247.

68. Goodrich, *What to Do*, p. 25.

69. See Richard I. Rabinowitz, "Soul, Character, and Personality: The Transformation of Personal Religious Experience in New England, 1790–1860" (Ph.D. diss., Harvard University, 1977).

70. Alcott, *Young Man's Guide*, p. 76.

71. Clark, *Lectures*, pp. 325–26.

72. Magie, *Spring-time*, p. 135.

73. Ibid.

74. Ibid., pp. 127–28.

75. Goodrich, *What to Do*, p. 68.

76. Clark, *Lectures*, p. 138.

77. Alcott, *Young Man's Guide*, p. 76.

78. See Leon Guilhamet, *The Sincere Ideal: Studies in Sincerity in Eighteenth-century English Literature.*

79. Quoted, ibid., p. 31.

80. Quoted, ibid., p. 16.

81. Ibid., chaps. 3, 4, 5, Appendix.

82. Quoted in Maximillian E. Novak, ed., *English Literature in the Age of Disguise*, p. 2.

83. Alcott, *Young Man's Guide*, p. 132.

84. Ibid., p. 76.

85. Robert Walsh, *Didactics: Social, Literary, and Political*, 1:47.

86. *Young Man's Own Book*, pp. 211, 212.

87. Ibid., pp. 162–63.

Chapter 3

1. Ian Watt, *The Rise of the Novel: Studies in Defoe, Richardson and Fielding*, pp. 181–82, 180, 200. In chapter 6, "Private Experience and the Novel," Watt offers a brilliant analysis of the connections between urban social life and the rise of the novel.

2. For discussions of American sentimental literature in the nineteenth century, see Herbert Ross Brown, *The Sentimental Novel in America, 1789–1860;* A. Douglas, *Feminization of American Culture;* Ann Douglas Wood, "The 'Scribbling Women' and Fanny Fern: Why Women Wrote," *American Quarterly* 23 (Spring 1971): 3–24; Helen Waite Papashvily, *All the Happy Endings;* E. Douglas Branch, *The Sentimental Years, 1836–1860: A Social History.*

3. John Davis, *Ferdinand and Elizabeth*, quoted in H. Brown, *Sentimental Novel*, p. 77.

4. J[oyce] M[arjorie] S[axter] Tompkins, *The Popular Novel in England, 1770–1800*, p. 96.

5. "The Female Sex," *Literary Magazine* 15 (1805), quoted in Cott, *Bonds of Womanhood*, p. 163.

6. H. Brown, *Sentimental Novel*, p. 80.

7. S. R. R., "Female Charms," *Godey's Lady's Book* 33 (1846), quoted in Barbara Welter, "The Cult of True Womanhood: 1820–1860," in Michael Gordon, ed., *The American Family in Social-Historical Perspective*, p. 317.

8. *Memoir of Miss Hannah Adams, written by Herself, with additional notices, by a friend,* quoted in Cott, *Bonds of Womanhood*, p. 164.

9. Clark, *Lectures*, p. 133.

10. Lydia H. Sigourney, "The Father," in Sigourney et al., *The Young Ladies' Offering; or Gems of Prose and Poetry* (Boston: Phillips and Sampson, 1849), p. 14.

11. Aileen S. Kraditor first applied the phrase *cult of domesticity* to prevailing ideas about woman's role in nineteenth-century American society, in the introduction to *Up from the Pedestal: Selected Writings in the History of American Feminism* (Chicago: Quadrangle Books, 1968). Also see Mary P. Ryan, *American Society and the Cult of Domesticity, 1830–1860* (Ann Arbor, Mich.: University Microfilms, 1972); Cott, *Bonds of Womanhood*, chap. 2; Kathryn K. Sklar, *Catharine Beecher: A Study in American Domesticity;* Welter, "Cult of True Womanhood."

12. Cott, *Bonds of Womanhood*, p. 64. Cott's discussion of the separation of the domestic sphere from the world at large is excellent; see chap. 2.

13. Charles Burroughs, *An Address on Female Education, Delivered in Portsmouth, N.H., Oct. 26, 1827,* quoted in Cott, *Bonds of Womanhood*, p. 64.

14. *The Mother's Assistant* 7 (July 1845): 33.

15. Catharine Beecher, *The Elements of Mental and Moral Philosophy, Founded upon Experience, Reason and the Bible,* quoted in Sklar, *Catharine Beecher*, p. 87.

16. *The Discussion: or the Character, Education, Prerogatives, and Moral Influence of Woman,* quoted in Cott, *Bonds of Womanhood*, p. 67.

17. Cott has pointed out the domestic convention that the air of the world is a poison, the antidote for which is domestic affection and religious faith; see *Bonds of Womanhood*, p. 68.

18. Sklar, *Catharine Beecher*, p. 137.

19. For a discussion of the concept of gentility during this period, see Stow Persons, *The Decline of American Gentility*, introduction and chaps. 1–4. Also see Leonore Davidoff, *The Best Circles: Society Etiquette and the Season.* Although Davidoff's study concerns only English middle-class "Society," her insights are often broadly applicable to the American Victorians; see especially her introduction.

20. See René König, *The Restless Image: A Sociology of Fashion*, trans. F. Bradley.

21. Joan Wildeblood and Peter Brinson, *The Polite World: A Guide to English Manners and Deportment from the 13th to the 19th Century,* pp. 33–38.

22. König, *Restless Image,* p. 146.

23. Tocqueville, *Democracy in America,* 2:227.

24. König, *Restless Image,* p. 153.

25. Harriett Martineau, *Society in America,* 3 vols. (New York: Saunders and Otley, 1837), 3:34.

26. Francis J. Grund, *Aristocracy in America,* p. 33.

27. Charles Dickens, *The Life and Adventures of Martin Chuzzlewit,* 2 vols. (Boston: Fields, Osgood and Co., 1861), 1:302.

28. Thomas Hamilton, *Men and Manners in America,* 2 vols. (Philadelphia: Carey, Lea, and Blanchard, 1833), 1:206.

29. Grund, *Aristocracy,* pp. 146, 55.

30. Ibid., p. 10.

31. Clark, *Lectures,* p. 50.

32. Todd, *Young Man,* p. 126.

33. Jared Bell Waterbury, *The Voyage of Life; Suggested by Cole's Allegorical Paintings,* pp. 112–13.

34. Clark, *Lectures,* p. 167.

35. Alcott, *Young Man's Guide,* pp. 145, 149. Alcott here voiced the belief of the American medical community that ambition and the pursuit of wealth were major causes of insanity among Americans during the antebellum years; see David J. Rothman, *The Discovery of the Asylum: Social Order and Disorder in the New Republic* (Boston: Little, Brown and Co., 1971), pp. 115–17.

36. Alcott, *Young Man's Guide,* p. 266. In this passage Alcott was warning his readers not to marry such worthless women.

37. "In nineteenth-century England upper- and middle-class women were used to maintain the fabric of society, as semi-official leaders but also as arbiters of social acceptance or rejection. By effectively preventing upper- and middle-class women from playing any part in the market, any part in public life whatsoever, the Victorians believed that one section of the population would be able to provide a haven of stability, of exact social classification in the threatening anonymity of the surrounding economic and political upheaval." Davidoff, *Best Circles,* p. 16. The role of American women in reigning over society was very similar to that described by Davidoff for the English woman.

38. See Robert Kunciov, ed., *Mr. Godey's Ladies: Being a Mosaic of Fashions and Fancies* (Princeton: Pyne Press, 1971), p. 1.

39. "St. Paul's Person," *Godey's Lady's Book* 1 (May 1831): 226 (hereafter cited as *GLB*).

40. "Personal Appearance," *GLB* 3 (August 1831): 115.

41. "Madame Cottlin's Pelisse," *GLB* 2 (June 1831): 291–92.

42. "Editor's Table," *GLB* 15 (August 1837): 95–96.

43. "Fashion-Principle," *GLB* 18 (January 1839): 8.

44. Mrs. Harrison Smith, "Who is Happy?" *GLB* 18 (May 1839): 214.

45. "A Life of Fashion," *GLB* 22 (January 1841): 23; "The Lady's Lesson," *GLB* 26 (January 1843): 28.

46. "A Life of Fashion," *GLB* 22 (January 1841): 23.

47. *GLB* 36 (March 1848): 180.

48. "Editor's Table," *GLB* 27 (December 1843): 285.

49. "Select Sentences," *GLB* 10 (June 1835): 285.

50. See, e.g., "Fashions of the Olden Time," *GLB* 11 (July 1835): 2; "Apparel," *GLB* 11 (October 1835): 145–49; "Editor's Table," *GLB* 27 (December 1843): 285–86; "Editor's Table," *GLB* 28 (March 1844): 149–50; "Old and New Fashions," *GLB* 35 (November 1847): 244–47; "A Sketch of the History of Female Costume, from the Death of Louis XIV to Our Own Days.—No. III," *GLB* 38 (March 1849): 196, and "No. IV," *GLB* 38 (April 1849): 287–90.

51. "A Sketch of the History of Female Costume, from the Death of Louis XIV to Our Own Days.—No. II," *GLB* 38 (January 1849): 123.

52. Caroline Lee Hentz, "The Fatal Cosmetic," *GLB* 18 (June 1839): 265, 266.

53. Ibid., p. 265.

54. Ibid., p. 273.

55. *GLB* 20 (February 1840): 76.

56. See Ruth E. Finley, *The Lady of Godey's: Sarah Josepha Hale* (Philadelphia: J. B. Lippincott Co., 1931); Sklar, *Catharine Beecher,* p. 163.

57. "Fashion," *GLB* 18 (February 1839): 96.

58. Florence Fashionhunter [pseud.], "Reminiscences of Bonnets—III," *GLB* 52 (May 1856): 416.

59. "The Prevailing Fashions," *GLB* 8 (January 1834): 1.

60. "Editor's Table," *GLB* 27 (December 1843): 285.

61. Ibid.

62. "Editor's Table," *GLB* 26 (January 1843): 56.

63. Ibid.

64. "The Gatherer," *GLB* 2 (February 1831): 109.

65. "Editor's Table," *GLB* 28 (April 1844): 198.

66. "The Gatherer," *GLB* 2 (May 1831): 278.

67. "Health and Beauty," *GLB* 35 (October 1847): 209.

68. "Mirror of the Graces," *GLB* 3 (August 1831): 105.

69. "The Toilet—No. 5—Eyes and Nose," *GLB* 10 (February 1835): 63.

70. "Man," *GLB* 3 (October 1831): 200.

71. "The Gatherer," *GLB* 5 (October 1832): 216.

72. *Young Ladies' Friend,* quoted in "Review of the Young Ladies' Friend," *GLB* 16 (May 1838): 227.

73. See C. Willett Cunnington, *English Women's Clothing in the Nine-teenth Century,* p. 4, 26; Doreen Yarwood, *European Costume: 4000 years of Fashion,* p. 215; R. Turner Wilcox, *Five Centuries of American Costume,* p. 137.

74. Cunnington, *English Women's Clothing,* p. 25.

75. See James Laver, *Taste and Fashion from the French Revolution until Today,* chap. 1; Geoffrey Squire, *Dress Art and Society, 1560–1970,* pp. 123–43; Cunnington, *English Women's Clothing,* chap. 2; Yarwood, *European Costume,* 229–34; Nancy Bradfield, *Costume in Detail: Women's Dress 1730–1930,* pp. 85–116; C. Willett Cunnington and Phillis Cunnington, *Handbook of English Costume in the Nineteenth Century,* pp. 353–81; C. Willett Cunnington, Phyllis Cunnington, and Charles Beard, *A Dictionary of English Costume.*

76. See Laver, *Taste and Fashion,* chap. 2; Squire, *Dress Art and Society,* pp. 123–63; Cunnington, *English Women's Clothing,* chap. 2; Bradfield, *Costume in Detail,* pp. 85–116; Cunnington and Cunnington, *Handbook of English Costume,* pp. 353–81; Lucy Barton, *Historic Costume for the Stage,* pp. 400–07; J. Anderson Black and Madge Garland, *A History of Fashion,* pp. 242–61.

77. See Laver, *Taste and Fashion,* chap. 2; Squire, *Dress Art and Society,* 141–57; Cunnington, *English Women's Clothing,* chap. 3; Brad-field, *Costume in Detail,* pp. 117–60; Cunnington and Cunnington, *Handbook of English Costume,* pp. 383–419; Cunnington, Cunnington, and Beard, *Dictionary of English Costume.*

78. Squire, *Dress Art and Society,* p. 155.

79. Cunnington, *English Women's Clothing,* p. 80.

80. See Laver, *Taste and Fashion,* chap. 3; Black and Garland, *History of Fashion,* pp. 242–61; Squire, *Dress Art and Society,* pp. 145–63; Cunnington, *English Women's Clothing,* chap. 4; Bradfield, *Costume in Detail,* pp. 162–208; Cunnington and Cunnington, *Handbook of English Costume,* pp. 420–62; Millia Davenport, *The Book of Costume,* 2:795; Barton, *Historic Costume for the Stage,* pp. 434–42.

81. Cunnington and Cunnington, *Handbook of English Costume,* p. 400.

82. Cunnington, *English Women's Clothing,* p. 131.

83. See Agnes Brooks Young, *Recurring Cycles of Fashion 1760–1937,* pp. 1–31.

84. Anne Hollander, *Seeing Through Clothes,* p. xii.

85. "Dress," *GLB* 45 (December 1852): 576.

86. See Laver, *Taste and Fashion,* chap. 2; Squire, *Dress Art and Society,* pp. 145–63.

87. Caroline H. Butler, "Affectations," *GLB* 28 (June 1844): 269.

88. Miss Leslie, "Henrietta Harrison; or, the Blue Cotton Um-brella," *GLB* 17 (July 1838): 28.

89. Ibid., p. 27.

90. "The History of a Hat," *GLB* 9 (August 1834): 90.

91. *GLB* 30 (May 1845): 238.

92. "Dress," *GLB* 20 (April 1840): 187.

93. "Female Education," *GLB* 16 (February 1838): 76.

94. Harriet Beecher Stowe, "Art and Nature," *GLB* 19 (December 1839): 243, 242.

95. H. T. Tuckerman, "Costume," *GLB* 30 (March 1845): 140.

96. Hentz, "The Fatal Cosmetic," p. 266.

97. Cunnington, *English Women's Clothing,* introduction and chap. 5.

98. "The Gatherer," *GLB* 4 (February 1832): 168.

99. "Toilet," *GLB* 62 (May 1861): 460–61.

100. "The Toilet,—No. 5—Eyes and Nose," *GLB* 10 (February 1835): 63.

101. Hentz, "The Fatal Cosmetic," pp. 265–66.

102. Tuckerman, "Costume," p. 140.

103. Laver, *Taste and Fashion,* chap. 10; Georgine de Courtais, *Women's Headdress and Hairstyles in England from AD 600 to the Present Day,* pp. 104–05; Richard Corson, *Fashions in Hair,* chap. 12; Black and Garland, *History of Fashion,* pp. 242–61; Jean Keyes, *A History of Women's Hairstyles, 1500–1965,* pp. 37–39.

104. "A Series of Papers on the Hair," *GLB* 50 (May 1855): 436.

105. Ibid.

106. Laver, *Taste and Fashion,* chap. 10; de Courtais, *Women's Headdress,* pp. 114–15; Corson, *Fashions in Hair,* chap. 12; Black and Garland, *History of Fashion,* pp. 242–61; Keyes, *Women's Hairstyles,* pp. 40–43.

107. "Old and New Fashions," *GLB* 35 (November 1847); 245.

108. Laver, *Taste and Fashion,* chap. 10; de Courtais, *Women's Headdress,* pp. 116–17; Squire, *Dress Art and Society,* pp. 145–63; Bradfield, *Costume in Detail,* p. 180; Cunnington and Cunnington, *Handbook of English Costume,* pp. 392–96, 434–36; Cunnington, Cunnington, and Beard, *Dictionary of English Costume,* p. 154.

109. "The Mirror of the Graces," *GLB* 4 (February 1832): 116.

110. Ibid.

111. Ibid., p. 115.

112. "The Gatherer," *GLB* 8 (February 1834): 120.

113. "Beauty and How to Gain It," *GLB* 62 (April 1861): 268.

114. "Personal Beauty," *GLB* 8 (February 1834): 115.

115. "Editors' Table," *GLB* 62 (April 1861): 367.

116. "The Gatherer," *GLB* 7 (December 1833): 310.

117. Squire, *Dress Art and Society,* pp. 159, 154.

118. Richard Sennett, *The Fall of Public Man: On the Social Psychology of Capitalism,* pp. 161–64.

119. Timothy S. Arthur, "Conformity to the World," *GLB* 31 (December 1845): 241–45.

120. Anna Wilmot, "The Spring Bonnet," *GLB* 40 (June 1850): 384.

Chapter 4

1. For statistics on antebellum American etiquette manuals see Arthur M. Schlesinger, *Learning How to Behave: A Historical Study of American Etiquette Books;* Esther B. Aresty, *The Best Behavior: The Course of Good Manners—from Antiquity to the Present—As Seen through Courtesy and Etiquette Books.* For my purposes, Aresty's estimate that 67 manuals were published in America during this period is more useful; Schlesinger's count of 102 includes many books that I have classified as advice manuals.

2. See Norbert Elias, *The Civilizing Process: The History of Manners,* trans. Edmund Jephcott, esp. pp. 53–84.

3. See Schlesinger, *Learning How to Behave,* chaps. 1, 2.

4. Persons, *Decline of American Gentility,* p. 35.

5. John Adams, Samuel Adams, James Warren et al., *Warren–Adams Letters,* 2: 129, quoted in Schlesinger, *Learning How to Behave,* p. 12.

6. See Schlesinger, *Learning How to Behave,* chap. 2; Wildeblood and Brinson, *Polite World,* chap. 2; John E. Mason, *Gentlefolk in the Making: Studies in the History of English Courtesy Literature and Related Topics from 1531 to 1774,* chap. 4; *Letters to His Son, by the Earl of Chesterfield: On the Fine Art of Becoming a Man of the World and a Gentleman,* 2 vols. (London: Navarre Society, 1926).

7. Schlesinger, *Learning How to Behave,* p. 17.

8. *The Art of Good Behaviour; and Letter Writer on Love, Courtship, and Marriage: A Complete Guide for Ladies and Gentlemen, particularly those who have not Enjoyed the Advantages of Fashionable Life,* pp. viii–ix.

9. Catharine M. Sedgwick, *Morals of Manners,* p. 61, quoted in Schlesinger, *Learning How to Behave,* p. 16; Sedgwick, *Means and Ends,* p. 150, quoted, ibid., p. 21.

10. *Ladies' Vase; or, Polite Manual for Young Ladies; Original and Selected,* p. 22.

11. Catharine M. Sedgwick, *Means and Ends,* pp. 149–50, quoted in Persons, *Decline of American Gentility,* p. 40.

12. *The Perfect Gentleman; or, Etiquette and Eloquence,* p. 212.

13. *The Laws of Etiquette, or, Short Rules and Reflections for Conduct in Society,* p. 10.

14. *The Handbook of the Man of Fashion,* p. 34.

15. Davidoff, *Best Circles,* pp. 15, 16.

16. Aresty, *Best Behavior,* p. 129.

17. *Chesterfield's Art of Letter-Writing Simplified . . . to which is appended the Complete Rules of Etiquette, and the Usages of Society . . .* , p. 43.

18. *A Manual of Politeness, Comprising the Principles of Etiquette, and Rules of Behavior in Genteel Society, for Persons of Both Sexes*, p. 55.

19. *The Habits of Good Society: A Handbook for Ladies and Gentlemen*, p. 285.

20. George Winfred Hervey, *The Principles of Courtesy: With Hints and Observations on Manners and Habits*, p. 39.

21. Elias, *Civilizing Process*, esp. pp. 53–84.

22. Magie, *Spring-Time*, p. 196.

23. C. P. Bronson, quoted in *How to Behave: A Pocket Manual of Republican Etiquette, A Guide to Correct Personal Habits . . .* , p. xi.

24. *Ladies' Vase*, p. 12.

25. Florence Hartley, *The Ladies' Book of Etiquette, and Manual of Politeness: A Complete Hand Book for the Use of the Lady in Polite Society*, p. 4.

26. Hervey, *Principles of Courtesy*, p. 93.

27. Henry T. Tuckerman, "Lord Chesterfield," *GLB* 44 (January 1852): 7–12.

28. *Ladies' Vase*, p. 13.

29. Rev. James Porter, *The Operative's Friend, and Defence: Or, Hints to Young Ladies, who are Dependent on their Own Exertions*, p. 120.

30. Hervey, *Principles of Courtesy*, p. xiii.

31. *The School of Good Manners: Composed for the Help of Parents in Teaching their Children How to Behave in their Youth*, p. 13.

32. Arthur Martine, *Martine's Hand-Book of Etiquette, and Guide to True Politeness*, p. 126.

33. Hervey, *Principles of Courtesy*, p. 89.

34. Ibid.

35. *School of Good Manners*, p. 13.

36. *Perfect Gentleman*, p. 208.

37. *Handbook of the Man of Fashion*, p. 40.

38. For a good discussion of the "natural gentleman," see Persons, *Decline of American Gentility*, chap. 3.

39. Henry Lunettes [pseud.], *The American Gentleman's Guide to Politeness and Fashion*, p. 145.

40. *Laws of Etiquette*, p. 87.

41. D. Mackellar, *A Treatise on the Art of Politeness, Good Breeding and Manners. With Maxims and Moral Reflections*, pp. 122–23.

42. *Habits of Good Society*, pp. 309–10.

43. Elias Howe, *Howe's Complete Ball-room Hand Book: Containing Upwards of Three Hundred Dances, including all the Latest and Most Fashionable Dances*, p. 23.

44. *Habits of Good Society*, p. 310.

45. F. Hartley, *Ladies' Book*, p. 55.

46. F. Hartley, *Ladies' Book*, pp. 151–52.

47. Mackellar, *Treatise*, p. 119.

48. *True Politeness; A Hand-book of Etiquette for Ladies*, p. 17.

49. See Goffman, *Presentation of Self*, chap. 3.

50. Ibid., p. 64.

51. *Habits of Good Society*, pp. 372–73.

52. Sarah J. Hale, *Manners; or, Happy Homes and Good Society All the Year Round*, p. 284.

53. F. Hartley, *Ladies' Book*, p. 93.

54. *Etiquette at Washington: and Complete Guide through the Metropolis and its Environs*, pp. 47–48.

55. *Mixing in Society. A Complete Manual of Manners*, p. 50.

56. *Mixing*, p. 181.

57. F. Hartley, *Ladies' Book*, p. 48.

58. *Habits of Good Society*, p. 358.

59. *Mixing*, p. 182.

60. Cecil B. Hartley, *The Gentleman's Book of Etiquette, and Manual of Politeness; being a Complete Guide for a Gentleman's Conduct in All His Relations towards Society*, p. 4.

61. Eliza Leslie, *Miss Leslie's Behaviour Book: A Guide and Manual for Ladies . . .* , pp. 47–48.

62. Ibid., p. 49.

63. *Chesterfield's Art*, p. 17.

64. F. Hartley, *Ladies' Book*, p. 84.

65. Henry P. Willis, *Etiquette, and the Usages of Society: containing the Most Approved Rules for Correct Deportment in Fashionable Life . . .* , p. 40.

66. Martine, *Martine's Hand-Book*, p. 35.

67. Mackellar, *Treatise*, p. 104.

68. Martine, *Martine's Hand-Book*, p. 29.

69. *Handbook of the Man of Fashion*, p. 79.

70. C. Hartley, *Gentleman's Book*, p. 22.

71. Charles William Day, *Hints on Etiquette and the Usages of Society; with a Glance at Bad Habits*, p. 11.

72. Willis, *Etiquette*, p. 10.

73. *Chesterfield's Art*, p. 30.

74. Martine, *Martine's Hand-Book*, p. 116.

75. Aresty, *Best Behavior*, chap. 21.

76. F. Hartley, *Ladies' Book*, p. 19.

77. C. Hartley, *Gentleman's Book*, p. 74.

78. *True Politeness*, p. 12.

79. *The Bazar Book of Decorum*, p. 152.

80. *Laws of Etiquette*, p. 61.

81. Grund, *Aristocracy*, p. 55.

82. *Chesterfield's Art*, p. 41.

83. Martine, *Martine's Hand-Book*, p. 161.

84. Mrs. C. Lee Hentz, "A Rainy Evening: A Sketch," *GLB* 25 (December 1842): 282–85.

85. Mrs. A. M. F. Annan, "The Cheap Dress," *GLB* 31 (September 1845): 88.

86. Porter, *Operative's Friend*, p. 123.

87. See Everett V. Stonequist, *The Marginal Man: A Study in Personality and Culture Conflict*, esp. chap. 9.

88. *Handbook of the Man of Fashion*, p. 34.

89. *Manual of Politeness*, pp. 124–25.

90. *Chesterfield's Art*, p. 8.

91. *The American Gentleman's Hand-book of Etiquette and Letter-writing* (Philadelphia: Henry F. Anners, 1847), p. 15; *Art of Good Behaviour*, pp. 114, 103.

92. *Art of Good Behaviour*, p. 94; *American Gentleman's Hand-book*, pp. 25, 33.

93. *The New Letter Writer, containing a Great Variety of Letters . . . selected from Judicious and Eminent Writers*, p. 184.

94. Ibid., p. 134.

95. Ibid., p. 71.

96. *Art of Good Behaviour*, p. 92.

97. *Ladies and Gentlemen's Letter Writer and Guide to Polite Behaviour, containing also Moral and Instructive Aphorisms, for Daily Use*, p. 42.

98. *The New Letter Writer*, p. 118.

99. *Art of Good Behaviour*, p. 11.

100. *The New Letter Writer*, p. 91.

101. *American Gentleman's Hand-book*, pp. 44–45.

102. *Chesterfield's Art*, p. 54.

103. *Ladies' Vase*, pp. 89–90.

104. *Chesterfield's Art*, p. 68.

105. *Ladies' Vase*, pp. 90–91.

106. *Chesterfield's Art*, p. 3.

107. John Higham, *From Boundlessness to Consolidation: The Transformation of American Culture, 1848–1860*.

Chapter 5

1. See David E. Stannard, *The Puritan Way of Death: A Study in Religion, Culture, and Social Change*, chap. 4; Edwin Dethlefsen and James Deetz, "Death's Heads, Cherubs, and Willow Trees," in Charles O. Jackson, ed., *Passing: The Vision of Death in America*, pp. 48–59.

2. Stannard, *Puritan Way of Death*, chap. 6; Dethlefsen and Deetz, "Death's Heads"; Ann Douglas, "Heaven Our Home: Consolation Literature in the Northern United States, 1830–1880," in David E. Stannard, ed., *Death in America*, pp. 49–68.

3. Philippe Ariès, *Western Attitudes toward Death: From the Middle Ages to the Present,* chap. 3; Dethlefsen and Deetz, "Death's Heads"; Edmund Vincent Gillon, Jr., *Early New England Gravestone Rubbings;* Harriette Merrifield Forbes, *Gravestones of Early New England and the Men Who Made Them 1653–1800;* Dickran and Ann Tashjian, *Memorials for Children of Change: The Art of Early New England Stonecarving;* Margaret M. Coffin, *Death in Early America: The History and Folklore of Customs and Superstitions of Early Medicine, Funerals, Burials, and Mourning,* pp. 211–17; Edmund V. Gillon, Jr., *Victorian Cemetery Art.*

4. Thomas Baldwin Thayer, *Over the River; or, Pleasant Walks into the Valley of Shadows, and Beyond* . . . , pp. 269–70. Also see Stanley French, "The Cemetery as Cultural Institution: The Establishment of Mount Auburn and the 'Rural Cemetery' Movement," in Stannard, ed., *Death in America,* pp. 69–91; Neil Harris, "The Cemetery Beautiful," in C. Jackson, ed., *Passing,* pp. 103–11; A. Douglas, *Feminization of American Culture,* chap. 6.

5. A. Douglas, "Heaven Our Home."

6. See Donald Meyer, *The Positive Thinkers: Religion as Pop Psychology from Mary Baker Eddy to Norman Vincent Peale,* chaps. 1, 3, 5.

7. John Keese, ed., *The Mourner's Chaplet: An Offering of Sympathy for Bereaved Friends. Selected from American Poets,* p. 23.

8. Nehemiah Adams, *Agnes and the Little Key: Or, Bereaved Parents Instructed and Comforted,* pp. 62–63.

9. J. B. Syme, ed., *The Mourner's Friend: Or Sighs of Sympathy for Those who Sorrow,* p. 166.

10. J. M. Mason, *Christian Mourning: A Sermon, Occasioned by the Death of Mrs. Isabella Graham: and Preached on the Evening of Sabbath, the 14th August 1814* (New York: Whiting and Watson, 1814), p. 15.

11. William Simonds, ed., *Our Little Ones in Heaven,* p. 174.

12. Francis Parkman, *An Offering of Sympathy to the Afflicted, especially to Parents Bereaved of their Children* . . . , p. 134.

13. Edwin Hubbell Chapin, *The Crown of Thorns: A Token for the Sorrowing,* p. 101.

14. *The Mourners' Book,* p. 219.

15. Ibid., p. 16.

16. Rufus Wilmot Griswold, *The Cypress Wreath,* p. 127.

17. *Triumphant Deaths; or Brief Notices of the Happy Deaths of Twenty Six Sabbath School Scholars,* p. 102.

18. Griswold, *Cypress Wreath,* p. 76.

19. *Mourners' Book,* p. 16.

20. Ibid., pp. 16–17.

21. Griswold, *Cypress Wreath,* p. 111; F.W.P. Greenwood, *Sermons of Consolation,* p. 107.

22. Mason, *Christian Mourning,* p. 16.

23. J. Duncan, *The Mourner's Friend: Or, Recognition of Friends in Heaven,* p. 51.

24. Griswold, *Cypress Wreath*, p. 32.

25. William Chalmers Whitcomb, *The True Consoler, or Balm for the Stricken, Original and Selected*, p. 18.

26. Adams, *Agnes*, p. 163.

27. Parkman, *Offering*, p. 194.

28. Whitcomb, *True Consoler*, pp. 19–20.

29. Chapin, *Crown of Thorns*, p. 211.

30. Frederick Rinehart Anspach, *The Sepulchres of Our Departed*, p. 196.

31. Thomas E. Vermilye, *A Funeral Discourse: Occasioned by the Death of Mrs. Cornelia Van Rensselaer (Relict of Hon. Stephen Van Rensselaer), delivered in the North Dutch Church, Albany, on Sabbath the 1st September, 1844* (New York: Henry Ludwig, 1844), p. 11.

32. Simonds, *Little Ones*, p. 161.

33. Syme, *Mourner's Friend*, p. 33.

34. Mackellar, *Treatise*, p. 12.

35. Syme, *Mourner's Friend*, p. 94.

36. *Mourners' Book*, p. 116; Mrs. M. A. Patrick, ed., *The Mourner's Gift*, p. 143; Daniel C. Eddy, *The Angels' Whispers; or, Echoes of Spirit Voices. Designed to Console the Mourning Husband and Wife, Father and Mother, Son and Daughter, Brother and Sister*, p. 91.

37. Keese, *Mourner's Chaplet*, p. 117.

38. *Mourners' Book*, p. 108.

39. Syme, *Mourner's Friend*, p. 171.

40. T. Thayer, *Over the River*, p. 249.

41. Keese, *Mourner's Chaplet*, pp. 22, 128; Patrick, *Mourner's Gift*, p. 52.

42. Patrick, *Mourner's Gift*, p. 143.

43. Greenwood, *Sermons*, p. 104.

44. *Mourners' Book*, p. 105.

45. Parkman, *Offering*, p. 89.

46. Anspach, *Sepulchres*, p. 52; T. Thayer, *Over the River*, p. 270.

47. Anspach, *Sepulchres*, pp. 452, 444, 444–45, 445.

48. Adams, *Agnes*, pp. 102, 115, 123–24.

49. Eddy, *Angels' Whispers*, p. 82.

50. Hervey, *Principles of Courtesy*, p. 154.

51. "The Fashion of Mourning," *GLB* 54 (March 1857): 286.

52. "Chitchat upon New York and Philadelphia Fashions for September," *GLB* 49 (September 1854): 287.

53. "Mourning," *GLB* 48 (February 1854): 190.

54. Phillis Cunnington and Catherine Lucas, *Costume for Births, Marriages and Deaths*, chap. 16; Coffin, *Death in Early America*, pp. 197–202; *GLB* 48 (February 1854): 190.

55. "Chitchat upon New York and Philadelphia Fashions for June," *GLB* 54 (June 1857): 574.

56. Cunnington and Lucas, *Costume*, chap. 16; Coffin, *Death in Early*

America, pp. 196–99; *GLB* 48 (February 1854): 90; Hervey, *Principles of Courtesy,* p. 154.

57. Timothy A. Taylor, *The Solace; Or, Afflictions Lightened,* pp. 90–91.

58. Hervey, *Principles of Courtesy,* p. 154.

59. Ibid.

60. T. Taylor, *Solace,* p. 82.

61. Coffin, *Death in Early America,* p. 201; Hervey, *Principles of Courtesy,* pp. 154–55.

62. *A New Letter-writer, for the Use of Ladies: Embodying Letters on the Simplest Matters of Life . . . ,* p. 87.

63. Orville Dewey, *On the Duties of Consolation, and the Rites and Customs Appropriate to Mourning,* p. 6.

64. T. S. Arthur, "Going Into Mourning," *GLB* 23 (October 1841): 170–74.

65. Ibid., p. 174.

66. "The Fashion of Mourning," *GLB* 54 (March 1857): 286.

67. Ibid.

68. Ibid.

69. "Chitchat upon New York and Philadelphia Fashions for September," *GLB* 49 (September 1854): 288.

70. "Editors' Table," *GLB* 28 (May 1844): 244–46.

71. "Chitchat upon New York and Philadelphia Fashions for September," *GLB* 49 (September 1854): 287.

72. Ibid.

73. Ibid., p. 288.

74. Augustus C. Thompson, *Last Hours, or Words and Acts of the Dying,* p. 15.

75. Hervey, *Principles of Courtesy,* p. 149.

76. Adams, *Agnes,* p. 35.

77. Dewey, *Duties of Consolation,* p. 1.

78. Ibid., pp. 1–2.

79. Syme, *Mourner's Friend,* p. 138.

80. Parkman, *Offering,* p. vii.

81. Simonds, *Little Ones,* p. 148.

82. *Mourners' Book,* p. 290.

83. Patrick, *Mourner's Gift,* p. 186.

84. *Mourners' Book,* p. 60.

85. See Charles O. Jackson, "American Attitudes to Death," pp. 297–312; Robert Habenstein and William Lamers, *The History of American Funeral Directing,* chap. 5.

86. C. Jackson, "American Attitudes to Death"; Habenstein and Lamers, *American Funeral Directing,* chap. 6.

87. Arthur Martine, *Martine's Hand-Book,* p. 122.

88. Ibid.

89. Adams, *Agnes,* pp. 68–69.

90. Dewey, *Duties of Consolation,* p. 4.

91. Ibid., p. 14.

92. Madame de Gasparin, *The Near and Heavenly Horizons*, p. 185.

93. *How to Behave*, p. 99.

94. *Laws of Etiquette*, p. 183.

95. Ibid.

96. Dewey, *Duties of Consolation*, p. 8.

97. Parkman, *Offering*, p. ix.

98. Ibid.

99. Dewey, *Duties of Consolation*, pp. 2–3.

100. Parkman, *Offering*, p. 56.

101. Hervey, *Principles of Courtesy*, p. 153.

102. Charles William Day, *The American Ladies and Gentleman's Manual of Elegance, Fashion, and True Politeness* (Auburn: Alden, Beardsley, and Co., 1854), p. 113.

103. Hervey, *Principles of Courtesy*, p. 151.

104. Mackellar, *Treatise*, p. 5.

Chapter 6

1. See Eric Wollencott Barnes, *The Lady of Fashion: The Life and the Theatre of Anna Cora Mowatt*; David Grimsted, ed., *Notions of the Americans, 1820–1860*, p. 161.

2. Anna Cora Mowatt, *Fashion; or, Life in New York: A Comedy, in Five Acts* (New York: Samuel French, 1849), p. 11.

3. Ibid., pp. 17, 24, 12, 39.

4. Ibid., pp. 19–61.

5. Ibid., p. 13, preface.

6. G. Wood, *Creation of the American Republic*, pp. 108–10, 113, 114; Neil Harris, *The Artist in American Society: The Formative Years, 1790–1860*, chap. 2; Edmund S. Morgan, "The Puritan Ethic and the American Revolution," *William and Mary Quarterly*, 3d ser. 24 (January 1967): 3–43.

7. Larzer Ziff, *Puritanism in America: New Culture in a New World* (New York: The Viking Press, 1973), pp. 3–7.

8. Richard Slotkin, *Regeneration through Violence: The Mythology of the American Frontier, 1600–1860* (Middletown, Conn.: Wesleyan University Press, 1973), p. 65.

9. Caroline Lee Hentz, "The Fatal Cosmetic," *GLB* 18 (June 1839): 265–74.

10. "Chitchat," *GLB* 42 (February 1851): 140.

11. Florence Fashionhunter [pseud.], "Rambles About the City," *GLB* 54 (January 1857): 11.

12. "Chitchat," *GLB* 42 (March 1851): 206.

13. "Fashion Plates," *GLB* 47 (October 1853): 369.

14. Mrs. Merrifield, "Dress—As a Fine Art," *GLB* 46 (April 1853):

323–27; 47 (July 1853): 20–22; 47 (September 1853): 238–40; 48 (January 1854): 25–26; 48 (April 1854): 346–48; 48 (May 1854): 412–14.

15. Mrs. Merrifield, "Dress—As a Fine Art," *GLB* 46 (April 1853): 324.

16. "Maternal Counsels to a Daughter: Dress," *GLB* 53 (November 1856): 413.

17. "Hints on the Art of Dress," *GLB* 54 (June 1857): 538.

18. "The Business of Being Beautiful," *GLB* 45 (July 1852): 105.

19. "Hints on the Art of Dress," *GLB* 54 (June 1857): 538.

20. "A Series of Papers on the Hair: Modes of Wearing the Hair," *GLB* 50 (May 1855): 436.

21. "A Chapter on Pigments, Patches, Masks, Etc.," *GLB* 45 (October 1852): 320.

22. Pauline Forsyth, "The Cosmetic: A Sketch of Southern Life," *GLB* 50 (January 1855): 16–22.

23. *GLB* 55 (September 1857): 216.

24. See Kunciov, ed., *Mr. Godey's Ladies;* Squire, *Dress Art and Society,* pp. 145–63; Laver, *Taste and Fashion,* chap. 4; C. W. Cunnington, *English Women's Clothing,* chaps. 6 and 7; Nancy Bradfield, *Costume in Detail,* pp. 187–200; Cunnington and Cunnington, *Handbook of English Costume,* pp. 442–62; Lucy Barton, *Historic Costume for the Stage,* chap. 16.

25. Richard Corson, *Fashions in Hair,* chap. 12; de Courtais, *Women's Headdress,* pp. 112–21; Black and Garland, *History of Fashion,* pp. 262–83; Squire, *Dress Art and Society,* pp. 145–63; Laver, *Taste and Fashion,* chap. 10.

26. Richard Corson, *Fashions in Makeup from Ancient to Modern Times;* Neville Williams, *Powder and Paint: A History of the Englishwoman's Toilet, Elizabeth I–Elizabeth II.*

27. Hervey, *Principles of Courtesy,* pp. 91–92.

28. Sarah J. Hale, *Manners,* p. 91.

29. Ibid., p. 89.

30. Hervey, *Principles of Courtesy,* pp. 116–44.

31. Emily Thornwell, *The Lady's Guide to Perfect Gentility . . . ,* p. 70.

32. F. Hartley, *Ladies' Book,* p. 3.

33. *Habits of Good Society,* p. 3.

34. See, e.g., *Hints on Common Politeness,* p. 92; Willis, *Etiquette,* p. iv; F. Hartley, *Ladies' Book,* p. 143.

35. *Bazar Book,* pp. 223, 224, 238.

36. *Habits of Good Society,* p. 272.

37. "Chitchat upon the Philadelphia Fashions for July—Authentic," *GLB* 37 (July 1848): 60.

38. "Chitchat upon New York and Philadelphia Fashions for June," *GLB* 54 (June 1857): 574.

39. "Chitchat upon New York and Philadelphia Fashions for February," *GLB* 54 (February 1857): 192.

40. Ibid.

41. Habenstein and Lamers, *American Funeral Directors*, p. 354.

42. Ibid., chaps. 9, 10.

43. Ibid., chaps. 7, 9.

44. Ibid., chap. 10. For a dramaturgical discussion of the role of the modern funeral director, see Vanderlyn R. Pine, *Caretaker of the Dead: The American Funeral Director.*

45. *The New Athenian Oracle; or Ladies' Companion. In Two Books, Book First, Containing an Extraordinary Variety of Questions in Prose, on Moral, Philosophical and Other Subjects, together with a Great Number of Enigmas, Paradoxes, Rebuses, Charades, etc.* . . . (London: A. Loudon, 1806), p. 56.

46. "Charades in Action," *GLB* 49 (December 1854): 515.

47. Ibid., pp. 517–19.

48. "Charades in Action," *GLB* 50 (May 1855): 425.

49. For a list of parlor entertainment manuals, see publisher's advertisement in the back of Martine, *Martine's Hand-Book.*

50. *The Sociable; or, One Thousand and One Home Amusements* . . . (New York: Dick and Fitzgerald, 1858), preface, p. 14.

51. Sarah Annie Frost, *Parlor Charades and Proverbs* (Philadelphia: J. B. Lippincott and Co., 1859), preface; Tony Denier, *Parlor Tableaux; or, Animated Pictures* (New York: Happy Hours Co., 1868), p. v.

52. *The Sociable*, pp. 10–11.

53. See *The Sociable;* Frost, *Parlor Charades;* Denier, *Parlor Tableaux;* and Sarah Annie Frost, *The Book of Tableaux and Shadow Pantomimes* (New York: Dick and Fitzgerald, 1869).

54. Denier, *Parlor Tableaux*, p. viii; Frost, *Parlor Charades;* Frost, *Book of Tableaux; The Sociable.*

55. *The Sociable*, p. 12.

56. Ibid., p. 121.

57. *The Sociable*, p. 12.

58. *The Sociable;* Denier, *Parlor Tableaux.*

59. "Charades in Action," *GLB* 49 (December 1854): 516.

60. "Charades in Action," *GLB* 53 (July 1856): 39.

61. *The Sociable;* Denier, *Parlor Tableaux;* Frost, *Book of Tableaux;* Frost, *Parlor Charades.*

62. *The Sociable;* Denier, *Parlor Tableaux;* Frost, *Book of Tableaux.*

63. Denier, *Parlor Tableaux*, p. 19.

64. *The Sociable*, p. 9.

65. Frank Cahill, "Irresistibly Impudent," in *The Sociable*, pp. 151, 152.

66. *The Sociable;* Frost, *Parlor Charades;* Denier, *Parlor Tableaux;* Frost, *Book of Tableaux.*

67. E. J. Hobsbawm, *The Age of Capital, 1848–1875*, esp. chap. 13.

68. Thorstein Veblen, "Conspicuous Consumption," from *The Theory of the Leisure Class*, in Max Lerner, ed., *The Portable Veblen* (New York: Viking Press, 1950), pp. 111–40.

69. Samuel Langhorne Clemens and Charles Dudley Warner, *The Gilded Age: A Tale of Today* (New York: Trident Press, 1964).

70. Mackellar, *Treatise*, p. 12.

71. Lionel Trilling, *Sincerity and Authenticity*, p. 9.

Conclusion

1. Tocqueville, *Democracy in America*, 1:3, 2:145, 2:144, 2:146, 2:147.

2. Rozwenc, ed., *Ideology and Power*, p. 92.

3. Ibid., p. xii.

4. Meyers, *Jacksonian Persuasion*, p. 37.

5. Tocqueville, *Democracy in America*, 2:106.

6. *American Whig Review*, in Rozwenc, ed., *Ideology and Power*, p. 49.

7. Quoted in Pessen, *Jacksonian America*, p. 79.

8. Grund, *Aristocracy*, p. 180 (Grund's emphasis).

9. Higham, *From Boundlessness to Consolidation*.

Epilogue

1. See John G. Cawelti, *Apostles*, chap. 4.

2. Horatio Alger, Jr., *Ragged Dick and Mark the Matchboy* (New York: Collier Macmillan, 1962), p. 216.

3. Ibid., pp. 49, 55, 210.

4. Ibid., pp. 40, 41, 114, 115.

5. Ibid., pp. 42, 61–62, 81, 82, 83, 106, 107.

6. See Cawelti, *Apostles*, chaps. 1 2; Irvin G. Wyllie, *Self-Made Man;* Richard Weiss, *The American Myth of Success from Horatio Alger to Norman Vincent Peale*, chap. 1; Daniel T. Rodgers, *The Work Ethic in Industrial America, 1850–1920*, chap. 1; Max Weber, *The Protestant Ethic and the Spirit of Capitalism*, trans. Talcott Parson.

7. Weiss, *American Myth of Success*, p. 49 and passim.

8. Cawelti, *Apostles*, p. 122.

9. Weiss, *American Myth of Success*, p. 97; Wyllie, *Self-Made Man*, p. 117.

10. William R. Alger, *The School of Life*, p. 64.

11. J. Wilson, *Practical Life and the Study of Man*, p. 10.

12. See, e.g., C. H. Kent, *Kent's New Commentary: A Manual for Young Men;* William M. Thayer, *Tact, Push, and Principle;* William Mathews, *Getting On in the World; or, Hints on Success in Life;* Matthew Hale Smith, *Successful Folks: How They Win;* Edwin P. Whipple, *Success and its Conditions*.

13. Kent, *Kent's New Commentary*, p. 76.

14. Mathews, *Getting On*, p. 178.

15. Smith, *Successful Folks*, p. 22; Theodore T. Munger, *On the Threshold*, p. 38; also see Orison S. Marden, *The Secret of Achievement*.

16. Smith, *Successful Folks*, p. 136.

17. See Cawelti, *Apostles*, p. 183.

18. Wilson, *Practical Life*, p. 208.

19. Oliver Addison Kingsbury, *Success or Hints for Living*, p. 85.

20. Smith, *Successful Folks*, p. 288; Wilson, *Practical Life*, p. 8. Also see Newell D. Hillis, *The Contagion of Character: Studies in Culture and Success*, p. 20.

21. Newell D. Hillis, *A Man's Value to Society: Studies in Self-Culture and Character*, p. 259.

22. Wilson, *Practical Life*, p. 7.

23. Ibid., p. 281.

24. Kent, *Kent's New Commentary*, pp. 73–74.

25. Benjamin Wood, *The Successful Man of Business*, p. 77.

26. Mathews, *Getting On*, pp. 178–79.

27. See, e.g., Francis Edward Clark, *Danger Signals: The Enemies of Youth, from the Business Man's Standpoint;* David J. Burrell, *The Lure of the City: A Book for Young Men;* Andrew James Symington, *Hints to Our Boys;* Robert South Barrett, *Character Building: Talks to Young Men;* J. M. Buckley, *Oats or Wild Oats? Common-sense for Young Men.*

28. Cawelti, *Apostles*, p. 183. For a provocative discussion of the transformation of "a culture of character" into "a culture of personality" in the first two decades of the twentieth century, see Warren I. Susman, " 'Personality' and the Making of Twentieth-century Culture," in John Higham and Paul K. Conkin, eds., *New Directions in American Intellectual History*, pp. 212–26. A good "personality," as Susman argues, was to be *"fascinating, stunning, attractive, magnetic, glowing, masterful, creative, dominant, forceful"* (p. 217). Susman emphasizes the theatrical dimension of the culture of personality: "The social role demanded of all in the new culture of personality was that of a performer. Every American was to become a performing self" (p. 220).

29. Weiss, *American Myth of Success*, pp. 9–10.

30. W. Thayer, *Tact, Push, and Principle*, p. 20.

31. Wilson, *Practical Life*, pp. 242–43.

32. B. Wood, *Successful Man*, p. 28. For general attitudes of the business community toward character formation, see Edward C. Kirkland, *Dream and Thought in The Business Community, 1860–1900.*

33. See Paul A. Carter, *The Spiritual Crisis of the Gilded Age.*

34. Weiss, *American Myth of Success*, chap. 1.

35. Cawelti, *Apostles*, chap. 6.

36. Ibid., p. 183.

37. See, e.g., Newell D. Hillis, *The Investment of Influence: A Study of*

Social Sympathy and Service: "Nature's forces carry their atmosphere. . . . Business men understand this principle; those skilled in promoting great enterprises bring the men to be impressed into a room and create an atmosphere around them" (p. 13).

38. Meyer, *Positive Thinkers,* p. 189.

39. Christopher Lasch, *The Culture of Narcissism: American Life in an Age of Diminishing Expectations* (New York: W. W. Norton and Co., 1978), pp. 57, 53, 58, 59, 66.

40. Meyer, *Positive Thinkers,* pp. 181, 184, 187, 180.

41. Dale Carnegie, *How to Win Friends and Influence People* (New York: Pocket Books, 1964), pp. 249–50.

42. Ibid., p. 250.

Selected Bibliography

Secondary Sources

Arden, Eugene. "The Evil City in American Fiction." *New York History* 35 (July 1954): 259–79.

Aresty, Esther B. *The Best Behavior: The Course of Good Manners—from Antiquity to the Present—As Seen through Courtesy and Etiquette Books.* New York: Simon and Schuster, 1970.

Ariès, Philippe. *Western Attitudes toward Death: From the Middle Ages to the Present.* Baltimore: Johns Hopkins University Press, 1974.

Asbury, Herbert. *Sucker's Progress: An Informal History of Gambling in America from the Colonies to Canfield.* New York: Dodd, Mead and Co., 1938.

Bailyn, Bernard. *Education in the Forming of American Society: Needs and Opportunities for Study.* Chapel Hill: University of North Carolina Press, 1960.

———. *The Ideological Origins of the American Revolution.* Cambridge: Harvard University Press, Belknap Press, 1967.

Barnes, Eric Wollencott. *The Lady of Fashion: The Life and the Theatre of Anna Cora Mowatt.* New York: Charles Scribner's Sons, 1954.

Barton, Lucy. *Historic Costume for the Stage.* Boston: Walter H. Baker Co., 1963.

Bercovitch, Sacvan. *The American Jeremiad.* Madison: University of Wisconsin Press, 1978.

Bergmann, Johannes Dietrich. "The Original Confidence Man." *American Quarterly* 21 (Fall 1969): 560–77.

Black, J. Anderson, and Garland, Madge. *A History of Fashion.* New York: William Morrow and Co., 1975.

Bledstein, Burton J. *The Culture of Professionalism: The Middle Class and the Development of Higher Education in America.* New York: W. W. Norton and Co., 1976.

Blumin, Stuart M. *The Urban Threshold: Growth and Change in a Nineteenth-century American Community.* Chicago: University of Chicago Press, 1976.

Bobbitt, Mary Reed. *A Bibliography of Etiquette Books Published before 1900.* New York: New York Public Library, 1947.

Bode, Carl. *The American Lyceum: Town Meeting of the Mind.* New York: Oxford University Press, 1956.

———. *Antebellum Culture.* Carbondale, Ill.: Southern Illinois University Press, 1970.

Boyer, Paul. *Urban Masses and Moral Order in America, 1820–1920.* Cambridge: Harvard University Press, 1978.

Bradfield, Nancy. *Costume in Detail: Women's Dress 1730–1930.* Boston: Plays Inc., 1968.

Branch, E. Douglas. *The Sentimental Years, 1836–1860: A Social History.* New York: Hill and Wang, 1934.

Brown, Herbert Ross. *The Sentimental Novel in America, 1789–1860.* Durham, N.C.: Duke University Press, 1940.

Brown, Richard D. "Modernization and the Modern Personality in Early America, 1600–1865: A Sketch of a Synthesis." *Journal of Interdisciplinary History* 2 (Winter 1972): 201–28.

Bruchey, Stuart. *The Roots of American Economic Growth 1607–1861: An Essay in Social Causation.* New York: Harper and Row, 1965.

Burn, W. L. *The Age of Equipoise: A Study of the Mid-Victorian Generation.* New York: W. W. Norton and Co., 1965.

Burns, Elizabeth. *Theatricality: A Study of Convention in the Theatre and in Social Life.* New York: Harper and Row, 1973.

Calhoun, Daniel. *Professional Lives in America: Structure and Aspiration, 1750–1858.* Cambridge: Harvard University Press, 1965.

Carson, Gerald. *The Polite Americans: A Wide-angle View of Our More or Less Good Manners over 300 Years.* New York: William Morrow, 1966.

Carter, Paul A. *The Spiritual Crisis of the Gilded Age.* Dekalb, Ill.: Northern Illinois University Press, 1972.

Cawelti, John G. *Apostles of the Self-made Man: Changing Concepts of Success in America.* Chicago: University of Chicago Press, 1965.

Coffin, Margaret M. *Death in Early America: The History and Folklore of Customs and Superstitions of Early Medicine, Funerals, Burials, and Mourning.* Nashville: Thomas Nelson, 1976.

Corson, Richard. *Fashions in Hair.* New York: Hastings House, 1965.

———. *Fashions in Makeup from Ancient to Modern Times.* London: Peter Owen, 1972.

Cott, Nancy F. *The Bonds of Womanhood: "Woman's Sphere" in New England, 1780–1835.* New Haven: Yale University Press, 1977.

Courtais, Georgine de. *Women's Headdress and Hairstyles in England from AD 600 to the Present Day.* London: B. T. Batsford, 1973.

Cunnington, C. Willett. *English Women's Clothing in the Nineteenth Century.* London: Faber and Faber, 1937.

———— and Cunnington, Phillis. *Handbook of English Costume in the Nineteenth Century.* Boston: Plays Inc., 1970.

Cunnington, C. Willett; Cunnington, Phillis; and Beard, Charles. *A Dictionary of English Costume.* London: Adam and Charles Black, 1960.

Cunnington, Phillis, and Lucas, Catherine. *Costume for Births, Marriages and Deaths.* London: Adam and Charles Black, 1972.

Curl, James Stevens. *The Victorian Celebration of Death.* London: David and Charles, 1972.

Davenport, Millia. *The Book of Costume.* 2 vols. New York: Crown Publishers, 1948.

Davey, Richard. *A History of Mourning.* London: McCorquodale and Co., n.d.

Davidoff, Leonore. *The Best Circles: Society Etiquette and the Season.* London: Croom Helm, 1973.

Davies, John D. *Phrenology, Fad and Science: A Nineteenth-century American Crusade.* New Haven: Yale University Press, 1955.

Davis, David B., ed. *The Fear of Conspiracy: Images of Un-American Subversion from the Revolution to the Present.* Ithaca: Cornell University Press, 1971.

Douglas, Ann. *The Feminization of American Culture.* New York: Alfred A. Knopf, 1977.

Douglas, Mary. *Natural Symbols: Explorations in Cosmology.* New York: Vintage Books, 1973.

————. *Purity and Danger: An Analysis of Concepts of Pollution and Taboo.* New York: F. A. Praeger, 1966.

Elias, Norbert. *The Civilizing Process: The History of Manners.* Translated by Edmund Jephcott. New York: Urizen Books, 1978.

Flaherty, David H. *Privacy in Colonial New England.* Charlottesville: University Press of Virginia, 1967.

Forbes, Harriette Merrifield. *Gravestones of Early New England and the Men Who Made Them 1653–1800.* New York: Da Capo Press, 1967.

Forgie, George. *Patricide in the House Divided: A Psychological Interpretation of Lincoln and His Age.* New York: W. W. Norton and Co., 1979.

Formisano, Ronald P. "Deferential-Participant Politics: The Early Republic's Political Culture, 1789–1840." *American Political Science Review* 68 (June 1974): 473–87.

Gillon, Edmund Vincent, Jr. *Early New England Gravestone Rubbings.* New York: Dover Publications, 1966.

————. *Victorian Cemetery Art.* New York: Dover Publications, 1972.

Goffman, Erving. *Frame Analysis: An Essay on the Organization of Experience.* New York: Harper Colophon Books, 1974.

————. *Interaction Ritual: Essays on Face-to-Face Behavior.* New York: Doubleday and Co., 1967.

————. *The Presentation of Self in Everyday Life.* Garden City, N.Y.: Doubleday Anchor Books, 1959.

————. *Relations in Public: Microstudies of the Public Order.* New York: Harper Colophon Books, 1971.

Gorer, Geoffrey. *Death, Grief, and Mourning.* Garden City, N.Y.: Doubleday Anchor Books, 1967.

Greven, Philip J. *Four Generations: Population, Land, and Family in Colonial Andover, Massachusetts.* Ithaca: Cornell University Press, 1970.

————. *The Protestant Temperament: Patterns of Child-rearing, Religious Experience, and the Self in Early America.* New York: New American Library, 1977.

Griffen, Clyde. "Making It in America: Social Mobility in Mid-nineteenth-century Poughkeepsie." *New York History* 51 (October 1970): 479–99.

Grimsted, David, ed. *Notions of the Americans, 1820–1860.* New York: George Braziller, 1970.

Guilhamet, Leon. *The Sincere Ideal: Studies in Sincerity in Eighteenth-century English Literature.* Montreal: McGill-Queens University Press, 1974.

Habenstein, Robert, and Lamers, William. *The History of American Funeral Directing.* Milwaukee: Bulfin Printers, 1955.

Hall, Edward T. *The Hidden Dimension.* Garden City, N.Y.: Doubleday, 1966.

————. *The Silent Language.* Garden City, N.Y.: Doubleday, Anchor Books, 1973.

Haller, William. *The Rise of Puritanism.* New York: Harper and Row, 1957.

Harris, Neil. *The Artist in American Society: The Formative Years, 1790–1860.* New York: Simon and Schuster, 1966.

————. *Humbug! The Art of P. T. Barnum.* Boston: Little, Brown and Co., 1973.

Henretta, James A. *The Evolution of American Society, 1700–1815: An Interdisciplinary Analysis.* Lexington, Mass.: D. C. Heath and Co., 1973.

————. "Families and Farms: Mentalité in Pre-industrial America." *William and Mary Quarterly* 35 (January 1978): 3–32.

Higham, John. *From Boundlessness to Consolidation: The Transformation of American Culture, 1848–1860.* Ann Arbor, Mich.: William L. Clements Library, 1969.

Hobsbawm, E. J. *The Age of Capital, 1848–1875.* New York: Charles Scribner's Sons, 1975.

Hollander, Anne. *Seeing Through Clothes.* New York: Viking Press, 1978.

Horlick, Allan Stanley. *Country Boys and Merchant Princes: The Social*

Control of Young Men in New York. Lewisburg, Pa.: Bucknell University Press, 1975.

Horne, Marilyn J. *The Second Skin: An Interdisciplinary Study of Clothing.* Boston: Houghton Mifflin Co., 1968.

Houghton, Walter E. *The Victorian Frame of Mind, 1830–1870.* New Haven: Yale University Press, 1957.

Huber, Richard M. *The American Idea of Success.* New York: McGraw-Hill Book Co., 1971.

Huizinga, Johan. *Homo Ludens: A Study of the Play-element in Culture.* Boston: Beacon Press, 1955.

Jackson, Charles O. "American Attitudes to Death." *Journal of American Studies* 11 (December 1977): 297–312.

―――, ed. *Passing: The Vision of Death in America.* Westport, Conn.: Greenwood Press, 1977.

Jackson, Kenneth T., and Schultz, Stanley K., eds. *Cities in American History.* New York: Alfred A. Knopf, 1972.

Johnson, Paul E. *A Shopkeeper's Millennium: Society and Revivals in Rochester, New York, 1815–1837.* New York: Hill and Wang, 1978.

Kammen, Michael. *A Season of Youth: The American Revolution and the Historical Imagination.* New York: Oxford University Press, 1978.

Katz, Michael B. *The People of Hamilton, Canada West: Family and Class in a Mid-Nineteenth-Century City.* Cambridge: Harvard University Press, 1975.

Kelley, Robert. "Ideology and Political Culture from Jefferson to Nixon." *American Historical Review* 82 (June 1977): 531–62.

Kett, Joseph F. "Growing Up in Rural New England, 1800–1850." In *Anonymous Americans: Explorations in Nineteenth Century Social History,* edited by Tamara K. Hareven. Englewood Cliffs, N.J.: Prentice-Hall, 1971.

―――. *Rites of Passage: Adolescence in America, 1790 to the Present.* New York: Basic Books, 1977.

Keyes, Jean. *A History of Women's Hairstyles, 1500–1965.* London: Methuen and Co., 1967.

Kirkland, Edward C. *Dream and Thought in the Business Community, 1860–1900.* Ithaca: Cornell University Press, 1956.

Knights, Peter R. *The Plain People of Boston, 1830–1860: A Study in City Growth.* New York: Oxford University Press, 1971.

König, René. *The Restless Image: A Sociology of Fashion.* Translated by F. Bradley. London: George Allen and Unwin, 1973.

Kuhlmann, Susan. *Knave, Fool, and Genius: The Confidence Man as He Appears in Nineteenth Century American Fiction.* Chapel Hill: University of North Carolina Press, 1973.

Lane, Roger. *Policing the City: Boston 1822–1885.* Cambridge: Harvard University Press, 1967.

Laver, James. *Taste and Fashion from the French Revolution until Today.* London: George G. Harrap and Co., 1937.

Lindberg, Gary. *The Confidence Man in American Literature*. New York: Oxford University Press, 1982.

Lockridge, Kenneth A. "Land, Population, and the Evolution of New England Society, 1630–1790." In *Class and Society in Early America*, edited by Gary B. Nash. Englewood Cliffs, N.J.: Prentice-Hall, 1970.

Lofland, Lyn. *A World of Strangers: Order and Action in Urban Public Space*. New York: Basic Books, 1973.

Ludwig, Allan. *Graven Images: New England Stonecarving and Its Symbols, 1650–1815*. Middletown, Conn.: Wesleyan University Press, 1966.

Marcus, Steven. *The Other Victorians: A Study of Sexuality and Pornography in Mid-Nineteenth-Century England*. New York: Basic Books, 1964.

Marshall, Lynn L. "The Strange Stillbirth of the Whig Party." *American Historical Review* 52 (January 1967): 445–68.

Mason, John E. *Gentlefolk in the Making: Studies in the History of English Courtesy Literature and Related Topics from 1531 to 1774*. Philadelphia: University of Pennsylvania Press, 1935.

McLoughlin, William G. *The Meaning of Henry Ward Beecher: An Essay on the Shifting Values of Mid-Victorian America, 1840–1870*. New York: Alfred A. Knopf, 1970.

Meyer, Donald. *The Positive Thinkers: Religion as Pop Psychology from Mary Baker Eddy to Norman Vincent Peale*. New York: Pantheon Books, 1980.

Meyers, Marvin. *The Jacksonian Persuasion: Politics and Belief*. Stanford: Stanford University Press, 1957.

Miller, Perry. *The New England Mind: From Colony to Province*. Boston: Beacon Press, 1953.

———. *The New England Mind: The Seventeenth Century*. Boston: Beacon Press, 1939.

Miller, Zane L. *The Urbanization of Modern America: A Brief History*. New York: Harcourt Brace Jovanovich, 1973.

Minnegerode, Meade. *The Fabulous Forties, 1840–1850: A Presentation of Private Life*. New York: G. P. Putnam's Sons, 1924.

Montgomery, David. "The Working Classes of the Preindustrial American City, 1790–1830." *Labor History* 9 (November 1968): 3–22.

Morgan, Edmund S. *The Puritan Family: Religion and Domestic Relations in Seventeenth-century New England*. New York: Harper and Row, 1966.

———. *Visible Saints: The History of a Puritan Idea*. Ithaca: Cornell University Press, 1963.

Newton, Stella Mary. *Health Reformers of the Nineteenth Century*. London: John Murray, 1974.

North, Douglass C. *The Economic Growth of the United States*. New York: W. W. Norton and Co., 1966.

Novak, Maximillian E., ed. *English Literature in the Age of Disguise*. Berkeley and Los Angeles: University of California Press, 1977.

Nye, Russell Blaine. *Society and Culture in America, 1830–1860.* New York: Harper Torchbooks, 1974.

Papashvily, Helen Waite. *All the Happy Endings.* New York: Harper and Bros., 1956.

Park, Robert. "The City: Suggestions for the Investigation of Human Behavior in the Urban Environment." In *Classic Essays on the Culture of Cities,* edited by Richard Sennett. New York: Meredith Corp., 1969, pp. 91–130.

Parker, Gail Thain. *Mind Cure in New England from the Civil War to World War I.* Hanover, N.H.: University Press of New England, 1973.

Persons, Stow. *The Decline of American Gentility.* New York: Columbia University Press, 1973.

Pessen, Edward. *Jacksonian America: Society, Personality, and Politics.* Homewood, Ill.: Dorsey Press, 1978.

―――. *Riches, Class, and Power before the Civil War.* Lexington, Mass.: D. C. Heath and Co., 1973.

―――, ed. *Three Centuries of Social Mobility in America.* Lexington, Mass.: D. C. Heath and Co., 1974.

Pierson, George W. "The M-Factor in American History." *American Quarterly* 14 (Summer 1962): 275–89.

Pine, Vanderlyn R. *Caretaker of the Dead: The American Funeral Director.* New York: Irvington Publishers, 1975.

Puckle, Bertram S. *Funeral Customs: Their Origins and Development.* Detroit: Singing Tree Press, 1968.

Rabinowitz, Richard I. "Soul, Character, and Personality: The Transformation of Personal Religious Experience in New England, 1790–1860." Ph.D. dissertation, Harvard University, 1977.

Richards, Leonard. *Gentlemen of Property and Standing: Anti-Abolition Mobs in Jacksonian America.* New York: Oxford University Press, 1970.

Roach, Mary Ellen, and Eicher, Joanne B., eds. *Dress, Adornment and the Social Order.* New York: John Wiley and Sons, 1965.

―――, eds. *The Visible Self: Perspectives on Dress.* Englewood Cliffs, N.J.: Prentice-Hall, 1973.

Rodgers, Daniel T. *The Work Ethic in Industrial America, 1850–1920.* Chicago: University of Chicago Press, 1979.

Rosenberg, Charles E. *The Cholera Years: The United States in 1832, 1849, and 1866.* Chicago: University of Chicago Press, 1962.

Rourke, Constance. *American Humor: A Study of the National Character.* New York: Harcourt, Brace and Co., 1931.

Rozwenc, Edwin, ed. *Ideology and Power in the Age of Jackson.* Garden City, N.Y.: Doubleday Anchor Books, 1964.

Schlesinger, Arthur M. *Learning How to Behave: A Historical Study of American Etiquette Books.* New York: Macmillan Co., 1946.

Sennett, Richard. *The Fall of Public Man: On the Social Psychology of Capitalism.* New York: Vintage Books, 1978.

Shalhope, Robert E. "Toward a Republican Synthesis: The Emergence of an Understanding of Republicanism in American Historiography." *William and Mary Quarterly* 29 (January 1972): 49–80.

Shea, Daniel B., Jr. *Spiritual Autobiography in Early America*. Princeton: Princeton University Press, 1968.

Simmel, Georg. "The Stranger." In *The Sociology of Georg Simmel*, pp. 402–08. Glencoe, Ill.: Free Press, 1950.

Sklar, Kathryn K. *Catharine Beecher: A Study in American Domesticity*. New Haven: Yale University Press, 1973.

Somkin, Fred. *Unquiet Eagle: Memory and Desire in the Idea of American Freedom, 1815–1860*. Ithaca: Cornell University Press, 1967.

Squire, Geoffrey. *Dress Art and Society, 1560–1970*. London: Studio Vista, 1974.

Stannard, David E., ed. *Death in America*. Philadelphia: University of Pennsylvania Press, 1975.

———. *The Puritan Way of Death: A Study in Religion, Culture, and Social Change*. New York: Oxford University Press, 1977.

Stern, Madeline B. *Heads and Headlines: The Phrenological Fowlers*. Norman, Okla.: University of Oklahoma Press, 1971.

Still, Bayrd. *Urban America: A History with Documents*. Boston: Little, Brown and Co., 1974.

Stonequist, Everett V. *The Marginal Man: A Study in Personality and Culture Conflict*. New York: Charles Scribner's Sons, 1937.

Strachey, Lytton. *Eminent Victorians*. New York: Capricorn Books, 1963.

Susman, Warren I. " 'Personality' and the Making of Twentieth-century Culture." In *New Directions in American Intellectual History*, edited by John Higham and Paul K. Conkin, pp. 212–26. Baltimore: The Johns Hopkins University Press, 1979.

Tanner, Tony. Introduction to *Mansfield Park*, by Jane Austen. Baltimore: Penguin Books, 1972.

Tashjian, Dickran, and Tashjian, Ann. *Memorials for Children of Change: The Art of Early New England Stonecarving*. Middletown, Conn.: Wesleyan University Press, 1974.

Taylor, William R. *Cavalier and Yankee: The Old South and American National Character*. New York: Harper and Row, 1961.

Tegg, William. *The Last Act, being the Funeral Rites of Nations and Individuals*. London: William Tegg and Co., 1876.

Thernstrom, Stephan. *Poverty and Progress: Social Mobility in a Nineteenth Century City*. Cambridge: Harvard University Press, 1964.

Tocqueville, Alexis de. *Democracy in America*. 2 vols. New York: Vintage Books, 1945.

Tompkins, J[oyce] M[arjorie] S[axter]. *The Popular Novel in England, 1770–1800*. Lincoln: University of Nebraska Press, 1961.

Trilling, Lionel. *Sincerity and Authenticity*. Cambridge: Harvard University Press, 1973.

Turner, Victor. *The Ritual Process: Structure and Anti-structure.* Ithaca: Cornell University Press, 1969.

Wadlington, Warwick. *The Confidence Game in American Literature.* Princeton: Princeton University Press, 1975.

Wallace, Michael. "Changing Concepts of Party in the United States: New York, 1815–1828." *American Historical Review* 74 (December 1968): 453–91.

Ward, John W. *Andrew Jackson: Symbol for an Age.* New York: Oxford University Press, 1962.

Warner, Sam Bass, Jr. *The Private City: Philadelphia in Three Periods of Its Growth.* Philadelphia: University of Pennsylvania Press, 1968.

———. *Streetcar Suburbs: The Process of Growth in Boston, 1870–1900.* Cambridge: Harvard University Press, 1962.

Watt, Ian. *The Rise of the Novel: Studies in Defoe, Richardson, and Fielding.* Berkeley and Los Angeles: University of California Press, 1967.

Weber, Max. *The Protestant Ethic and the Spirit of Capitalism.* Translated by Talcott Parson. New York: Charles Scribner's Sons, 1958.

Weiss, Richard. *The American Myth of Success from Horatio Alger to Norman Vincent Peale.* New York: Basic Books, 1969.

Welter, Barbara. "The Cult of True Womanhood: 1820–1860." In *The American Family in Social-Historical Perspective,* edited by Michael Gordon, pp. 313–33. New York: St. Martin's Press, 1978.

Wilcox, R. Turner. *Five Centuries of American Costume.* New York: Charles Scribner's Sons, 1963.

Wildeblood, Joan, and Brinson, Peter. *The Polite World: A Guide to English Manners and Deportment from the 13th to the 19th Century.* London: Oxford University Press, 1965.

Williams, Neville. *Powder and Paint: A History of the Englishwoman's Toilet, Elizabeth I–Elizabeth II.* London: Longmans, Green and Co., 1957.

Wohl, R. Richard. "The 'Country Boy' Myth and Its Place in American Urban Culture: the Nineteenth-century Contribution." *Perspectives in American History* 3 (1969): 77–156.

Wood, Gordon S. *The Creation of the American Republic, 1776–1787.* New York: W. W. Norton and Co., 1969.

Wyatt-Brown, Bertram. "Prelude to Abolitionism: Sabbatarian Politics and the Rise of the Second Party System." *Journal of American History* 58 (September 1971): 316–41.

Wyllie, Irvin G. *The Self-Made Man in America: The Myth of Rags to Riches.* New Brunswick, N.J.: Rutgers University Press, 1954.

Yarwood, Doreen. *European Costume: 4000 Years of Fashion.* London: B. T. Batsford, 1975.

Young, Agnes Brooks. *Recurring Cycles of Fashion 1760–1937.* New York: Harper and Bros., 1937.

Primary Sources

Abbott, John Stevens Cabot. *The School-boy; or, A Guide for Youth to Truth and Duty.* Boston: Crocker and Brewster, 1839.

Abell, Mrs. L. G. *Woman in her Various Relations: containing Practical Rules for American Females.* New York: William Holdredge, 1851.

Adams, Nehemiah. *Agnes and the Little Key: Or, Bereaved Parents Instructed and Comforted.* Boston: S. K. Whipple and Co., 1857.

Advice to a Young Gentleman on Entering Society. Philadelphia: Lea and Blanchard, 1839.

Alcott, William A. *Familiar Letters to Young Men on Various Subjects. Designed as a Companion to the Young Man's Guide.* Buffalo: George H. Derby and Co., 1850.

———. *The Young Man's Guide.* Boston: Lilly, Wait, Colman, and Holden, 1834.

———. *The Young Woman's Guide to Excellence.* Boston: George W. Light, 1840.

Alger, William R. *The School of Life.* Boston: Roberts Bros., 1881.

The American Chesterfield. Philadelphia, 1828.

Anspach, Reverend Frederick Rinehart. *The Sepulchres of Our Departed.* Philadelphia: Lindsay and Blakiston, 1854.

The Art of Good Behaviour; and Letter Writer on Love, Courtship, and Marriage: A Complete Guide for Ladies and Gentlemen, particularly those who have not Enjoyed the Advantages of Fashionable Life. New York: C. P. Huestis, 1846.

Arthur, Timothy Shay. *Advice to Young Ladies on their Duty and Conduct in Life.* Boston: Phillips, Sampson, and Co., 1854,

———. *Advice to Young Men on their Duties and Conduct in Life.* Boston: Phillips, Sampson, and Co., 1851.

Barrett, Robert South. *Character Building: Talks to Young Men.* New York: Thomas Whittaker, 1882.

The Bazar Book of Decorum. New York: Harper and Bros., 1870.

Beadle's Dime Book of Practical Etiquette for Ladies and Gentlemen: being a Guide to True Gentility and Good-breeding, and a Complete Directory to the Usages and Observances of Society. New York: Irwin P. Beadle, and Co., 1859.

Beecher, Henry Ward. *Seven Lectures to Young Men, on Various Important Subjects; Delivered Before the Young Men of Indianapolis, Indiana, During the Winter of 1843–4.* Indianapolis: Thomas B. Cutler, 1844.

Blunders in Behavior Corrected; a Concise Code of Deportment for Both Sexes. New York: Dick and Fitzgerald, n.d.

Bohn's Manual of Etiquette in Washington and Other Cities in the Union. Washington: Casimir Bohn, 1857.

Bowker, Richard Rogers. *The Arts of Life.* Boston: Houghton Mifflin Co., 1900.

Buckley, James Monroe. *Oats or Wild Oats? Common-sense for Young Men.* New York: Harper and Bros., 1885.

Burgess, George. *The Last Enemy: Conquering and Conquered.* Philadelphia: H. Hooker, 1850.

Burrell, David J. *The Lure of the City: A Book for Young Men.* New York: Funk and Wagnalls Co., 1908.

Butler, Charles. *American Gentlemen.* Philadelphia: Hogan and Thompson, 1836.

———. *The American Lady.* Philadelphia: Hogan and Thompson, 1839.

Celnart, Madame. *The Gentleman's and Lady's Book of Politeness and Propriety of Deportment, dedicated to the Youth of Both Sexes.* Boston: Allen and Ticknor, and Carter, Hendee and Co., 1833.

Chapin, Edwin Hubbell. *The Crown of Thorns: A Token for the Sorrowing.* Boston: A. Tompkins, 1860.

———. *Duties of Young Men, Exhibited in Six Lectures; with an Anniversary Address, Delivered before the Richmond Lyceum.* Boston: Abel Tompkins, and B. B. Mussey, 1840.

———. *Duties of Young Women.* Boston: George W. Briggs, 1851.

Chesterfield's Art of Letter-writing Simplified . . . to which is appended the Complete Rules of Etiquette, and the Usages of Society . . . New York: Dick and Fitzgerald, 1857.

Childs, Charles Francis. *Essays on Education and Culture.* St. Louis: E. P. Gray, 1867.

Clark, Francis Edward. *Danger Signals: The Enemies of Youth, from the Business Man's Standpoint.* Boston: Lee and Shepard, 1885.

Clark, Reverend Rufus W. *Lectures on the Formation of Character, Temptations and Mission of Young Men.* Boston: John P. Jewett and Co. 1853.

Clarke, James Freeman. *Self-Culture: Physical, Intellectual, Moral, and Spiritual.* Boston: James R. Osgood and Co., 1880.

Cooley, Eli Field. *A Description of the Etiquette at Washington City.* Philadelphia: L. B. Clarke, 1829.

Dana, Joseph. *The Mourner's Relief: A Sermon at Ipswich to Console Mourning Relatives and Friends of Rev. Joseph McKean.* Newburyport: William Hastings, 1818.

Day, Charles William. *Hints on Etiquette and the Usages of Society; with a Glance at Bad Habits.* Boston: William D. Ticknor and Co., 1844.

DeMotte, John B. *The Secret of Character Building.* Chicago: S. C. Griggs and Co., 1893.

Dewey, Orville. *On the Duties of Consolation, and the Rites and Customs Appropriate to Mourning.* New Bedford: B. Lindsey, 1825.

Drysdale, William. *Helps for Ambitious Boys.* New York: Thomas Y. Crowell Co., 1899.

Duncan, Reverend J. *The Mourner's Friend: Or, Recognition of Friends in Heaven.* Lowell, Mass.: N. L. Dayton, 1850.

Eddy, Daniel C. *The Angels' Whispers; or, Echoes of Spirit Voices. Designed to*

Console the Mourning Husband and Wife, Father and Mother, Son and Daughter, Brother and Sister. Boston: G. W. Cottrell, 1866.

Eggleston, George Cary. *How to Make a Living: Suggestions upon the Art of Making, Saving, and Using Money.* New York: G. P. Putnam's Sons, 1875.

Emerson, Ralph Waldo. *The Conduct of Life.* Boston: Ticknor and Fields, 1861.

Etiquette at Washington: and Complete Guide through the Metropolis and its Environs . . . Baltimore: Murphy and Co., 1857.

Etiquette for Gentlemen. London and New York: George Routledge and Sons, n.d.

Etiquette of the Ball-room; or the Dancer's Companion. Boston: Oliver Ditson and Co., n.d.

Farrar, Mrs. John. *The Young Lady's Friend.* New York: Samuel S. and William Wood, 1849.

Fiske, Lewis R. *Man-building: A Treatise on Human Life and its Forces.* New York: Charles Scribner's Sons, 1901.

Friswell, James Hain. *The Gentle Life: Essays in Aid of the Formation of Character.* New York: W. Low, 1864.

Gasparin, Madame de. *The Near and Heavenly Horizons.* New York: Robert Carter and Bros., 1862.

Gilman, Nicholas P. *The Laws of Daily Conduct.* Boston: Houghton Mifflin Co., 1891.

Godey's Lady's Book, vols. 1–63. Philadelphia, 1830–1861.

Goodrich, Samuel G. [Peter Parley]. *What to Do, and How to Do It; or, Morals and Manners Taught by Examples.* New York: Lamport, Blakeman and Law, 1844.

Greenleaf, Reverend Patrick Henry, ed. *Consolatio: Or Comfort for the Afflicted.* Boston and Cambridge: James Munroe and Co., 1849.

Greenwood, Francis William Pitt. *Sermons of Consolation.* Boston: Little, Brown and Co., 1864.

Griswold, Reverend Rufus Wilmot. *The Cypress Wreath.* Boston: Gould, Kendall and Lincoln, 1844.

Grund, Francis J. *Aristocracy in America.* New York: Harper Torchbooks, 1959.

The Habits of Good Society: A Handbook for Ladies and Gentlemen. New York: Carleton, 1869.

Haines, Thomas Louis, and Yaggy, Levi W. *The Royal Path of Life: or, Aims and Aids to Success and Happiness.* Chicago: Western Publishing House, 1876.

Hale, Sarah J. *Manners; or, Happy Homes and Good Society All the Year Round.* 1868. Reprint. New York: Arno Press, 1972.

The Hand-book of Carving; with Hints on the Etiquette of the Dinner Table. London: Robert Tyas, 1839.

The Handbook of the Man of Fashion. Philadelphia: Lindsay and Blakiston, 1846.

Hardy, Edward J. *The Business of Life.* New York: Charles Scribner's Sons, 1891.

Hartley, Cecil B. *The Gentleman's Book of Etiquette, and Manual of Politeness; being a Complete Guide for a Gentleman's Conduct in All His Relations towards Society.* Boston: G. W. Cottrell, 1860.

Hartley, Florence. *The Ladies' Book of Etiquette, and Manual of Politeness. A Complete Hand Book for the Use of the Lady in Polite Society.* Boston: G. W. Cottrell, 1860.

Hawes, Joel. *Lectures Addressed to the Young Men of Hartford and New-Haven.* Hartford: Oliver D. Cooke and Co., 1828.

Herron, S. P. *Thoughts on Life and Character.* Philadelphia: J. B. Lippincott and Co., 1873.

Hervey, George Winfred. *The Principles of Courtesy: With Hints and Observations on Manners and Habits.* New York: Harper and Bros., 1852.

Hillgrove, Thomas. *A Complete Practical Guide to the Art of Dancing.* New York: Dick and Fitzgerald, 1866.

Hillis, Newell D. *The Contagion of Character: Studies in Culture and Success.* Chicago and New York: Fleming H. Revell Co., 1911.

———. *The Investment of Influence: A Study of Social Sympathy and Service.* Chicago and New York: Fleming H. Revell Co., 1897.

———. *A Man's Value to Society: Studies in Self-Culture and Character.* Chicago and New York: Fleming H. Revell Co., 1896.

Hints on Common Politeness. Boston: D. C. Colesworthy, 1867.

Hitchcock, Edward. *A Wreath for the Tomb: Or, Extracts from Eminent Writers on Death and Eternity.* Amherst: J. S. and C. Adams, 1839.

Holland, Josiah Gilbert. *Plain Talks on Familiar Subjects.* New York: C. Scribner, 1863.

———. *Titcomb's Letters to Young People, Single and Married.* New York: C. Scribner, 1863.

How to Behave. A Pocket Manual of Republican Etiquette, A Guide to Correct Personal Habits . . . New York: Fowler and Wells, 1856.

Howe, Elias. *Howe's Complete Ball-room Hand Book: Containing Upwards of Three Hundred Dances, including all the Latest and Most Fashionable Dances.* Boston: Brown, Taggard and Chase, 1858.

Huntington, Frederic Dan. *Good Talking and Good Manners: Fine Arts.* Syracuse: Wolcott and West, 1887.

The Illustrated Manners Book; a Manual of Good Behavior and Polite Accomplishments. New York: Leland Clay and Co., 1855.

Jackson, Edward P. *Character Building: A Master's Talks with his Pupils.* Boston and New York: Houghton Mifflin Co., 1891.

James, John Angell. *The Young Man from Home.* New York: American Tract Society, 1840.

Jay, Reverend William. *The Happy Mourner: or Sympathy for the Bereaved, Presenting the Consolations of God to his Afflicted Children.* Boston: James Loring, 1838.

Keese, John, ed. *The Mourner's Chaplet: An Offering of Sympathy for Bereaved Friends. Selected from American Poets.* Boston: Gould, Kendall and Lincoln, 1844.

Kendig, John A. J. "Intellect or Character?" Chicago: Chicago Legal News Print, 1878.

Kent, Charles H. *Kent's New Commentary: A Manual for Young Men.* Davenport, Iowa: C. H. Kent, 1880.

Kingsbury, Oliver Addison. *Success; or, Hints for Living.* Boston: D. Lothrop and Co., 1886.

Kirkland, Caroline Matilda. *The Evening Book; or, Fireside Talk on Morals and Manners.* New York: C. Scribner, 1852.

Ladies and Gentlemen's Letter Writer and Guide to Polite Behavior, containing also Moral and Instructive Aphorisms, for Daily Use. Boston: G. W. Cottrell, 1859.

Ladies and Gentlemen's Pocket Companion of Etiquette and Manners, with the Rules of Polite Society, to which is added Hints on Dress, Courtship, Etc. New York, n.d.

Ladies' Indispensable Assistant. New York: Nassau-Street, 1851.

The Ladies Pocket Book of Etiquette. 1838. Reprint. New York: The Golden Cockerel Press, 1928.

The Ladies Science of Etiquette. New York: Wilson and Co., 1844.

Ladies' Vase; or, Polite Manual for Young Ladies; Original and Selected. Lowell, Mass.: N. L. Dayton, 1843.

The Laws of Etiquette, or, Short Rules and Reflections for Conduct in Society. Philadelphia: Carey, Lea, and Blanchard, 1836.

Leslie, Eliza. *Miss Leslie's Behaviour Book: A Guide and Manual for Ladies* . . . Philadelphia: Willis P. Hazard, 1857.

Lieber, Francis. *The Character of the Gentleman.* Philadelphia: J. B. Lippincott and Co., 1864.

Lunettes, Henry [pseud.]. *The American Gentleman's Guide to Politeness and Fashion.* New York: Derby and Jackson, 1858.

MacConaughy, Julia E. *Capital for Working Boys.* Boston: James H. Earle, 1883.

Mackellar, D. *A Treatise on the Art of Politeness, Good Breeding, and Manners. With Maxims and Moral Reflections.* Detroit: George E. Pomeroy and Co., 1855.

Magie, Reverend David. *The Spring-time of Life; or, Advice to Youth.* New York: Robert Carter and Bros., 1853.

Mann, Horace. *A Few Thoughts for a Young Man: A Lecture, Delivered Before the Boston Mercantile Library Association, on its 29th Anniversary.* Boston: Ticknor, Reed, and Fields, 1850.

Manners, Mrs. [pseud.]. *At Home and Abroad; or, How to Behave.* New York: Evans and Brittan, 1853.

A Manual of Politeness, Comprising the Principles of Etiquette, and Rules of Behaviour in Genteel Society, for Persons of Both Sexes. Philadelphia: W. Marshall and Co., 1837.

Marden, Orison S. *The Secret of Achievement*. New York: Thomas Y. Crowell and Co., 1898.

Martine, Arthur. *Martine's Hand-Book of Etiquette, and Guide to True Politeness*. New York: Dick and Fitzgerald, 1866.

Mathews, William. *Getting On in the World; or, Hints on Success in Life*. Chicago: S. C. Griggs and Co., 1873.

Meditations for the Afflicted, Sick and Dying. Boston: Samuel G. Simpkins, 1833.

Mixing in Society. A Complete Manual of Manners. London and New York: George Routledge and Sons, 1870.

Mogridge, George. *Learning to Act*. Philadelphia: American Sunday-School Union, 1846.

Moore, George. *Man and His Motives*. New York: Harper and Bros. 1848.

Mountford, William. *Euthanasy; or Happy Talk Towards the End of Life*. Boston: William Crosby and H. P. Nichols, 1848.

The Mourners' Book. Philadelphia: William Marshall and Co., 1836.

Moxom, Philip S. *The Aim of Life: Plain Talks to Young Men and Women*. Boston: Roberts Bros., 1894.

Munger, Theodore T. *On the Threshold*. Boston: Houghton Mifflin Co., 1881.

Muzzey, Artemus B. *The Young Maiden*. Boston: William Crosby and Co., 1840.

——. *The Young Man's Friend*. Boston: J. Munroe, 1838.

The New Letter Writer, containing a Great Variety of Letters . . . selected from Judicious and Eminent Writers. New York: Richard Marsh, 1853.

A New Letter-writer, for the Use of Ladies: Embodying Letters on the Simplest Matters of Life . . . Philadelphia: Porter and Coates, n.d.

Parkman, Francis. *An Offering of Sympathy to the Afflicted, especially to Parents Bereaved of their Children . . .* Boston: Lilly, Wait, Colman, and Holden, 1833.

Patrick, Mrs. M. A., ed., *The Mourner's Gift*. New York: Charles S. Francis, 1837.

Payne, Charles Henry. *Guides and Guards in Character-Building*. New York: Phillips and Hunt, 1883.

Peabody, Andrew P. *Character-Building*. Boston: James H. Earle, 1886.

The Perfect Gentleman; or, Etiquette and Eloquence. New York: Dick and Fitzgerald, 1860.

Porter, Reverend James. *The Operative's Friend, and Defence: Or, Hints to Young Ladies, who are Dependent on their Own Exertions*. Boston: Charles H. Peirce, 1850.

Richards, Mrs. Cornelia Holroyd (Bradley). *Springs of Action*. New York: Harper and Bros., 1863.

Routledge's Etiquette for Gentlemen. New York: George Routledge and Sons, n.d.

Schmidt, F. Leopold, Jr. *An Object in Life, and How to Attain It.* New York: Fowler and Wells, 1889.

The School of Good Manners. Composed for the Help of Parents in Teaching their Children How to Behave in their Youth. Boston: Massachusetts Sabbath School Society, 1837.

Sigourney, Lydia Howard (Huntley). *How to be Happy, Written for the Children of Some Dear Friends.* Hartford: D. F. Robinson and Co., 1833.

Simonds, William, ed. *Our Little Ones in Heaven.* Boston: Gould and Lincoln, 1864.

Smith, Matthew Hale. *Successful Folks: How They Win.* Hartford: American Publishing Co., 1878.

Syme, J. B., ed. *The Mourner's Friend: Or Sighs of Sympathy for Those who Sorrow.* Worcester, Mass.: William Allen, 1852.

Symington, Andrew James. *Hints to Our Boys.* New York: Thomas Y. Crowell and Co., 1884.

Taylor, Isaac. *Youth's Own Book: Character Essential to Success in Life.* Hartford: Canfield and Robins, 1836.

Taylor, Reverend Timothy Alden. *The Solace; Or, Afflictions Lightened.* Boston: Congregational Board of Publication, 1849.

Thayer, Thomas Baldwin. *Over the River; or, Pleasant Walks into the Valley of Shadows, and Beyond . . .* Boston: Tompkins and Co., 1864.

Thayer, William Makepeace. *Ethics of Success: A Reader for the Higher Grades of Schools.* New York: Silver, Burdett, and Co., 1897.

———. *Tact, Push, and Principle.* Boston: James H. Earle, 1880.

Thompson, Augustus C. *Last Hours, or Words and Acts of the Dying.* Boston: Perkins and Whipple, 1851.

Thornwell, Emily. *The Lady's Guide to Perfect Gentility . . .* New York: Derby and Jackson, 1856.

Todd, John. *The Young Man: Hints Addressed to the Young Men of the United States.* Northampton, Mass.: n.p., 1850.

Triumphant Deaths; or Brief Notices of the Happy Deaths of Twenty Six Sabbath School Scholars. New Haven: Jeremy L. Cross, 1831.

True Politeness; a Hand-book of Etiquette for Ladies. New York: Leavitt and Allen, 1847.

Walsh, Robert. *Didactics: Social, Literary, and Political.* 2 vols. Philadelphia: Carey, Lea, and Blanchard, 1836.

Waterbury, Reverend Jared Bell. *Considerations for Young Men.* New York: American Tract Society, 1851.

———. *The Voyage of Life; Suggested by Cole's Celebrated Allegorical Paintings.* Boston: Massachusetts Sabbath School Society, 1852.

Weaver, Reverend George Sumner. *Hopes and Helps for the Young of Both Sexes.* New York: Fowler and Wells, 1853.

———. *The Ways of Life Showing the Right Way and Wrong Way; Contrasting the High Way and the Low Way; the True Way and the False Way; the*

Upward Way and the Downward Way; the Way of Honor and the Way of Dishonor. New York: Fowler and Wells, 1855.

The Well-bred Boy and Girl; or, New School of Good Manners. 2 vols. Boston: B. B. Mussey and Co., 1850.

Whipple, Edwin P. *Character and Characteristic Men.* Boston: Ticknor and Fields, 1866.

————. *Success and its Conditions.* Boston: James R. Osgood and Co., 1871.

Whitcomb, William Chalmers. *The True Consoler, or Balm for the Stricken, Original and Selected.* Boston: Charles C. P. Moody, 1861.

Willard, Mrs. Emma (Hart). *Morals for the Young; or, Good Principles Instilling Wisdom.* New York: A. S. Barnes and Co., 1857.

Williams, Theodore C. *Character-Building.* New York: E. P. Dutton and Co., 1893.

Willis, Henry P. *Etiquette, and the Usages of Society: containing the Most Approved Rules for Correct Deportment in Fashionable Life . . .* New York: Dick and Fitzgerald, 1860.

Wilson, Jacob. *Practical Life and the Study of Man.* Newark, N. J.: J. Wilson and Sons, 1882.

Wood, Benjamin. *The Successful Man of Business.* New York: Brentano's, 1899.

Wood, Wallace, ed. *Ideals of Life: Human Perfection, How to Attain It.* New York: E. B. Treat, 1892.

The Young Lady's Mentor. Philadelphia: H. C. Peck and Theo. Bliss, 1851.

The Young Man's Own Book: A Manual of Politeness, Intellectual Improvement, and Moral Deportment, calculated to Form the Character on a Solid Basis, and to Insure Respectability and Success in Life. Philadelphia: Key and Biddle, 1833.

The Young Man's Sunday Book: a Practical Manual of the Christian Duties of Piety, Benevolence and Self-Government. Philadelpnia: Key and Biddle, 1834.

The Young Mechanic. New York: Saxton and Miles, 1843.

The Young Merchant. Boston: George W. Light, 1841.

Index